DATA PROTECTION –
THE NEW LAW

DATA PROTECTION –
THE NEW LAW

Susan Singleton LLB, Solicitor
Principal, Singletons Solicitors

JORDANS

1998

Published by
Jordan Publishing Limited
21 St Thomas Street, Bristol BS1 6JS

British Library Cataloguing-in-Publication Data
A catalogue record for this book is available from the British Library.

ISBN 0 85308 421 8

Typeset by Mendip Communications Ltd, Frome, Somerset
Printed by MPG Books Ltd, Bodmin, Cornwall

DEDICATION

To my husband, Martin, and our children, Rachel, Rebecca, Benjamin and our new twins, Joseph and Samuel, whose gestation coincided with the writing of this book.

THE AUTHOR

Susan Singleton LLB, Solicitor, founded her own solicitors practice, Singletons, in 1994. The firm provides specialist advice to almost 200 companies, both large and small, on intellectual property, computer, competition and commercial law. She is the author of several books within those fields.

Singletons Solicitors
The Ridge
South View Road
Pinner
Middlesex
HA5 3YD

Tel: 0181 866 1934
Fax: 0181 429 9212
e-mail: essingleton@link.org

PREFACE

The holding of personal data on individuals brings tremendous benefits for consumers and businesses. Few would deny, however, that such power should be used responsibly; this is what data protection law seeks to ensure. This guide to the Data Protection Act 1998 examines the new law as it is implemented. The Act received Royal Assent on 16 July 1998. Case-law will show how the law will be interpreted henceforth.

At first sight, the new Act is in many ways similar to the 1984 Act. Data controllers must follow certain principles in relation to the data that they hold. Individuals have rights of access to data which is held on them and rights to sue for damages if various offences occur. However, it is in the detail that this legislation differs from the 1984 Act. The UK has had more flexibility than with implementation of some other EU Directives in that the Directive on which the 1998 Act is based contains options and choices for Member States. There are areas highlighted in the text where the new law is not clear. For some, data protection will remain a great regulatory burden and, indeed, some years ago the then Conservative Government did moot the abolition of the registration requirement. Readers will know that those who hold personal data have to register and must pay fees every three years. It is unfortunate that in many areas of industry this requirement is more honoured in the breach, but it was and will remain the law. Indeed, the new Act requires that those holding certain categories of manual (non-computerised) data about data subjects must register so that its scope is wider than that of the 1984 Act. Some countries such as the USA manage with a voluntary system of regulation and no registrations.

One controversial aspect of the 1998 Act is the restriction on export of data to countries without the same data protection safeguards as those in the EU. The UK, however, has been obliged to follow the regulatory route which, in any event, mirrors the 1984 regime.

For ease of reference, the book follows the order of the various Parts of the Act, which is reproduced, together with the Directive on which it is based, in the Appendices at the end of the book. However, readers will always need to watch out for new case-law, and for regulations and guidance notes, of which there are expected to be many issued by the Data Protection Commissioner in due course. As at 1 November 1998, only consultation on draft regulations was taking place. These will have considerable impact on the interpretation of the Act. The book refers to debates in Parliament because, under *Pepper v Hart* [1993] AC 593, reports in *Hansard* may be used as an aid to the interpretation of the Act where the meaning is unclear. Equally important is the EU law principle that, in the event of a conflict between an EU Directive and the UK implementing legislation, in this case, the 1998 Act, the terms of the Directive will prevail. The consequence of this is that individuals can, as against government bodies, treat as the law the Directive rather than the 1998 Act. However, as against private sector companies, they must treat the 1998 Act as the law and sue the Government for damages if an incorrect implementation of the Directive has led to their suffering loss. In addition, the late implementation of the Act in early 1999 will leave the Government open to legal actions for breaches of the Directive's requirements. Having said that, the Act is a very good attempt by the Government to implement the Directive as it stands and conflicts are likely to be few and far between. Indeed, some of the less clear wording in the Act is present because of the need to implement the 'euro-compromise' which flows from all new EU legislation.

Finally, the book also examines briefly the related 1998 Directive on telecommunications and data protection, and that Directive is also reproduced, in Appendix 3. Readers should also consider the implications of the UK's implementation into English law of the European Convention on Human Rights by means of the Human Rights Act 1998, which is likely to have general privacy law implications.

In this book, the term 'data' is used in its correct plural form as used by the Data Protection Registrar (to be retitled Data Protection Commissioner) and in the Act, even though this may not accord with common parlance.

The Commissioner is referred to as 'she' since Mrs Elizabeth France looks set to remain as Commissioner when her title alters from Data Protection Registrar.

The law is stated as at 1 November 1998.

Susan Singleton
Pinner
November 1998

CONTENTS

TABLES

References are to paragraph numbers.

Table of Cases

Table of Statutes

Table of Statutory Instruments

Table of EC Materials

Chapter 1

APPLICATION OF THE ACT AND DEFINITIONS

INTRODUCTION

1.1   The Data Protection Act 1998 ('the Act') replaces the Data Protection Act 1984. The Act received Royal Assent on 16 July 1998 but the regulations to bring it into force will be drafted later. Only those provisions relating to definitions and giving power to the Secretary of State to make regulations have come into force immediately. In broad terms, the Act follows much the same principles as the 1984 Act, but the difference is in the detail and this is the subject-matter of this book. The 1998 Act implements the EU Data Protection Directive 95/46 ('the Directive') in the UK although it has missed the 24 October 1998 deadline. The Act and the Directive are reproduced in Appendices 1 and 2 respectively. The Act applies to data controllers and data processors who process personal data about data subjects. All these terms are defined in the legislation, and this chapter looks at when the Act applies and, in particular, at the definitions. Later chapters examine the substantive provisions in detail.

1.2   Under the 1984 Act, the Data Protection Registrar, from time to time, issued guidance or guidelines indicating her interpretation of the Act in relation to particular areas of activity. Examples include guidance as to the Act's operation in relation to optical character readers (scanners) and also in respect of the internet. It is likely that similar guidance will be issued by the Data Protection Commissioner (the new title for the Data Protection Registrar under the 1998 Act) in relation to those matters which are dealt with in this chapter but no such guidance was available at the time of writing. Readers should look out for such guidance to appear in due course.

DEFINITIONS

Data

1.3   The Act, as its title implies, deals with data. Under s 1(1), this is information which:

'(a)   is being processed by means of equipment operating automatically in response to instructions given for that purpose,

(b)   is recorded with the intention that it should be processed by means of such equipment,

(c)   is recorded as part of a relevant filing system or with the intention that it should form part of a relevant filing system, or

(d)   does not fall within paragraph (a), (b) or (c) but forms part of an accessible record as defined by section 68.'

1.4　　　These provisions constitute four alternatives. In most cases, there will be no problem with what is meant by paras (a) and (b) above. 'Equipment operating automatically which processes data' would include a computer system. However, 'processing' must take place. This is also defined (see **1.23** below). Paragraph (c) of the definition above is the important new provision. Under the 1984 Act, there was no protection for data held manually.

1.5　　　It is too simplistic to state that the new Act also applies to manual data. As readers can see from para (c) of the definition above, the important point, where there is no automatic processing, is that the information is 'recorded as part of a relevant filing system' or that it is intended that this will be the case.

1.6　　　Paragraph (d) of the definition was added only as the Bill went through its last parliamentary stages. Section 68 defines an 'accessible record' as a health record, an educational record or an accessible public record, all of which are defined elsewhere. Such records may not fall within paras (a)–(c): hence the addition of para (d) to ensure that certain rights of access to information held in manual records were covered by the Act. These are rights under the Personal Files Act 1987, the Access to Health Records Act 1990 and the Education (School Records) Regulations 1989 and corresponding legislation in Scotland and Northern Ireland. They relate to local authority housing and social services records, health records, and records held by schools on pupils and former pupils.

1.7　　　The case of *Gaskin v United Kingdom* (1989) 12 ECHR 36, under the European Convention on Human Rights required that access to such records be given and the Government sensibly wanted the rights of access to be consolidated in the new Act rather than in the other legislation mentioned above. The measure was discussed in the House of Lords debate of 10 July 1998. 'Accessible' records are health records, defined in s 68(2); educational records, defined in Sch 11; and accessible public records, defined in Sch 12. The full definitions in Schs 11 and 12 are not repeated here but for those involved in the areas affected by those provisions, careful note should be taken of those Schedules.

Personal data

1.8　　　The Act defines 'personal data' in s 1(1). Not all data are personal under the Act and it is the processing of personal data and no other form of data which is caught by the Act. Personal data are 'data', as defined above, which relate to a living individual who can be identified from the data, or from the data and other information which is in the possession of, or is likely to come into the possession of, the data controller. It also includes any expression of opinion about the individual and any indication of the intentions of the data controller or any other person in respect of the individual. It must relate to a living individual. As soon as a person dies, many of his or her 'rights' are lost at law: for example, under the law of defamation, the deceased's estate cannot bring an action for libel or slander. The Act follows this principle too. Therefore, no privacy rights or rights akin to privacy are given to individuals after their death.

1.9　　　The Act will not apply where the individual cannot be identified from the data on its own or with other information. The Act does not apply to information about limited companies – who by definition are not living individuals. However, it does apply to expressions of opinion about a person. So, for example, a solicitors firm might have a secret internal directory of barristers they have used and what the staff think of them. It might name Mr Z and say: 'I would never work with him again, pompous and slow' or 'absolutely brilliant, great with clients'. This would be information about a living individual and an expression of opinion about that person. It would therefore be 'personal data' under the definition in s 1(1).

Relevant filing system

1.10 Section 1(1) also defines a relevant filing system. This means:

> '... any set of information relating to individuals to the extent that, although the information is not processed by means of equipment operating automatically in response to instructions given for that purpose, the set is structured, either by reference to individuals or by reference to criteria relating to individuals, in such a way that specific information relating to a particular individual is readily accessible.'

Application of the Act to manual records

1.11 One of the problems commentators have had with the Act is in deciding what manual records are covered by the legislation. In order to determine whether specific manual records are covered, it is necessary to apply the above definition to them.

It is only a limited category of manual records which are caught:

- they form part of a structured set;
- the structuring is by reference to individuals, such as by means of unique personal identification numbers;
- structuring is done so that specific information about individuals is readily available.

Example
The following example was used by Lord Williams of Mostyn in a House of Lords debate on 16 March 1998 on the Bill:

> 'We do not wish the definition to apply to miscellaneous collections of paper about individuals, even if the collections are assembled in a file with the individual's name or other unique identifier on the front, if specific data about the individual cannot be readily extracted from that collection.
>
> An example might be a personnel file with my name on the front. Let us assume that the file contains every piece of paper or other document about me which the personnel section has collected over the course of my career; and those papers are held in the file in date order, with no means of readily identifying specific information about me except by looking at every document. The Government's clear intention is that such files should not be caught. We want to catch only those records from which specific information about individuals can be readily extracted.'

Lord Williams then went on to contrast this example with a sickness record which is part of a structured set as it gives specific information about the person it relates to. It would appear that those whose manual files are well ordered and structured are caught, whereas the disorganised will be outside the scope of the Act.

1.12   If a garage places customer information into an unsorted filing tray then it is not caught by the Act because this is not a relevant filing system. The information is not ordered in such a way that it is readily accessible. However, if it had a set of index cards with customers' names and addresses in alphabetical order, then the Act would apply and for the first time there will be an obligation to comply with data protection legislation in relation to that information and to register under the 1998 Act in due course.

1.13   The Act refers to processing by reference to 'criteria relating to individuals', which is not an easy phrase to interpret. All manner of things relate to individuals such as their hair colour or qualifications, postcodes or national insurance numbers.

1.14   'Specific information' on a file means information which is distinguished from other information in the file and accessible separately. Presumably, this could be by attaching yellow stickers, for example, to particular documents labelling them as 'sickness record', 'wage rises', 'appraisals', etc, or by inserting dividers in the file. It is still not clear exactly what will amount to a sufficient structure to make the Act apply.

1.15   The provisions in respect of manual records, however, are not expected to come into force until 24 October 2001 as the Government has indicated that there will be a three-year transitional period beyond the date by which the Directive should have been implemented (24 October 1998) before the data protection regime is extended beyond computer records. Potentially, the definition of 'relevant filing system' and thus 'data' could extend to handwritten notes, entries in a diary, voice mail and telephone calls which are recorded. Such items would not have been covered by the 1984 Act. There is doubt as to whether new manual records created after the Act comes into force will benefit from the three-year transitional period. The Commissioner's regulations/guidance are awaited with interest in this regard.

Action on manual records

1.16   All data controllers will need to ascertain which records held within their company will be caught by the Act, in particular the provisions relating to manual records. They will need to identify what relevant filing systems they hold and determine how they propose to control the use of the systems and the information in them once the manual records provisions are in force. Since individuals have a right of access to their personal data and this will extend to manual records, the controller will need to be able to provide such access. If Mrs Bloggs wants to see the handwritten notes Mr Smith from the personnel department made when he was taking down her details and which he then filed, the company will need to know that they exist and ensure that copies can be provided, if such handwritten notes fall within the relevant definitions described in this chapter.

Transitional provisions and manual records: Sch 8

1.17   Schedule 8 provides that 'eligible manual data', other than data forming part of an accessible record, are exempt for the first transitional period (which ends on

23 October 2001). 'Eligible manual data' are defined in Sch 8, para 1(2) as eligible data which are not eligible automated data. 'Eligible automated data' are data which fall within paras (a) and (b) of the definition of 'data' in s 1(1) of the Act (discussed above) – which would cover data held on computer, for example, but not manual data.

1.18   Most importantly of all, data are 'eligible data' under para 1(1) of Sch 8:

> 'at any time if, and to the extent that, they are at that time subject to processing which was already under way immediately before 24th October 1998.'

1.19   During the first transitional period, the data are exempt from the data protection principles in Sch 1, Part I and from Parts II and III of the Act, except that they are not exempt from the sixth principle (processing in accordance with data subject's rights) as far as it relates to ss 7 and 12A (see further Chapter 3). However, the transitional provision here does not apply to eligible manual data which is 'information relevant to the financial standing of the data subject and in respect of which the data controller is a credit reference agency' (Sch 8, para 4).

1.20   Eligible manual data held before 24 October 1998 are given exemption for the second transitional period too (ie until 24 October 2007). This exemption is from the first to the fifth data protection principles, with one exception, and from certain other provisions. There are special provisions for eligible manual data processed for the purposes of historical research.

1.21   It is confusing that the definition of eligible data refers to data being subject to processing before 24 October 1998 and then provides an extra transitional period for data held before that date. The definition of eligible data appears to apply only to data held before that date. The answer is in the wording of Sch 8. To be eligible, the data do not have to be held before 24 October 1998. Instead, they must be subject to processing, and the processing (presumably not necessarily of the same data) must have begun before that date.

1.22   Readers must read Sch 8 as regards the transitional provisions when considering what to do about existing and new manual data. The provisions are much more complex than briefly summarised above and in the early stages of all new legislation the transitional provisions are often the most important of all. The Commissioner's guidelines will assist in due course.

Processing

1.23   According to s 1(1) of the Act, 'processing':

> 'in relation to personal data, means obtaining, recording or holding the information or data or carrying out any operation or set of operations on the information or data, including –
>
> (a)   organisation, adaptation or alteration of the information or data,
> (b)   retrieval, consultation or use of the information or data,
> (c)   disclosure of the information or data by transmission, dissemination or otherwise making available, or
> (d)   alignment, combination, blocking, erasure or destruction of the information or data.'

1.24   It is only where personal data is processed that the Act applies. However, as 'processing' includes the holding and obtaining of data, most of the activities which may be undertaken in relation to data will be covered. It is not clear whether this definition would include simple erasure or destruction of data by someone who has not been involved with the data. In the *Questions to Answer* document (April 1996), the Data Protection Registrar raised the question of whether the Directive would cover a company which recycled computer disks where there was personal data on those disks. The position remains unclear.

1.25   'Obtaining' or 'recording' of personal data is defined in s 1(2) in relation to personal data as including obtaining or recording the information to be contained in the data. 'Using' or 'disclosing' in relation to personal data includes using or disclosing the information contained in the data. There is no express inclusion of data-matching activities in the Act, although given the broad wording of the definition of processing this may well be included.

Processing under enactments

1.26   Where data is processed because of an enactment such as an Act of Parliament or statutory instrument and this is done solely for that purpose, the person on whom the obligation to process the data is imposed by the relevant law is the person who is deemed to be the data controller.

CCTV and related systems

1.27   When the Bill was before the House of Lords Committee on 23 February 1998, debate ensued about whether amendments were required to clarify whether the Act applied to CCTV surveillance systems used to prevent crime and civil disorder and other digital technology. In Recital 14 of the Directive, it is provided that:

> 'in the framework of the information society, of the techniques used to capture, transmit, record, store or communicate sound and image data relating to natural persons, this Directive should be applicable to processing involving such data.'

1.28   The Government therefore believed that the Bill, as it then was, already encompassed such data held on such systems. Indeed, Lord Williams of Mostyn (Parliamentary Under-Secretary of State to the Home Office) commented that the words 'operating automatically in response to instructions given for that purpose' covered 'text or image, and storage and other processing'. The Government also believed that the 'processing' covers storage, and therefore the new definitions are broad enough to catch not only 'sophisticated types of CCTV but much simpler equipment also, for example the sort of equipment which merely projects images of individuals passing a shop into the shop window, without recording those images'. Therefore, no amendment to the Bill was required.

1.29   The conclusion therefore must be, given the clear wording in the recital to the Directive, and the intention of Parliament, that CCTV and similar systems are caught by the Act, notwithstanding that the images stored are people's faces rather than text descriptions about the individuals. It follows that the Act could also apply to other information so stored, such as DNA profiles of individuals, photographs held by photography agencies or museums, or even pictures of oil paintings of live individuals which are scanned onto a computer system or sold as postcards at the relevant museum. However, if the effect of the application of the Act is analysed, in most cases, the relevant body using the information will already be registered under the Act and therefore will simply need to ensure that it follows the principles set out in the Act so that the burden of application will not be onerous.

1.30   The defeated amendment referred to above would have limited the definition to information which is text or image. It is therefore likely that it would have removed from the scope of the Act items such as the processing of binary codes by computer and other forms of information processing such as radio waves which the Government was specifically trying to cover.

Word processing

1.31   The definition of 'processing' in the 1998 Act and indeed in the Directive is much broader than that under the 1984 Act. For example, s 1(8) of the 1984 Act allowed an exclusion for simple word processing which the Government has been constrained to include in the 1998 Act because of the provisions of the Directive. In the House of Lords debate on the Bill on 23 February 1998, the Government did comment however that:

> 'We wonder whether there is a problem in practice. Text preparation in the form of word processing will be, to a considerable extent – possibly almost always – done as an adjustment to other processing which itself is likely to be caught by the Bill. Therefore, the application of the Bill to word processing is unlikely to bring any additional significant burdens.'

Processing for export from the EEA

1.32   If the information were to be processed or to form part of a filing system only after being transferred to a country outside the European Economic Area (EEA), the Act would still apply. Section 1(3) states that such an intention is immaterial to whether or not the Act applies. The countries of the EEA are:

–   Austria;
–   Belgium;
–   Denmark;
–   Finland;
–   France;
–   Germany;
–   Greece;
–   Holland;
–   Iceland;
–   Ireland;
–   Italy;
–   Liechtenstein;
–   Luxembourg;
–   Norway;
–   Portugal;

– Spain;
– Sweden; and
– the UK.

1.33   Someone who discloses personal data to a person in a country or territory or who otherwise makes the information contained in the data available to a person in a country or territory is taken to have transferred the data to that country or territory. As there are restrictions on the export of personal data to countries where data protection laws are not as tight as in the EU, this is a very important provision. For example, there may be cases where a data controller puts personal data on its internet web site. This can be accessed in any country in the world using the internet. Many, probably most, of these countries will not fulfil the provisions necessary to permit the export of such data and therefore that data controller who originally put the data on the internet will be in breach of the Act.

Web sites and data
1.34   Everyone should therefore check thoroughly the information they have on their web sites and whether it amounts to personal data; in many cases it will not. It is not currently possible to block internet access to particular countries, although some countries such as China have sought by local laws to restrict access to the internet for certain sections of their community. In order to overcome the difficulty of compliance with all local laws in relation to the content of their internet web pages, businesses often specify that: (i) English law applies; and (ii) orders are not accepted from certain States – such as those where the product might be illegal (alcohol in Muslim countries, for example). However, this does not overcome the data export problem. It is anticipated that the European Commission may produce a list of approved countries for export of data, similar to that produced by the US, of countries which meet its requirements for intellectual property protection locally, or that it may even draw up instead a blacklist of those countries to which export is prohibited. At the date of writing, EU discussions on this are continuing. Discussions of this sort would be very useful for those seeking to place personal data on the internet as they will find it hard technically to restrict access to data to those from countries with adequate data protection laws. The eighth data protection principle which prohibits data export from the EEA to countries without an adequate level of data protection is discussed in more detail at **2.40–2.42**.

1.35   In the House of Lords debate on the Bill on 10 July 1998, Lord Avebury raised this issue, asking what the situation was concerning dissemination of information via the worldwide web:

'A case has recently come to my attention where information relating to the sexual orientation and religious beliefs of an individual was placed on a website. The service provider was approached by the individual and asked to take the information off the web. He did so in circumstances where, I understand, the interpretation of s 1 of the Defamation Act was not clear as applying to service providers. He was afraid that litigation against him might ensue as the publisher of that material. If we disregard that and the application of this clause to service providers, is there not an additional danger that where those operating websites place information in relation to an individual on a page it becomes available to anyone in any country and would seem to be caught by this part of the Bill?'

Sensitive personal data

1.36   'Data' and 'personal data' were defined above. Section 2 of the Act defines 'sensitive personal data'. This is personal data which consists of information as to:

'(a)   racial or ethnic origin of the data subject,

(b)   his political opinions,

(c)   his religious beliefs or other beliefs of a similar nature,

(d)   whether he is a member of a trade union (within the meaning of the Trade Union and Labour Relations (Consolidation) Act 1992),

(e)   his physical or mental health or condition,

(f)   his sexual life,

(g)   the commission or alleged commission by him of any offence, or

(h)   any proceedings for any offence committed or alleged to have been committed by him, the disposal of such proceedings or the sentence of any court in such proceedings.'

1.37   The Act and Article 8 of the Directive prohibit processing of sensitive data except in specified cases where safeguards are imposed. Under s 2(3) of the 1984 Act, the Secretary of State was allowed to modify the level of data protection for certain similar types of sensitive data but this authority was never used, which means that the new Act is therefore stronger than the 1984 Act. The detail of how such sensitive data may be used will be examined later. Here, the definitions are considered.

Racial or ethnic origin

1.38   It will normally be clear what this means. There are many employment law cases concerning whether discrimination is 'racial' in nature, determining such questions as whether 'gypsies' are a race, whether Irish jokes breach the legislation, etc.

Political opinions

1.39   Britain is known throughout the world as being tolerant of different political opinions, even to the extent of being accused by certain Arab States of harbouring terrorists. This provision will ensure continued protection for those whose political beliefs may be extreme or simply different from those of the majority.

Religious or other beliefs

1.40   Although religious discrimination is not prohibited under any UK statute, except in certain specific legislation in Northern Ireland or where it may also amount to racial or sexual discrimination, there is no need in many cases for information about religious beliefs to be held by data controllers – hence the inclusion of this type of information in the list of sensitive data. However, in some cases it is perfectly proper to hold such data, such as where a Roman Catholic school is amassing information about prospective parents of children applying for entry to the school.

1.41   In earlier drafts of the Bill, the section referred simply to 'religious or other beliefs' which could have covered any beliefs – such as whether the government of the day was bad. This was sensibly changed in the Act to 'religious or other beliefs of a similar nature'. There is no definition of 'belief of a similar nature'. It may, for example, include the information that an individual is an atheist or practises witchcraft. Is vegetarianism a belief similar to religion, or beliefs about the rightness or otherwise of abortion or whether children should be smacked? It is submitted that in order to be caught by the Act the belief in question must be related to the meaning of religion in some way or another rather than being of the kind of more general beliefs described in the examples above.

1.42   Article 8 of the Data Protection Directive refers to 'religious or philosophical beliefs', and it is a pity that the Government has not used the same words although this wording was referred to in the debate of 10 July 1998. The Government believes that 'of a similar nature' 'captures more precisely the data which the Directive requires to be treated as sensitive'.

Membership of trade unions

1.43   Many employers have historically tried to weed out troublemakers in their midst by seeking either not to recruit, or else to choose for redundancy or dismissal, those who are active in or who are simply members of a trade union. The White Paper *Fairness at Work* (May 1998), if and when it is implemented by legislation, will require an employer to recognise trade unions where a majority of those voting in a ballot, and at least 40% of those eligible to vote, are in favour of recognition where there are more than 20 employees working for that employer. Membership of a trade union is therefore a category of sensitive data.

Health

1.44   This covers physical and mental health. Not only is it broadly illegal to discriminate on the grounds of disability under the Disability Discrimination Act 1995, in relation to the processing of their personal data, it is irrelevant whether or not someone has a disability.

Sexual life

1.45   Whether an individual is homosexual, has taken a vow of chastity or is happily married is to be treated as sensitive personal data. There are no current laws prohibiting discrimination on the grounds of sexual orientation, so, for example, a fundamentalist Christian employer could require that only non-homosexual members of staff who were either married or celibate be recruited as long as no racial discrimination or sexual discrimination was found to have occurred. It is also contrary to the Sex Discrimination Act 1975 to discriminate on the grounds of marital status. The House of Lords was not happy with the expression 'sexual life' as the Bill went through Parliament. Indeed, Viscount Astor commented that it is not clear what this includes:

> 'It might include lots of different things in Scotland than it might not include in England, as we know.'

Offences or proceedings regarding offences

1.46   Criminal convictions are treated in a special way under the Act but are regarded as sensitive personal data for these purposes.

Data controllers and processors

1.47　Many of the obligations under the Act fall upon the person who controls personal data. The 'data controller' is defined as a person who either alone, or jointly, or in common with other persons, determines the purposes for which, and the manner in which, any personal data are, or are to be, processed subject to s 1(4). Section 1(4) provides that, where personal data are processed only for purposes required by an enactment (law), the person on whom the obligation to process the data is imposed by or under the enactment is taken to be the data controller for the purposes of the Act.

1.48　Under s 1(1), 'data processors' are those who, in relation to personal data, process data on behalf of a data controller. However, this does not apply to people who are employees of the data controller. If employees carry out the processing for their employer, then the employer is both the data controller and the data processor.

Controllers and internet service providers

1.49　When the Bill was debated in the House of Lords on 23 February 1998, consideration was given to identifying the person doing the processing when messages are sent by internet or by telephone. Lord Williams of Mostyn said:

> '[If] I used the internet to send a message, I, not the internet service provider, would be the controller for any personal data used in the system underpinning the message. … The internet service provider has no part in the determination of the process so he cannot be controller for the message content. However he does determine the process and manner of processing of any personal data used in the support of the message – for instance if I am to be billed for use of the service. In the billing context, the service provider is the controller not I who simply use the service which the service provider provides.'

1.50　Case-law in the USA has held that in some States where the internet service provider controls the content of discussion groups, such as by vetting, editing and checking, it can be liable in damages for the content of those messages whereas if it acts simply like a telephone company and allows all calls through without checks, no liability ensues.

No exemption for back-up data

1.51　The Government did consider whether it had power to include an amendment exempting back-up data from the Act but decided that it did not have power to do so. There was such an exemption in the 1984 Act. It believes that, in practice, it will be unlikely that a data subject will want access to back-up data and there is nothing to prevent a controller confirming that a data subject wishes to access only the most recent records. There is a mention of back-up data in Sch 8, para 12, which provides that eligible automated data processed to replace other data which has been lost, destroyed or impaired are exempt from s 7 during the first transitional period (ending on 23 October 2001); but this is not a general exemption for back-up data in the traditional sense.

Data subjects

1.52　The term 'data subject' is used throughout the Act and is defined in s 1(1) as 'an individual who is the subject of personal data'. A data subject cannot be a limited company or other legal entity but only an individual. Of course, since a partnership comprises individuals it can be subject to the Act in the sense that information held about the partners will be personal data about those individuals.

Special purposes

1.53   The final definition is that of 'special purposes' in s 3. This means the purposes of journalism, artistic purposes and literary purposes, and these are the subject of special provisions discussed later in this book.

1.54   In the later chapters of this book, the very important definitions discussed above will be considered in the context of the provisions to which they relate. They are terms used throughout the Act and in some instances case-law will be required to clarify the definitions. In addition, guidance by the Data Protection Commissioner (formerly the Data Protection Registrar) will also assist in construing the relevant provisions.

TO WHOM WILL THE ACT APPLY?

1.55   Section 5 establishes that the Act will apply to data controllers in relation to data only if:

– the data controller is established in the UK and the data are processed 'in the context of that establishment'; or
– the data controller is established neither in the UK nor in any other EEA State but uses equipment in the UK for processing the data otherwise than for the purposes of transit through the UK.

1.56   Thus, since someone processing personal data in Australia would not be established in the UK and would not be using equipment in the UK, the Act would not apply. However, a UK company processing data in the UK would be caught.

Establishment in the UK

1.57   Section 5(2) defines establishment in the UK. Individuals ordinarily resident in the UK are established there. Bodies incorporated under laws of the UK such as a Welsh or English limited company are established here. Partnerships and unincorporated associations formed under the law of any part of the UK would also be caught by the Act. This would include a body set up in the UK, for example a charity or a company limited by guarantee or a members' club to improve the rights of the Kurds or the position of women in Afghanistan. Also classed as established in the UK is anyone who maintains in the UK an 'office, branch or agency through which he carries on any activity, or a regular practice'. The equivalent meaning is given to establishments in other EEA States. Thus, a US company with a commercial agent acting in the UK (although not an independent distributor) would be classed as established in the UK for these purposes, as would a Japanese company with an office in the UK. If orders for goods are taken from the UK through advertising in UK journals, but the orders are placed, in, say, Japan or over the internet, then it seems that there is no office, branch or agency. Lord Renton in the House of Lords debate on the Bill of 10 August 1998 raised the point that 'established' is a rather vague word: 'It could mean "residing" or someone who has an office in the UK but moves about the world'. He did not think s 5(2) was adequate. The Government's response was that the term has the same meaning as in EC law generally.

1.58   However, if a 'regular practice' is maintained in the UK, then the Act applies. What is a 'regular practice'? Can it mean a course of conduct such as soliciting sales via the internet or through internationally sold journals via mail order, or must it mean practising from an establishment in the traditional sense of bricks and mortar, or through a local agent? The Act is not clear.

1.59   The definitions of 'data', 'personal data' and 'processing' make no reference to activities taking place in the UK or relating to UK or EEA nationals. Today, much processing is carried out outside the country to which the data relates. When self-assessment tax was introduced in the UK, the Inland Revenue first intended that all processing would be carried out in the UK, but this was quickly abandoned on cost grounds and data was shipped abroad. Section 1(3) provides that it is immaterial if the information is to be processed only once it has left the EEA: the Act still applies. On the other hand, a Japanese company might have its personal data about Japanese mail order customers processed in the UK. For the purposes of this example, it will be assumed that the Japanese company has a small data processing operation in north east England where many other Japanese companies have set up operations and taken advantage of regional grants. Thus, as the Japanese company has 'an establishment, office, agent or other practice in the UK', even though the data relates solely to Japanese citizens, the 1998 Act must be followed. The company is treated as established in the UK.

1.60   Section 54 exempts certain international operations from these provisions, including where the Secretary of State orders the Commissioner (the Data Protection Registrar's title under the 1998 Act: see **1.61** below) to carry out an international obligation of the UK in relation to data protection.

THE COMMISSIONER

1.61   As a final introductory subject in Part I of the Act, s 6 provides that the Data Protection Registrar's office shall continue, but shall be known as the office of the Data Protection Commissioner. The head will be known as the Commissioner and will be appointed by Her Majesty. It is anticipated that Mrs Elizabeth France, the current Data Protection Registrar, will continue as the first Commissioner.

1.62   Schedule 5 sets out more detailed provisions concerning the Commissioner. The Commissioner continues to be a corporation sole in law, and she and her officers are not to be regarded as servants or agents of the Crown. The initial term of service of the Commissioner shall not exceed five years and a Commissioner must retire at the age of 65 or after a maximum of 15 years of service. No one can be reappointed for a third or subsequent term unless this is desirable in the public interest. A salary will continue to be paid as now and it will be set by the House of Commons. The Commissioner decides on and appoints the deputy commissioners and other members of staff and decides on their remuneration. Other parts of Sch 5 deal with payments to the Commissioner, accounts, the Commissioner's seal and the authenticity of documents issued by the Commissioner.

THE TRIBUNAL

1.63   There will continue to be a data protection tribunal which consists of a chairman appointed by the Lord Chancellor, and deputy chairmen and members appointed by the Secretary of State. To be appointed members of the tribunal, individuals must have seven years of legal service as defined in s 6(5) of the Act. The members shall be appointed either to represent the interests of data subjects or the interests of data controllers.

1.64   Schedule 5 also provides more detail on the tribunal. Members may resign; and the chairman and deputy chairman must do so at the age of 70. The Secretary of State decides what remuneration or allowances are paid to members of the tribunal.

Chapter 2

THE DATA PROTECTION PRINCIPLES

INTRODUCTION

2.1 This chapter examines the data protection principles which lie at the heart of the 1998 Act and, in particular, the obligations which they impose on data controllers and data processors. As under the 1984 Act, the 1998 Act imposes general and, in some cases, fairly loosely worded obligations on those handling data as to how they obtain and use that data. Section 4(4) provides that it is the duty of the data controller to comply with the data protection principles in relation to all personal data in respect of which he is the data controller. This obligation is subject to s 27 which exempts certain data which is covered by Part IV of the Act. This Part provides a total exemption for some data, whilst other data is exempt from only some of the obligations.

2.2 The data protection principles are set out in Sch 1 to the Act.

THE FIRST PRINCIPLE: FAIR AND LAWFUL PROCESSING

2.3 Schedule 1, Part I, para 1 states:

'Personal data shall be processed fairly and lawfully and, in particular, shall not be processed unless –

(a) at least one of the conditions in Schedule 2 is met, and
(b) in the case of sensitive personal data, at least one of the conditions in Schedule 3 is also met.'

2.4 Fair and lawful processing was also a principle in the 1984 Act. Part II of Sch 1 provides that regard should be had to the method by which the data are obtained, including whether any person from whom they are obtained is deceived or misled as to the purpose or purposes for which they are to be processed. Data controllers therefore have to be constantly vigilant to ensure they do not deceive data subjects about the use to which their data will be put. Data are deemed to be fairly obtained if they consist of information obtained from a person who is authorised by a law (enactment) or an international obligation to supply them.

2.5 Where data are obtained from the data subject, they are not fairly obtained *unless* the data controller ensures that 'so far as practicable that the data subject has, is provided with, or has made readily available to him' the following information as specified in Sch 1, Part II, para 2(3):

(a) the identity of the data controller;

(b) the identity of any representative appointed for the purposes of the Act by that data controller;

(c) the purpose or purposes for which the data are intended to be processed; and

(d) any further information which is necessary, having regard to the specific circumstances in which the data are to be processed, to enable the processing in respect of the data subject to be fair.

2.6   Where the data are obtained otherwise than from the data subject they must be provided to him before or as soon as reasonably practicable after 'the relevant time' – ie the time when the data are first processed or when data are disclosed to that third party within the time envisaged. If the data controller becomes aware that the data will not be disclosed within that period of time, then the 'relevant time' is the time when the data controller becomes aware of this delay or should have become aware of it or, at the latest, at the end of the reasonable period after which the data are to be disclosed to a third party.

2.7   Whilst this may seem a complicated provision it should not cause difficulties in practice except for the problem of determining what is a 'reasonable time'. Data controllers should be advised to specify a period in writing when obtaining information from data users.

Example

Company A Ltd sends out surveys about shopping habits to thousands of people in the UK. Respondents are asked to provide personal data including their names and addresses, personal income details, whether they smoke, have pets, have private health insurance, etc. Company A should include a statement on the form such as the following:

Data Protection Act 1998

The Data Controller is Company A Ltd.

The data you provide will be passed on to companies involved with the marketing of goods or services who may contact you about other goods and services in which you might be interested [*expand purpose where possible to comply with the second principle – see* **2.11** *below*].

Your data will be processed for market research purposes [*it may be necessary to expand on this*].

2.8   However, readers should also note that the Commissioner is likely to issue guidance on the first principle in due course, and this should be noted since guidance is often fuller than the wording in the Act. Note that the information does not have to be provided to the data subject but only made 'readily available' to him. 'Readily available' is not, unfortunately, defined in the Act, but may be assumed to cover the information being made available on demand in response to a telephone call or, where personal data are solicited in an internet survey, the data subject could access the information by clicking on an information box.

2.9   Information need not be provided at all where it is not obtained from the data subject where the provision of that information would involve a 'disproportionate' effort or where the data are recorded or disclosed for the purposes of compliance with a legal obligation to which the data controller is subject, other than an obligation imposed by contract.

General identifiers

2.10   A general identifier is an indication such as a number or code used for identification purposes which relates to an individual and forms part of a set of similar identifiers which is of general application. The issue has arisen as to whether the use of general identifiers complies with the requirements of fair and lawful processing (the first principle). The Secretary of State, by Sch 1, Part II, para 4, may specify that certain conditions are met when data which are subject to a general identifier are processed. At the date of writing, no such regulations have been drafted.

THE SECOND PRINCIPLE: PURPOSES

2.11   Under Sch 1, Part I, para 2:

> 'Personal data shall be obtained only for one or more specified and lawful purposes, and shall not be further processed in any manner incompatible with that purpose or those purposes.'

2.12   The information about the purposes to which the data will be put may be notified to the data subject by way of a notice or in a notification to the Commissioner under Part III of the Act (which is discussed in Chapter 4 below). An example of a notice which fulfils the requirements of the first principle was given at **2.7** above. In deciding whether a disclosure of personal data is compatible with the purpose(s) for which they were obtained, regard is had to the purpose(s) for which the personal data are intended to be processed by any person to whom they are disclosed. For example, Company A may obtain data from mail order customers so that it can supply goods and then send them an annual catalogue and details of special offers throughout the year. They may also sell on the list of customers to other non-competing companies so that they can do likewise. Company A must inform the customer of all the purposes for which the data may be used, including any purposes for which they may be used by other companies.

2.13   Recital 27 of the Data Protection Directive requires that the purposes for which the data are held must be 'explicit and legitimate and must be determined at the time of collection of the data'.

THE THIRD PRINCIPLE: ADEQUATE, RELEVANT AND NOT EXCESSIVE DATA

2.14   Under Sch 1, Part I, para 3:

> 'Personal data shall be adequate, relevant and not excessive in relation to the purpose or purposes for which they are processed.'

2.15   There is no explanation of this provision in Part II of Sch 1. However, this principle is virtually identical to the fourth principle of the 1984 Act. It means that data controllers must make sure that they obtain enough data, but not too much, and not irrelevant data. Data controllers need to ascertain the minimum amount of information which they require in order to carry out the purpose for which the data is to be held. In *Runnymede Community Charge Registration Officer v Data Protection Registrar* [1990] RVR 236, the Data Protection Tribunal, in considering the similar provisions of the 1984 Act, held that where information is required in relation to certain individuals, it is not reasonable to hold such additional data in relation to all individuals. As the Registrar said in her *Guidelines* under the 1984 Act (November 1994 issue) at p 62:

> 'Where a data user holds an item of information on all individuals which will be used or useful only in relation to some of then, the information is likely to be excessive and irrelevant in relation to those individuals in respect of whom it will not be used or useful and should not be held in those cases. It is not acceptable to hold information on the basis that it might possibly be useful in the future without a view of how it will be used. This is to be distinguished from holding information in the case of a particular foreseeable contingency which may never occur, for example, where a data user holds blood groups of employees engaged in hazardous occupations.'

2.16   The factors which the Registrar considered under the 1984 Act, in relation to this principle where an item of data is held for all, but not required for all, data subjects were:

–   the number of individuals on whom it is held;
–   the number of individuals for whom it is used;
–   the nature of that item of personal data;
–   the length of time for which it is held;
–   the way it was obtained;
–   the possible consequences for individuals of its holding or erasure;
–   the way in which it is used;
–   the purpose for which it is held.

2.17   The Registrar also had regard to Codes of Practice under the 1984 Act for particular industries.

2.18   The Registrar has taken an objective view on whether information is relevant and this approach is likely to continue under the new law.

THE FOURTH PRINCIPLE: ACCURATE AND UP-TO-DATE DATA

2.19   The fourth principle, as set out in Sch 1, Part I, para 4, states:

> 'Personal data shall be accurate and, where necessary, kept up to date.'

It is a matter of fact whether data are incorrect or misleading in each case. Data are not treated as inaccurate for these purposes where the data subject himself supplies inaccurate information nor where a third party does so if, having regard to the purposes for which the data have been obtained and further processed, the data controller has taken reasonable steps to ensure the accuracy of the data and, if the data subject has notified the data controller of the data subject's view that the data are inaccurate, the data indicate that fact.

2.20   This fourth principle uses exactly the words of the fifth principle of the 1984 Act and so will be familiar to those already operating under existing English law. Under the old law and, it is submitted, the new, an expression of opinion cannot be challenged on the grounds of inaccuracy.

2.21   When considering compliance with the fourth principle, the Commissioner will examine whether the data controller has taken steps necessary to ensure inaccuracies do not occur in the data in deciding what action to take. Factors under the 1984 Act which are also likely to be relevant under the new include:

– the significance of the inaccuracy. Has it caused or is it likely to cause damage or distress to the data subject?
– the source from which the inaccurate information was obtained. Was it reasonable for the data user to rely on information from that source?
– any steps taken to verify the information. Did the data user attempt to check its accuracy with another source? Would it have been reasonable to ask the data subject, either at the time of collection or at another convenient opportunity, whether the information was accurate?
– the procedures for data entry and for ensuring that the system itself does not introduce inaccuracies into the data;
– the procedures followed by the data user when the inaccuracy came to light. Were the data corrected as soon as the inaccuracy became apparent? Was the correction passed on to any third parties to whom the inaccurate data may already have been disclosed? Did the inaccuracy have any other consequences in the period before it was corrected? If so, what has the data user done about those consequences?

2.22   The obligation to keep data up to date applies only 'where necessary' and this was also the case under the 1984 Act. It is sensible for mail order companies, for example, when they send mailings to customers, to include a slip or notice for customers to send in changes of address. This is normal practice. If the data were intended as an historical record only, then updating would not be necessary and, indeed, would defeat the object of the exercise. The Commissioner will be concerned to see:

– whether any record has been kept of the date when the information was recorded or last updated;
– whether those involved will be aware or will have been made aware that the data do not necessarily reflect the current position;
– whether the data controller takes steps at regular intervals to update data and whether those steps are adequate; and
– whether the fact data may be out of date is likely to cause damage or distress to the data subject.

THE FIFTH PRINCIPLE: DATA NOT TO BE KEPT LONGER THAN PURPOSES REQUIRE

2.23   Under Sch 1, Part I, para 5:

'Personal data processed for any purpose or purposes shall not be kept for longer than is necessary for that purpose or those purposes.'

2.24   There is no elaboration on this principle in Part II of Sch 1. The wording, however, is the same as in the sixth principle of the 1984 Act and so does not change the law. Under the 1984 Act, and thus under the new Act, there is an obligation to review data regularly and delete what is no longer required. The Registrar has recommended that users have a systematic policy of data deletion. Users may have a standard policy of retaining particular categories of data for a specified duration. The appropriate period for keeping data is a difficult and important issue. The Institute of Chartered Secretaries and Administrators has issued guidance on the topic but all companies should take advice from their solicitors. It is desirable that some types of records are kept for very long periods. In a case of alleged fraud, for example, the Inland Revenue may wish to consult records from earlier than the normal six-year retention period. In respect of a document signed as a deed there is a 12-year limitation period after which legal actions cannot be brought and, consequently, it is advisable for the documents in this category to be held for at least this period. There are different rules for such information as health and safety records and employee records generally. If the data has only a short-term value to the data controller then it may be right for the data to be deleted after a matter of days or months. The important consideration is that the data controller must analyse its reasonable requirements and decide what is or is not an appropriate period in each case.

2.25   The Registrar has always recognised that, even where the relationship between the data subject and the data controller has come to an end, there are good reasons for retaining data, for instance, because they may be relevant to a legal action mounted at a later date. However, only information relevant to a potential claim should be kept and the rest should be destroyed. Once the possibility of a claim has passed then the data should be deleted unless there is another good reason why they should be retained. Remember that, although the limitation period for contract actions is six years from when the contract was made, for actions in tort such as negligence, the limitation period may only begin to run from the date on which the damage occurs (or is discovered). (See Limitation Act 1980.) Therefore, the data controller should assess its retention policies on the basis of the latest date at which an action could be brought in relation to that particular data.

THE SIXTH PRINCIPLE: DATA PROCESSED IN ACCORDANCE WITH DATA SUBJECTS' RIGHTS

2.26   The sixth principle, set out at Sch 1, Part I, para 6, states:

'Personal data shall be processed in accordance with the rights of data subjects under this Act.'

This provision is breached if, but only if, a person contravenes:

- s 7 of the Act by failing to supply information which has been duly requested in accordance with that section;
- s 10 or s 11 by failing to comply with a notice duly given under those sections; or
- s 12 by failing to give a notice under that section.

These provisions are considered in Chapter 3 below.

THE SEVENTH PRINCIPLE: MEASURES TO STOP LOSS: SECURITY MEASURES

2.27   Under Sch 1, Part I, para 7:

> 'Appropriate technical and organisational measures shall be taken against unauthorised or unlawful processing of personal data and against accidental loss or destruction of, or damage to, personal data.'

This principle means that those holding data must take steps to stop that data being unlawfully processed. For instance, they must take reasonable measures to stop hackers getting into their system and to prevent other breaches of security. Part II of Sch 1 provides that in assessing compliance with this principle regard is to be had to the state of technological development and the cost of implementing measures. Accordingly, a large company holding a substantial amount of highly secret data would be expected to have more expensive protective measures in place than a one-man garage in a back street with a set of index cards. However, even a local newsagent must take measures to ensure that the details of names and home addresses of data subjects on its computer screens and paper records cannot be seen by other customers. Such a breach led to censure by the Registrar under the 1984 Act in an earlier case involving visibility of a computer screen by other customers.

2.28   Having regard to technical and costs factors, the data controller must ensure security of a level which is appropriate to the nature of the data to protect against unauthorised or unlawful processing or accidental loss, destruction or damage as required by the seventh principle. Data controllers must also take reasonable steps to ensure that staff who have access to the personal data are reliable. For example, before recruiting a data entry clerk, it would be sensible to take up references and to check whether applicants have a police record. The old guidelines under the 1984 Act suggested that data protection controllers should consider the following questions:

- Is proper weight given to the discretion and integrity of staff when they are being considered for employment or promotion or for a move to an area where they will have access to personal data?
- Are the staff aware of their responsibilities? Have they been given adequate training and is their knowledge kept up to date? For example, even expert data protection managers in large companies dealing with a substantial amount of data will need education on the changes to the law under the 1998 Act; in-house seminars should be held for staff. It should not be assumed that new staff will have any knowledge at all of data protection law.
- Do disciplinary rules and procedures take account of the Act's requirements and are they enforced? If everyone knows that the company's rules in this area are more honoured in the breach then the rules may as well not exist.

–   If an employee is found to be unreliable, is his authority to access personal data immediately withdrawn?

2.29   Much processing will be carried out by data processors rather than the data controller. The definitions of these terms were examined in Chapter 1. Where the processing is carried out by a data processor on behalf of a data controller, then the data controller must, in order to comply with the seventh principle, ensure that the data processor provides sufficient guarantees in respect of the technical and organisational security measures governing the processing to be carried out and must take reasonable steps to ensure compliance with those measures. Thus, the principal responsibility for security resides with the data controller. The data controller cannot simply blame the data processor for inadequate security, although the controller could escape liability for breach of the seventh principle by showing that the controller has taken all reasonable steps to ensure that the processor has appropriate measures in place. Indeed, Sch 1, Part II, para 12 provides that where a data processor is entrusted with the processing, the data controller is not to be regarded as complying with the seventh principle unless:

–   the processing is carried out under a contract in writing under which the data processor is to act only on instructions from the data controller; and
–   the contract requires the data processor to comply with obligations equivalent to those imposed on a data controller by the seventh principle.

2.30   This provision has implications for those involved in the drafting of contracts in this field. First, there must be a written contract. Secondly, the contract must require the data processor to act on behalf of the data controller in regard to the processing of data and the contract should provide that the data processor must comply with the seventh principle. Companies which have contracts with data processors should revise these contracts now to ascertain whether they need alteration to ensure compliance with this provision.

2.31   The eighth principle under the 1984 Act was somewhat similar, although not identical, to the seventh principle under the new Act. The Guidelines to the 1984 Act stated that checks should be made on which staff have access to any building or room where the data were stored. Data controllers might like to formulate a survey or questionnaire for completion by prospective data processors including the following questions:

(1) Are passwords known only to authorised persons, and are passwords frequently changed?
(2) Does a password allow access to all parts of a system or just to those parts which hold the personal data with which the employee is concerned? Clearly, it is better if there is limited access only, although whether this is possible or practicable depends on the nature of the data controller or processor and the data itself.
(3) Is the system able to check that the data are valid and does it produce back-up copies? It is also necessary to check whether full use is made of the system's facilities. It is not enough that the system is able to produce back-up copies if no one bothers to make them.
(4) Does the system keep an audit trail so that all access to personal data can be logged and traced back to the person originally gaining access?

2.32   Other relevant questions might concern the precautions which the processor has taken against burglary, fire or natural disaster, and whether passers-by can read data from screens or print-outs. Enquiries should also be made as to whether back-up copies are stored off-site.

2.33   Although these provisions are not expressly included in the new Act they remain as relevant as under the old law. It should also be established whether there is a procedure for cleaning tapes and disks before they are reused or whether they are simply overwritten. It is safer and better to clean rather than overwrite. If they are not cleaned there may be a risk that the data may reach someone who is not authorised to have access to them and such a risk should be assessed. This will become even more important under the 1998 Act when data stored manually are also covered.

2.34   Companies also need to assess their waste disposal arrangements. On a regular basis, news stories appear about building societies or banks whose waste contractors, for whatever reason, have dumped confidential papers in a street or on a rubbish tip when they should have been shredded or disposed of in some other more confidential way. The data controller should look carefully at the contractual conditions it has with waste disposal companies and ensure that they are well-drafted. It is unlikely to be sufficient to engage a contractor with no written conditions or on the contractor's standard conditions of supply, because in either of these circumstances this will be of advantage to the contractor and may exclude or severely limit his liability. Similarly, if waste disposal is outsourced under an outsourcing agreement, the data controller must ensure that the contract for such outsourcing addresses issues of confidentiality and imposes on the outsourcing company corresponding obligations. Clauses on data protection law are quite common in such agreements. The Commissioner believes that shredding is often the best means of disposing of documents which contain personal data.

2.35   A very important security issue arises where personal data, for example, a bank balance, are requested by telephone. It is essential that steps are taken to ensure that the purported identity of the enquirer is genuine. In most instances, it will probably be sufficient to establish the fact by asking questions about the enquirer's date of birth and mother's maiden name or by requiring him to give a particular password. However, the data controller may hold data so secret that disclosure by telephone should not be allowed at all. Staff need precise guidance in this field. They should not assume, for example, that it is acceptable for a husband to be given information about his wife: they may be estranged or may simply want to keep their financial affairs separate.

2.36   It is also wise to have a defined hierarchy amongst those concerned with security of data so that ultimate responsibility lies with one named person. Many larger companies have a 'data protection manager' or 'data protection officer'. This person must be allocated sufficient funds and time to carry out his duties in this regard. He may also be responsible for educating other staff in this field. Data protection law is not very well known in the UK despite the efforts of the Data Protection Registrars over the years. For example, staff should be instructed that although they may have a right to check data on an individual for business purposes they do not have the right to access information for other purposes, such as looking up the name of someone who happens to live down their road or whose wife works with their spouse.

2.37   With the increase in teleworking, some staff now work on data at home. In many ways, jobs relating to processing and use of personal data are very well adapted to such ways of working. However, the employer still needs to ensure that adequate security measures are taken. If the employee is working at the kitchen table with people coming in and out all day able to read information on the screen, then home working for certain particularly sensitive data may not be permissible. A vigilant employer should check the suitability of staff homes (including locks, etc) for these purposes and if arrangements are unsuitable it may be more appropriate for staff to work at a local 'tele-cottage' if there is one or to set aside a dedicated room for their work at home.

2.38   Where breaches do occur, there should be a full investigation. In any contract with a data processor it should be made clear which of the parties is responsible for security of the data. In guidance under the old Act, the Registrar did not regard it as acceptable to use real data for staff training purposes and it is almost certain that fictitious details should continue to be used instead under the 1998 Act. In the 1994 Guidelines, the Registrar also states:

> 'Data users should also ensure that their contracts with computer suppliers and maintenance organisations with regard to the supply and maintenance of equipment and development of programmes, contain adequate safeguards regarding access to personal data by such organisations and their subsequent dealing with it.'

2.39   Data controllers need to assess the harm which may be caused by particular security breaches. In some cases, very little harm will be caused but, in others, considerable damage will result and the security measures taken should reflect these consequences.

THE EIGHTH PRINCIPLE: TRANSFER OF DATA ABROAD

2.40   The eighth principle, as set out at Sch 1, Part I, para 1, states:

> 'Personal data shall not be transferred to a country or territory outside the European Economic Area unless that country or territory ensures an adequate level of protection for the rights and freedoms of data subjects in relation to the processing of personal data.'

This principle was examined in Chapter 1. Paragraph 13 of Sch 1, Part II provides that protection may be determined as adequate having regard in particular to the nature of the data, the country or territory of origin of the information contained in the data, the final destination of the information, the purposes for which and period during which the data are intended to be processed, the law in force in the country in question, the international obligations of that country, any relevant codes of conduct or other rules in force in that country and security measures taken in respect of the data in that country.

Schedule 4

2.41   The eighth principle does not apply in circumstances specified by Sch 4 except as provided by the Secretary of State by order. These exclusions are broad and important. They are:

(1) The data subject has given consent to the transfer. It is not clear if this must be express consent or may also be consent by default. For instance, is it enough to include the following statement when requesting details from data subjects: 'By supplying this information you consent to its being processed in the USA. If you object tick the box below'?

(2) There is a contract between the data subject and the data controller, and to perform that contract the export of the data is necessary or the transfer is necessary for the taking of steps at the request of the data subject with a view to his entering into a contract with the data controller.

(3) The transfer is necessary to conclude a contract between the data controller and someone other than the data subject which the data subject has asked the data controller to enter into or which is in the interests of the data subject. (This is rather broad wording.) There is also an exception where the transfer is necessary for the performance of such a contract.

(4) The transfer is necessary for reasons of substantial public interest. The Secretary of State is given powers to formulate Orders which set out what may fall within this category.

(5) The transfer is necessary for the purpose of or in connection with any legal proceedings, including prospective legal proceedings; for the purpose of obtaining legal advice; or for the purposes of establishing, exercising or defending legal rights.

(6) The transfer is necessary to protect the vital interests of the data subject.

(7) The transfer is of part of the personal data on a public register and any conditions subject to which the register is open to inspection are complied with by any person to whom the data are or may be disclosed after the transfer.

(8) The transfer is made on terms which are of a kind approved by the Commissioner as ensuring adequate safeguards for the rights and freedoms of data subjects.

(9) The transfer has been authorised by the Commissioner as being made in such a manner as to ensure adequate safeguards for the rights and freedoms of data subjects.

2.42   As mentioned in Chapter 1, it is possible that the European Commission will produce an approved list of countries to which the export of data is allowed and whose internal laws suffice. However, even where the local laws are not strong enough for a country to be included on such a list many companies will find the nine exceptions set out here to be useful in ensuring that they are not restricted in their export of data because of the provisions of the eighth principle. In October 1998, the Commissioner was still discussing the issue and the International Chamber of Commerce was producing guidelines.

THE PRINCIPLES: CONCLUSION

2.43   The data protection principles in both the old Act and the new are rather general and very different from the clear legal wording which is often to be found in English statutes. However, they have worked adequately in the past, as supplemented by guidelines from the Registrar (and, no doubt, the Commissioner will issue similar guidelines in future), and where there has been doubt then the courts have laid down the relevant principles. It is assumed that the new rules will operate in the same way with the added advantage of achieving harmonisation with the other EC Member States in most areas of the law.

Chapter 3

RIGHTS OF DATA SUBJECTS

INTRODUCTION

3.1   This chapter examines the rights given by the Act to data subjects, ie those whose data is held subject to the provisions of the Act. Their principal right is one of access: the right to see the data held about them. They also have a right to prevent processing which may cause damage or distress, and for certain direct marketing purposes. Rights are given to data subjects to seek compensation for damage and/or distress caused by a failure to comply with the Act. All these provisions are contained in Part II of the Act.

RIGHTS OF ACCESS

3.2   Individuals are given the following rights by s 7(1) of the Act:

- to be informed by any data controller as to whether personal data of which they are the data subject are being processed by or on behalf of that data controller;
- where the above applies, to be given by the data controller a description of the personal data concerned, the purposes for which they are being processed and the recipients or classes of recipients to whom they are disclosed or may be disclosed;
- to have communicated to them in an intelligible form the information constituting the personal data, and any information available to the controller as to the source of the data; and
- where the processing by automatic means has constituted or is likely to constitute the sole basis for a decision significantly affecting the data subject, to be informed by the data controller of the 'logic involved in that decision-taking'. This includes data concerning an individual's performance at work, his creditworthiness, his reliability or his conduct.

There are certain exceptions given in ss 7 and 8 dealt with below.

The right to be informed

3.3   The first right is straightforward: a data subject has a right to be told by a data controller if that data controller is processing personal data about him. So Mr B can contact a bank, for example, and find out if it holds personal data about him. The answer may be negative, in which case his rights stop there, although he could contact the bank again later. The right applies where a data controller is processing the data (Chapter 1 examined the definition of processing in s 1 of the Act. It includes obtaining, recording or holding the data, or carrying out operations such as retrieval, consultation or use, disclosing it, organising or adapting it, and activities such as alignment, combination, blocking, erasure or destruction of the data.)

Description of the data

3.4   If personal data are being processed by or on behalf of a data controller, the data subject must be given a description of the data. In many cases, this will be a copy of the entry whether it consists of simply that person's name and address or a detailed profile of that person built up over the years through a market research organisation.

Purposes for which the data are being processed

3.5   A data subject should be told why data are held on him. He should be told, for example, that the data are held so that a company can post him its new catalogue every year or so that his details, together with those of other people, can be sold to list companies, etc.

Recipients of the data

3.6   By whom will the data be received? It may be the data controller alone who will receive the data, or the data may be shared with or sold to other companies. In either case, the data subject has a right to be informed. He could be given the names of the individual recipients of the data or simply the classes of recipient, such as credit card companies and banks.

The data held

3.7   The data subject is entitled to a copy of all the information which constitutes the personal data about that data subject. This is wider than the right to be given a description of the data. The data must be supplied in an intelligible form. Under the 1984 Act the information to be supplied was all that was contained in the personal data at the time the request was received and this is still the case under the new Act. However, by s 8(6) the information to be supplied may include amendments or deletions which would have been made regardless of the receipt of the request.

3.8   The data controller must not alter the data by making any special amendment or deletion which would not otherwise have been made. The data must not be tampered with to make them suitable for the data subject, although they must be intelligible. If the data are held in code, for example, the data subject is entitled to have the code translated. Section 8(2) provides that the copy of the information must be supplied in permanent form. It is presumed that this means that it must not be given over the telephone. An e-mail may be regarded as a permanent form although the legislation does not make this clear. However, if supply in permanent form is not possible or would involve disproportionate effort or the data subject agrees otherwise, then supply in a non-permanent form is permissible.

3.9   Sometimes an explanation will be needed so that the data user can understand what is supplied. Where the information is so technical that the data subject will not understand it, the accompanying explanation must be sufficient for the data subject to take the information to an expert who can then explain it.

Source of the data

3.10   The data controller must tell the data subject where the data have come from, as far as he is aware of their source.

Automatic means of processing

3.11   Section 12 (discussed below) provides that no decision which significantly affects a data subject may be based solely on the processing of data by automatic means. By s 7, the data subject must be given information, on request, as to whether such processing is likely to be the sole basis for a decision which significantly affects him and must be told about the logic involved in that decision-taking. However, the data subject is not entitled to be told information which constitutes a trade secret (s 8(5)).

Procedure for dealing with subject access requests

Fees and forms

3.12   In practice, one of the most important issues will concern the mechanics of dealing with a data subject's requests for access (subject access requests). Under s 7, the Act provides that a request will only be complied with where:

–   the individual makes the request in writing; and
–   he pays a fee not exceeding the prescribed maximum; and
–   the data controller is given the information he may reasonably require in order to satisfy himself as to the identity of the person making the request and to locate the information which that person seeks.

3.13   At the time of writing, the new maximum fee had not been prescribed. Under the 1984 Act, it has been £10 (although some companies have not charged a fee at all) but it may be higher under the new Act. Provided that the sum charged does not exceed the prescribed maximum, the fee is left to the discretion of the data controller.

3.14   If a data controller receives a telephone request for information, he cannot simply ignore it, but should notify the caller that the request should be put in writing. Some companies have their own forms for completion, and this is a recommended practice as it should ensure that the data subject supplies all the information needed in order to assist the data controller in locating the relevant data. For example, it may be helpful if the data subject quotes the data controller's reference but many data subjects writing with a request to the data controller may leave that information out, making the job of the data controller much more difficult.

Further information requested

3.15   The types of questions the data controller may ask the user could include whether the data subject is a past or present customer, which branch the data subject has used, whether the data subject is related to an employee of the data controller, the full name of the data subject and/or his date of birth.

Checking identities

3.16 There are important confidentiality issues at stake in relation to the provision of requested data because the data controller must be satisfied as to the identity of the data subject. Estranged husbands and wives may seek to find out information about their spouse, or private investigators or investigative journalists may make requests ostensibly as the data subject. If the data controller is not given all the information needed to identify the data or the individual requesting the data then he should notify the data subject of the further information required.

Under the old Act, the Registrar has said that:

> 'If the information held is not very sensitive and the reply is to be sent to an address known to the data user to be that of the individual, the usual signature of the individual should be sufficient proof of identity. If the information is more sensitive – so that its accidental disclosure to an individual impersonating the data subject would be likely to cause damage or distress to the real data subject – the data user might reasonably require better proof.'

It is expected that this advice will continue to apply under the new Act.

3.17 It will be the responsibility of each company to ensure that it has taken appropriate steps to ensure that information is not disclosed to those to whom it should not be disclosed. Most large companies who deal with many requests will have in place already sufficient steps to ensure this. Most readers will be familiar with the requirement when requesting, for example, banking details over the telephone to give information such as their date of birth, mother's maiden name, etc. Sometimes a password is required. The Registrar has suggested under the 1984 Act examples of steps companies may take to identify individuals requesting information and these suggestions should also hold good under the new law. They include asking the individual about his personnel record, his date of birth and/or his national insurance number. Other steps may be a requirement on a request form that the data subject's signature be witnessed by another person over 18, who is not a relative, who must also give his full name and address and certify that the data subject is who he says he is – although presumably a fraudulent applicant could simply invent a witness. The data controller would perhaps have to check with the witness before accepting the request as valid. A third measure might be asking the applicant to produce a document which is in his possession, such as a communication from the data user, a driving licence or a benefit book. If the data controller has grounds to suspect that the applicant is making an illegal request, the controller should notify the police.

Information about other people

3.18 Sometimes information relates to two or more people and only one has made a subject access request. Section 7(4) provides that where the data controller cannot comply with a request without disclosing information relating to another individual who can be identified by the information then he is not obliged to comply with the request unless:

(a) the other individual has consented to the disclosure; or

(b) it is reasonable in all the circumstances to comply with the request without the consent of the other individual.

3.19 Section 7(5) provides that the data controller must supply those parts of the information which do not disclose the third party's identity. In such a case, the data controller might blank out information about the third party. For example, a husband and wife may have filled out a mortgage application form, of which the wife now wants a copy. She is considering suing her spouse because of a dispute over a bank loan. She had not realised she was putting her marital home in jeopardy when her husband persuaded her to sign certain mortgage deeds. If the bank were to give her a copy of the application form it would reveal details about her husband. It might not be the case that she would know all those details, even though they both signed the original form, although that might be a reasonable assumption. However, even if the data controller believes that the data subject will already know the information about a third party whose data will be disclosed with the original data, that does not excuse the disclosure of such information to the data subject. In each case, the data controller must assess whether it is reasonable in all the circumstances to supply the information requested. In this example, it might be possible to copy the form and then blank out the husband's details.

3.20 Section 7(6) provides assistance on when it will be reasonable to disclose information about another individual in response to a subject access request from a third party. Regard must be paid to:

–   any duty of confidentiality owed to the other individual;
–   any steps taken by the data controller to seek the consent of the other party;
–   whether the other individual is capable of giving a consent;
–   any express refusal to give consent.

3.21 In the example above, the husband might refuse to give consent to disclosure when approached. In that case, rather than supplying the whole of the relevant form, the bank would have to blank out the parts relating to the husband. Of course, in that case, if the matter goes to litigation the document will be subject to discovery in any event. It would not be a document which would be privileged in any way.

3.22 By s 7(5), information revealed about an individual other than the data subject includes information identifying that individual as the source of the information which is sought by the data subject.

Court action

3.23 If a data controller is in breach of the requirement to supply information requested about a data subject then the data subject can apply to the court for an order that the data controller comply with the request. Note that the data subject's rights in this regard exist in relation to the data controller and not the data processor. However, it is not a criminal offence to refuse to comply with a subject access request under the 1998 Act. In this respect, the law has not changed.

Example of form for subject access request

3.24 The form below is given as an example only. It is not prescribed by statute. Every business has different information about data subjects and the information that each will require for a form will vary.

Data Protection Act 1998
FORM FOR SUBJECT ACCESS REQUEST

Please complete this form if you want us to supply you with data we hold about you and to which you are entitled to access under the Data Protection Act 1998. Keep a copy of this form for yourself. Send a cheque for [£10] payable to [XYZ Ltd] and, within 40 days of receipt of a properly completed form and provided your cheque has been cleared, we will send you the information required.

Your full name:

Address:

Previous address if moved in last 3 years:

Address when we would have obtained your information if more than 10 years ago:

Date of birth:

Our reference number:

Your account number with us:

The information we hold which you are seeking (write 'all information' if everything is required):

Any other information which might assist us in fulfilling the request:

Date when you last made a similar request to us:

Signed: ....

Full name:..

Date:..

Return form to: Data Protection Manager, XYZ Ltd, [address]

If you have any questions call our data protection manager on [direct line telephone number].

Notes:
1. For confidential personal information, further forms of identification may be required, such as a signature which is witnessed or sight of a driving licence.
2. The fee of £10 was the maximum chargeable under the old Act. It may well be higher under the new – check with the Data Protection Commissioner.
3. Many businesses will need further information than that requested on the form in order to: (a) ascertain the proper identity of the data subject, and (b) locate the relevant information.
4. The form does not address the situation where a request may involve disclosure of information about a third party. Where that is very likely to be the case then perhaps the form could be drafted to provide for signatures by both parties (partners/spouses etc).

40-day time period for requests

3.25   Under the 1984 Act the data controller had to supply the information requested within 40 days of receipt of such information as was necessary to comply with the request. Under the 1998 Act, s 7(8) there is an obligation on the data controller to respond promptly and in any event before the end of the prescribed period beginning with the relevant day. The prescribed period is likewise 40 days, or such other period as the Secretary of State may stipulate by regulation. To date, no such regulations have been made. The prescribed period begins on the 'relevant day', which is defined in s 7(10). This is the day on which the data controller receives the request or, if later, the day he receives the fee or, if later, the day the relevant information he needs to comply with the request is received.

Repeated requests

3.26   As under the 1984 Act, there are provisions to protect the data controller against time wasters. Section 8(3) says that if the data controller has complied with a s 7 request he is not obliged to comply with a 'subsequent identical or similar request' by that individual unless a reasonable interval has elapsed between compliance with the previous request and the making of the current request. There may be circumstances when a s 7 request leads the data subject to notice that the data as held are wrong and ask for them to be corrected. It may in such cases be reasonable for a data subject to make an identical request soon after the original request, after allowing the data controller time to correct the data. The data subject should make clear the reason for making a repeat request so quickly. In deciding whether a reasonable period of time has passed, generally s 8(4) requires that regard be had to the purpose for which the data are processed and the frequency with which the data are altered.

Consumer credit and credit reference agencies

3.27   Where the data controller is a credit reference agency and individuals make requests for personal data relevant to their financial standing, they shall be assumed to have limited such requests to that area unless the request shows a contrary intention.

3.28   Where a request is made under s 7 and the individual is also entitled to information under s 159 of the Consumer Credit Act 1974, then this information should be provided (s 9(3)).

Credit agencies must reveal names of referees

3.29   This amendment (s 9(3)) was introduced late into the Bill. Lord Falconer of Thoroton (10 July 1998) commented that there are about one million requests per year to credit reference agencies for access to personal data. These requests will continue to be treated under the cheap and quick provisions of the 1974 Act rather than under the more expensive and slower provisions of the 1998 Act unless the data subject requests otherwise. The section does require that data subjects be told their rights under s 159 and if the Secretary of State draws up an order then there may also be a duty on controllers to give data subjects in such cases information about their rights under the 1998 Act.

3.30   The House of Commons debated this provision at length and MPs expressed concerns about its effect on small businesses. Concerns were expressed about the situation where a credit reference agency asks a bank, insurance company or other trader about an individual data subject such as a sole trader or someone trading in partnership under investigation. The referee may say that the individual has low creditworthiness. The data subject concerned can ask to see details of the information held about him. Banks and others may be discouraged from giving such information because the data subject will see their reference and the referee might be sued if that reference is wrong. The Government has said that it will review this provision after three years in order to see whether such concerns have proved correct. During the passage of the Bill, the Institute of Credit Management said that 'many referees will either decline to give a reference, or will not give a meaningful one. This would leave many businesses unable to obtain meaningful information about sole traders and partnerships'. Under consumer credit legislation, the Director General of Fair Trading has allowed credit reference agencies not to disclose the names of referees.

Exclusions

3.31   There are exclusions to the right of subject access which are dealt with in Chapter 4.

RIGHT TO PREVENT PROCESSING WHICH MAY CAUSE DAMAGE OR DISTRESS

3.32   Data subjects are given a right by s 10 to prevent processing of their data which is causing or is likely to cause substantial damage or distress to themselves or to another person which is unwarranted. Thus, if the processing of data about Mr X can be proved to cause distress to Mrs X then Mr X can prevent it. However, the section does not apply in certain conditions set out in Sch 2 and in such other circumstances as may be prescribed by the Secretary of State. Schedule 2 provides that there is no right to object under s 10 where the data subject has given his consent to the processing or where the processing is necessary to perform a contract or so that the data subject can enter into a contract. Nor can the data subject stop the processing when it is necessary in order for the data controller to comply with a legal obligation or it is necessary to protect the vital interests of the data subject. Note that this does not include protecting the vital interests of the person who may suffer the distress, ie in the example above, the data subject's wife.

Example
A national newspaper obtains details of a credit card payment by a Member of Parliament, perhaps relating to the purchase of lingerie for his mistress. The publication of this information could cause the MP damage and distress. He has obviously not given consent. The MP's right to prevent processing depends on whether the processing is 'unwarranted'. If he were a Minister for Family Matters it might be warranted – on public interest grounds. Otherwise, there are strong grounds for claiming that that damage and distress caused would be

unwarranted and the processing should be prevented. The right may therefore be very significant. The position may change under the Human Rights Bill after enactment and implementation.

3.33   The Government intends that the damage or distress caused or likely to be caused must be to another individual or natural person. It did consider extending this to companies where processing of data about an individual causes damage to a company but decided not to do so:

> 'It seems to us, on reflection, that to restrict the availability of compensation to natural persons – "individuals" – is entirely consonant with the stated objectives and the language of the directive taken as a whole, and is in general the better solution.' (Lord Falconer of Thoroton, 24 June 1998).

The extent of damage or distress caused must be substantial, but 'substantial damage' is not defined. The Home Office used the term as its interpretation of Article 14 of the Directive which instead refers to 'compelling legitimate grounds'. There is 'no hidden agenda behind the wording of the section' (HL Deb, 16 March 1998). The data subject must prove that he has been damaged: 'physically, in monetary terms or by way of distress . . . This is a high threshold and is intended to be such. The Directive indicates that.' (Lord Williams of Mostyn, HL Deb, 16 March 1998).

3.34   If a data controller fails to comply with a notice issued under s 10, the individual can apply to court for an order. The court may order the data controller not to process the data or, if the processing has already begun, to stop. The individual may use other provisions of Part II of the Act as an alternative to s 10 (s 10(5)).

The nature of consent

3.35   Schedules 2 (processing of personal data) and 4 (transfer of data) require the consent of the data subject whilst Sch 3 (processing of sensitive personal data) refers to explicit consent. This difference must be intentional. It was a point picked up in the House of Lords by Viscount Chelmsford, director of the parliamentary group EURIM, which is closely involved with data protection and other IT policy issues on behalf of corporate and not-for-profit associations. He said:

> 'Let me turn to another example. One of EURIM's members is busy trying to put an electronic directory around the globe. There is concern as to whether it has the right to put up the personal data represented by employees: names, jobs, telephone numbers, fax numbers and E-mail numbers. If that becomes part of the standard employment contract will that be an acceptable form of consent under the Bill? If it were limited, for example, to the fact that anyone becoming an employee agreed that they should put their business details out to countries which otherwise would be excluded by the Eighth Protection Principle, would that be acceptable?'

Case-law may be required to determine the nature of the consent actually required.

RIGHT TO PREVENT PROCESSING FOR DIRECT MARKETING PURPOSES

3.36   Section 11 entitles a data subject to serve a notice on data controllers requiring them within a reasonable time to cease, or not to begin, processing personal data about him 'for the purposes of direct marketing'. This is an important change in the 1998 Act. If the data controller fails to comply with such a notice then the data subject may apply for a court order requiring the data controller to comply. 'Direct marketing' is defined as a means of communication of any advertising or marketing material which is directed to particular individuals (s 11(3)). It would include what is commonly called 'junk mail', whether by post, fax or e-mail, and telesales. In this respect, there is some overlap with other legislation such as the European Directive 97/66/EC on the processing of personal data and the protection of privacy in the telecommunications sector (which is discussed in Chapter 7).

3.37   Reasonable notice must be given to the data controller to enable him to comply with these provisions. This was discussed when the Bill was before the House of Lords. Lord Williams of Mostyn said (16 March 1998):

> 'The amendments, however, do not say that it will never be right to expect a data controller to bring his plans to an instant halt. In some cases it may well be reasonable to expect a data controller not to begin at very short notice, but not always. Much will depend on individual circumstances.'

3.38   An amendment was proposed (but not adopted) that data controllers should respond within 21 days to written notices from individuals seeking to prevent or stop processing likely to cause substantial damage or distress or to prevent the processing of their data for direct marketing purposes. This provision led to some discussion in Parliament. The Earl of Northesk said:

> 'As the Minister will be aware, a widely used practice in the direct marketing industry is that of offering the customer the opportunity of indicating his wish not to have his data further processed by means of an opt-out tick box. That methodology has distinct advantages. It is simple, concise and clear to both the customer and the business concerned. At issue here is whether it is intended that such tick boxes should be interpreted as being data subject notices [see **3.40** below]. Legal advice obtained for the British Retail Consortium indicates that they should be. If that is the case, it will have the inevitable effect of adding considerably to the administrative costs of, for instance, the mail order catalogue industry.' (HL, 16 March 1998.)

Isolating negative option ticks from a huge volume of orders within 21 days would comprise a significant workload for companies.

AUTOMATED DECISION-TAKING

3.39   Section 12 relates to 'automated decision-taking'. Decisions which significantly affect data subjects must not be solely based on the processing by automatic means of personal data for the purpose of evaluating that person *where an individual has given a notice in writing to the data controller to this effect*. Note that the prohibition applies only where the individual has given such notice. Such decisions might relate, for example, to:

– judging performance at work;
– creditworthiness;

– reliability; or
– conduct.

An example might be a system which enables a computer to assess the speed at which a supermarket check-out operator scans goods. Her performance might then be evaluated on the basis of such data processed by automatic means. If the operator has given the requisite notice and the decision taken on the basis of this evaluation has a significant effect on her (ie she does not get a pay rise or is sacked because she is too slow), then there is a breach of s 12. Section 12 is a useful check against the power of computer systems where staff do not double-check the output.

3.40   Where the individual has not given notice under s 12(1) (which will presumably normally be the case), then by s 12(2), where a decision based on automated decision-taking is made:

– the data controller must as soon as reasonably practicable notify the individual that the decision has been taken on that basis; and
– the individual is entitled within 21 days of receiving such notification to give notice in writing to require the data controller to reconsider the decision or to take a new decision otherwise than on that basis. A notice such as this is called a 'data subject notice'. The data controller has 21 days after receipt of the data subject notice to give the individual a written notice specifying the steps that he intends to take to comply with the data subject notice.

Section 12 does not apply where the decision is taken for the purpose of considering whether to enter into a contract with a data subject, for example an applicant for a job as a secretary might be given a computer test with the results assessed automatically by the computer. Nor does the section apply where a decision is taken with a view to entering into such a contract. (It is not clear what the difference is between 'for the purpose of considering whether to enter into a contract' and 'with a view to entering into a contract'.) Nor does it apply in the course of performing a contract with the data subject. Again it is not clear what this covers – for example, in the employment example above, there will be a contract between employer and employee and the assessment of the employer's skills through such automated decision-taking will be for the purposes of that contract. The wise employer will include in the contract a clause stating that the employee may be evaluated using data based on automated decision-taking.

3.41   The exception in relation to contracts or proposed contracts described above applies only where steps have been taken to safeguard the legitimate interests of the data subject, for example by allowing him to make representations, or where the effect of the decision is to grant a request of the data subject. In the example of the supermarket checkout operator above, the computer system may have been defective or the person scanning the relevant groceries on the test day may have been Mrs Jones not Mrs Brown because Mrs Brown was off sick. If Mrs Brown is given the chance to make representations then an error of that type can be corrected.

3.42   There is also an exception to s 12 where the automatic processing is permitted by an enactment or in other circumstances prescribed by order.

3.43   Where the court is satisfied that a person taking a decision has failed to comply with s 12(1) then the court may order that person (known as the 'responsible person') to reconsider the decision or take a new decision otherwise than on the basis of the automated processing. Such a court order does not affect the rights of anyone other than the data subject and the responsible person.

COMPENSATION FOR FAILURE TO COMPLY

3.44   Section 13 provides that an individual who suffers damage by reason of any contravention by a data controller of any of the requirements of the Act is entitled to compensation from the data controller for that damage. This applies to contravention of any provision, for example: processing without consent; failure to abide by any of the eight principles, etc. If an individual suffers both damage and distress, he can make a claim in respect of both. If an individual does not suffer damage but only distress, he may still claim compensation where the contravention relates to processing data for a special purpose. Special purposes is defined in s 3 as one or more of: the purposes of journalism; artistic purposes; or literary purposes. Therefore, where data are processed for the purposes of, say, publication in a newspaper, then the individual has the right to claim compensation for distress alone.

3.45   However, there is a complete defence where the data controller can prove that it has taken such care as in all the circumstances was reasonably required to comply with the requirement concerned (s 13(3)). This emphasises the importance of companies having in place proper and effective data protection procedures which they can cite when relying on the s 13(3) defence.

RECTIFICATION, AND BLOCKING, ERASURE AND DESTRUCTION

3.46   Data subjects are given the right, by s 14, to obtain a court order where inaccurate data are held about them. In such cases, the court can order that the data controller rectifies, blocks, erases or destroys those data and any other personal data in relation to which that person is the data controller and which contain inaccurate expressions of opinion. This applies even if the data were obtained in inaccurate form from the data subject or a third party. However, in those cases covered by Sch 1, Part II, para 7, the court can order that the data be supplemented by the true facts. That paragraph says that the fourth principle ('Personal data shall be accurate and, where necessary, kept up to date') is not contravened where the data controller has taken reasonable steps to ensure the accuracy of the data, and the data indicate that the data subject thinks the data are inaccurate where the data subject has notified the controller of this.

3.47   For example, Mrs Y tells a credit reference agency that she does not have a bad debt on her Marks & Spencer account, but the agency has reason to believe she has and that she is lying. If the agency has taken all reasonable steps to ensure the data obtained from a third party are accurate then it can keep the data on record but must also note Mrs Y's comment on the data.

3.48   The court also has powers to order that third parties to whom the data has been disclosed must be told of the blocking, destruction, etc, of the data where reasonably practicable. This is assessed by considering the number of people who would have to be notified (s 14(3)).

3.49   The court has power under s 14(4) to order the erasure, destruction or blocking of data where a data subject has suffered damage through the data processing under s 13 and where there is a substantial risk of further contravention of the requirements of the Act. In deciding whether data are inaccurate the test is whether they are incorrect or misleading as to any matter of fact.

3.50   The courts with jurisdiction in relation to matters covered by Part II are the High Court or county courts in England and Wales, and in Scotland, the Court of Session or the sheriff.

Chapter 4

REGISTRATION AND EXEMPTIONS

INTRODUCTION

4.1   This chapter begins by examining registration by data controllers. In practice, this is the most important practical issue for most businesses. Those who are familiar with registration under the 1984 Act will find the system is not radically different under the 1998 Act. Whilst, broadly, the new system is simpler, at the date of writing, the notification regulations have not yet been made available. Once published, these should be available from the Commissioner, The Stationery Office and on the Commissioner's web page (http://www.open.gov.uk/dpr/dprhome.htm).

It is hoped that more of the organisations required to register will actually do so under the new Act. Under the 1984 Act in some sectors the requirement to register has been more honoured in the breach, partly encouraged by the small number of prosecutions for non-registration.

The rest of the chapter is devoted to the various Part IV exemptions under the Act.

Note that where major changes to the law have taken place, most notably where earlier exemptions, for example for manual data, have been removed, data controllers will usually have three years to prepare for these changes.

KEY DIFFERENCES BETWEEN THE OLD AND NEW LAWS

Enforcement against non-registrants

4.2   Under the old law, the Registrar had no power to enforce the data protection principles against those who were exempt from registration. Under the new Act, the Commissioner will have the power to do so even where a business is exempt from the notification requirement. This is a key difference between the old and the new law, and one which has been welcomed by the Commissioner.

Publicity over processing

4.3   Another key difference between the old and the new law is that data controllers will be required on request to make public details of their processing, and this will apply even if they are not required to notify.

REGISTRABLE PARTICULARS

4.4   The registrable particulars for a data controller are:

–   his name and address – where the data controller is a limited company this is the address of the registered office and, otherwise, it is the principal place of business in the UK;

–   whether the data controller has a nominated representative for the purposes of the Act and, if so, the name and address of that representative (the representative might be a data protection director or manager whose address may differ from that of the company's registered office);

–   a description of the personal data being processed or to be processed by or on behalf of the data controller, and the category or categories of data subject to which they relate;

–   a description of the purpose or purposes for which the data are being or are to be processed;

–   a description of recipients to whom the data will be disclosed;

–   the names of countries outside the European Economic Area to which the data controller will directly or indirectly transfer the data; and

–   whether the data fall under s 17 (see below) and whether the notification does not extend to those data.

It can thus be seen that the data controller can relatively easily complete the information required. At the date of writing, new forms for registration have not yet been issued by the Commissioner but those seeking registration after the Act is in force should obtain the forms from the Commissioner who will also provide advice on their completion and timing. In most cases there will be at least a three-year period before those who are already registered under the 1984 Act will have to alter existing registrations although some will want to do so sooner as the new requirements are simpler than the old. As under the old Act it is important to ensure that the description of the data is comprehensive.

4.5   Processing of data should not take place until an entry in respect of the data controller has been made in the data protection register. Section 17(2) contains a limited exception to this (except where an order or statutory instrument under s 22 applies where the data are not information which falls within the definition of 'data' in s 1(1)(a) or (b) (see Chapter 1 for definitions). If it is not 'data' then the Act does not apply in any event. There may be certain data, the processing of which is not likely to prejudice the rights and freedoms of data subjects. In such cases, there are powers for the Secretary of State to issue regulations stating that processing may occur before registration. It is not yet clear whether and when this power will be used.

4.6   There is another important exception under s 17(4). The requirement to register before processing does not apply to processing 'whose sole purpose is the maintenance of a public register'. 'Public register' is not defined but it would be presumed to apply to the electoral roll and similar registers open to the public.

MAKING A NOTIFICATION

4.7   Those companies which require to be registered under the Act should make a notification to the Commissioner. In addition to providing the registrable particulars above, the data controller is obliged to give a general description of measures to be taken for the purpose of complying with the seventh data protection principle, ie that appropriate technical and organisational measures shall be taken against unauthorised or unlawful processing of personal data and against accidental loss or destruction of, or damage to, personal data.

4.8   It is likely that s 18 of the Act which deals with notification will be supplemented by detailed guidance from the Commissioner and clear forms for completion. Notification regulations will be issued which will specify the form to be used in making an application, how the data are to be described and the details to be provided. Regulations are also likely to include details of how partnerships should give notification and also how notification should be made where two or more persons are data controllers in relation to the same personal data. Notification regulations will also prescribe the fee which should be paid at the same time as the notification is made and will state prescribed circumstances when the fee may be refunded. It is possible that this will include the situation where a company registers without realising that it had no obligation to do so.

THE REGISTER OF NOTIFICATIONS

4.9   The Commissioner keeps a register of people who have given a notification under s 17. Every time someone makes a notification they will be entered on the register. The register entry contains the registrable particulars listed at **4.4** above. The notification regulations will state the date from which someone is to be taken as having placed the information on the register. No one can remain on the register for more than 12 months or such other period as may be prescribed in the regulations. This period may be different for different cases in the regulations. It is to be hoped that the minimum period prescribed will be greater than 12 months, as otherwise companies will find their data protection compliance requirements very onerous and expensive since it is likely that a new fee will have to be paid for each renewal. It is suggested that a period of 3–5 years would be more reasonable for renewals.

4.10   The public are entitled to view the information contained in these register entries in legible and visible form free of charge at reasonable hours, and the Commissioner may provide such other facilities for making the information contained in those entries available to the public as she considers appropriate. This might, for example, include viewing the register on the internet. Note that the register will not contain the personal data but just the registrable particulars of the data controller mentioned above. Even so, it is a useful service to be able to check whether a company is registered or not. For example, solicitors advising a client on the purchase of a business or company need to check for compliance with the Data Protection Act. Under the old law, frequently, companies which should have registered were discovered not to have done so, and registration was then undertaken before the sale. Warranties need to be drafted, in business purchase agreements, to deal with the data protection issues which arise from this and in general, such as to the effect that the vendor is registered under, and has not breached, the Act. Under s 19(7), members of the public who pay a fee prescribed in the regulations (if the regulations prescribe a fee) are entitled to a certified copy in writing of the particulars contained in each entry made in the register.

CHANGING REGISTRATION DETAILS

4.11   By s 20, data controllers must notify the Commissioner of changes to the registrable particulars and the measures they take to comply with the seventh principle. Regulations will be made to expand on s 20 in due course. The aim is to ensure that at any relevant time the register contains up-to-date names and addresses and describes the current practices or intentions of data controllers in relation to the processing of personal data. There is obviously also a duty on the Commissioner to ensure that any changes notified are made to the relevant entry in the register.

OFFENCE

4.12   Section 21 makes it an offence for a data controller to process data in breach of s 17, ie without registering (subject to the exemptions mentioned above). A second offence occurs where someone fails to comply with the duty imposed by the notification regulations. However, there is a defence, to the second offence only, under s 21(3), if it can be shown that all due diligence was used to comply with the duty. Companies with comprehensive data protection compliance programmes are less likely to contravene the Act than others without such policies and, even if they do so, may be able to use this and other due diligence defences in the Act. Those without such policies will find it hard to show that they exercised the necessary due diligence.

ASSESSMENTS BY THE COMMISSIONER

4.13   The Secretary of State may determine by order descriptions of processing of data which appear likely to cause significant damage or distress to data subjects or which might significantly prejudice the rights and freedoms of data subjects. Where a data controller notifies the Commissioner that certain data are to be processed, the Commissioner is under an obligation to consider whether s 22 of the Act applies to the processing of the data. The Commissioner is given 28 days to notify the data controller of the extent to which the Commissioner is of the opinion that the proposed processing is likely or unlikely to comply with the Act. Where there are 'special circumstances', the Commissioner may extend the 28-day period on one occasion only by one further period of up to 14 days.

4.14   The data controller must not process the data until the 28-day period has elapsed or before the end of that period if the Commissioner has given notice that the data controller may proceed in respect of the processing.

Section 22 will not be brought into effect until an order is made by the Secretary of State and it is not yet clear what types of processing which might cause significant damage or distress to data subjects will be caught by its provisions. If the data controller proceeds to process data within the 28-day period without receiving notice from the Commissioner then an offence is committed. Section 22(7) gives the Secretary of State the power to amend by regulation the periods for notice given in the section.

DATA PROTECTION SUPERVISORS

4.15   Under s 23, the Secretary of State may make an order making provision for data controllers to appoint someone to act as a data protection supervisor who will be responsible for monitoring in an independent manner the data controller's compliance with the provisions of the Act. The data protection supervisor may also have other roles. The Secretary of State may also provide that any data controller who has appointed a data protection supervisor and who complies with conditions in the relevant order may be subject to exemptions or other modifications from the provisions of Part III of the Act. It is difficult to anticipate the content of such an order. If it truly brings useful exemptions for data controllers then it will be a welcome provision, but, if not, it would appear to create additional and unnecessary bureaucracy and a duplication of the Commissioner's role as supervisor of compliance. Many companies already have internal data protection officers who are charged with ensuring compliance with the Act on behalf of their employer, although as employees, they do not provide 'independent' monitoring as would be required by this section.

INFORMATION TO BE MADE AVAILABLE

4.16   As was seen at **4.5** above, under s 17 where no 'data' as defined under s 1(1)(a) or (b) are processed, ie where the data are simply recorded as part of a relevant filing system or with the intention that they should form part of a relevant filing system, then there is no restriction on the processing of such data. Where this applies, and the data controller has not registered the holding of the data under s 18, then under s 24 the data controller has to make the relevant particulars (these are identical to the registrable particulars under s 18 (see **4.4** et seq)) available to any person who makes a written request free of charge within 21 days of receipt of the request. This is likely to apply to those who hold data manually who, until the implementation of the 1998 Act, were not subject to any registration requirement at all. It is an offence to fail to comply with s 24, but a defence exists where a person can show that he exercised all due diligence to comply with the duty.

REGULATIONS

4.17   The first regulations which the Commissioner will draft for the Secretary of State once the Act is passed will relate to notifications. The Commissioner will keep such regulations under review. It is likely that improvements upon procedures may be made once the Commissioner is able to see how notifications are proceeding when the

Act is brought into force. The Secretary of State must consult the Commissioner before regulations may be made (s 25(4)(b)).

4.18   There will also be specific regulations setting out the fees to be paid under the Act. These again have not been drafted at the date of writing. The aim of the fees charged will be to cover the costs of the Commissioner and the Tribunal in discharging their functions and also to cover the costs of the Secretary of State in relation to the Commissioner and the Tribunal.

EXEMPTIONS

4.19   It was noted at the start of this chapter that the Commissioner still has powers to enforce the data protection principles against those who do not have to register under the Act, and this is a major departure from the old law. However, particular types of data have been exempted from the data protection principles and these are described below.

The exemptions are many and varied under the 1998 Act and need to be studied carefully in each case because none are blanket exemptions. Some involve exemption only from the subject information provisions but others grant wider exemptions.

National security

4.20   Personal data are exempt from the data protection principles, from the provisions of Parts II, III and V (rights of data subjects, notification by data controllers and enforcement) and from s 55 (the offence of unlawful obtaining for personal data) if the exemption is required for the purposes of safeguarding national security.

4.21   A Minister will sign a certificate saying that the exemption applies, or at the time was required, and this is to be taken as conclusive evidence of that fact (s 28(2)). National security is not defined. These are wide-ranging powers given to Government which is why they are reserved to Ministers alone. The certificate may identify the data only by a general description if the Minister wishes and may have prospective effect. Rights to appeal to the Tribunal against the issuing of a certificate are, however, given to those who are affected by the issuing of the certificate. Note that this does not apply only to data subjects, so, for example, a national newspaper wishing to publish data could appeal as well as the data subject himself.

4.22   The Tribunal's powers to quash a certificate are set out in s 28(5). If, on appeal, it is found that, applying the normal judicial review procedures, the Minister did not have reasonable grounds to issue the certificate then it can be quashed. If the certificate relates to the wrong person then that too is grounds for appeal to the Tribunal. It is for someone challenging the validity of a document purporting to be such a certificate to prove that it is not so, otherwise the presumption under s 28(8) is that it is valid. It is possible to use a certified copy of a certificate in any proceedings under s 28(9).

4.23   To ensure that there is no abuse of the wide powers given under this section, the certificate must be signed by a Minister who is a member of the Cabinet, or the Attorney-General or the Lord Advocate.

4.24 A similar exemption in the interests of national security existed under the 1984 Act, and the operation of this exemption has not significantly changed.

Appeals regarding such certificates on national security

4.25 Schedule 6 sets out the procedure in relation, inter alia, to appeals in national security cases. It is the responsibility of the Lord Chancellor from among the chairman and deputy chairmen appointed by him to appoint those people who will hear appeals and also for the Secretary of State from time to time to designate members appointed by him who may hear appeals. The Lord Chancellor and the Secretary of State have powers to revoke the appointment of people who may hear appeals.

Crime and taxation

4.26 A second exemption, under s 29, applies to personal data processed for:

– the prevention or detection of crime;
– the apprehension or prosecution of offenders; or
– the assessment or collection of any tax or duty or of any imposition of a similar nature.

4.27 Exemption for these purposes is an exemption from the first data protection principle (that data shall be processed fairly and lawfully) and from s 7 (right of access) but only:

'in any case to the extent to which the application of those provisions to the data would be likely to prejudice any of the matters mentioned in this subsection.'

4.28 This clause is broadly worded. The police may decide, for example, that it would prejudice their ability to investigate a crime if suspected criminals were entitled to access to all data held about them in police files. The Inland Revenue could prevent taxpayers reading the files held on them. Nor would these institutions have to show they had obtained the data fairly and lawfully. For example, an Inland Revenue observation could be set up on an individual's house to ascertain whether his lifestyle and assets conflicted with his declared income for tax purposes, and the Inland Revenue would be within the law in keeping the data they found out secret until such time as they proceeded with a prosecution. Section 29 would also protect police and Inland Revenue informants. It is not clear if social security payments would fall under 'collection of any tax or duty or of any imposition of a similar nature', but this seems unlikely.

4.29 Data processed for the purpose of discharging a statutory function and consisting of information obtained for such purpose from a person who had in his possession the information for the purposes of detection of crime or taxation is also exempt, but only from the rights of subject access.

4.30 Personal data are exempt from the non-disclosure provisions of the Act in any case where a disclosure is for any purpose mentioned in s 29(1) (crime and taxation) *and* the application of those provisions in relation to disclosure would be likely to prejudice any of the matters mentioned in the section, such as detection of crime. Section 27 defines the 'non-disclosure provisions' of the Act to mean the first, second, third, fourth and fifth data protection principles, although the first principle is only included except to the extent to which it requires compliance with the conditions of Schs 2 and 3. Therefore, although at first sight the exemption regarding tax and crime may appear to apply only to the first principle (fair and lawful processing) and s 7 (subject access), it will also apply to all the other principles mentioned above if the aims of the section would be prejudiced if the body concerned did follow these principles. Note that the seventh principle, which states that appropriate measures should be taken to prevent unauthorised or unlawful processing, is not included in the exemption, as measures taken to prevent 'hacking', etc, will always be necessary.

4.31   It should be emphasised that the non-disclosure exemptions apply only where the functions described in s 29(1) are 'likely to be prejudiced' (unless the relevant provisions of the Act do not apply). This is the same phrase as used in the 1984 Act. Under the old law, the Registrar took the view that for the exemption to apply:

> 'there would have to be a substantial chance, rather than a mere risk, that, in a particular case, the purposes would be noticeably damaged. A data user needs to make a judgement as to whether or not prejudice is likely in relation to the circumstances of each individual case. The exemption cannot justify the disclosure of personal data relating to a number of individuals, when in fact those purposes would only be likely to be prejudiced by a failure to make the disclosure in the case of some of them.' (Registrar's Guidelines, 1994, p 99.)

4.32   The Secretary of State is also given powers to exempt personal data of a specified description from any of the following provisions:

(a)   the first data protection principle;
(b)   s 7;
(c)   the non-disclosure provisions as defined above,

where the exemption is required for the purposes of this section.

Health and social work

4.33   The Act does not contain express, immediate exemptions for health and social work data. It does provide that the Secretary of State may by order exempt from the subject information provisions, or modify those provisions in relation to:

–   'personal data consisting of information as to the physical or mental health or condition of the data subject';
–   personal data in respect of which the data controller is the proprietor of, or a teacher at, a school and which consist of information relating to persons who are or who have been pupils at the school (with equivalent provisions for Scotland);
–   information processed by government departments or local authorities or by voluntary organisations or other bodies designated by or under the order which appear to the Secretary of State to be processed in the course of carrying out social work in relation to the data subject or other individuals. Where this relates to social work, the Secretary of State may grant an exemption only insofar as he considers that the application to the data of those provisions would prejudice the carrying out of social work.

There is no definition of health or social security.

4.34   Under the 1984 Act, a modification of the right to subject access relating to health and social work data was made by statutory instrument. (Modifications were also extended to information protected by the law, data held by financial regulatory bodies and identifying data relating to individuals born as a consequence of fertilisation or embryology treatment.) The health data provisions were contained in the Data Protection (Subject Access Modification) (Health) Order 1987 (SI 1987/1903) and the social work provisions in the Data Protection (Subject Access Modification) (Social Work) Order 1987 (SI 1987/1904). It is likely that Orders made under the new Act will be broadly similar to these 1987 Orders. For example, data could be withheld from a person where its disclosure might cause serious harm to his physical or mental health or lead him to identify another person who has not consented to the disclosure.

Regulatory activity

4.35   Section 31 contains an exemption from the subject information provisions for personal data processed for the purpose of discharging one or more of the following functions where the disclosure would be likely to prejudice the proper discharge of those functions:

– protection of members of the public against financial loss due to dishonesty, malpractice or other seriously improper conduct by, or the unfitness or incompetence of, persons concerned in the provision of 'banking, insurance, investment or other financial services or in the management of bodies corporate';
– protection of members of the public against financial loss due to the conduct of discharged or undischarged bankrupts;
– protection of members of the public against dishonesty, malpractice or other seriously improper conduct by those authorised to carry on any profession or other activity;
– protection of charities against misconduct or maladministration whether by trustees or others;
– protecting the property of charities from loss and misapplication;
– recovering the property of charities;
– securing the health, welfare and safety of persons at work;
– protecting people other than persons at work against any risk to health or safety arising out of, or in connection with the actions of persons at work.

4.36   The functions exempt include those conferred by an enactment, the functions of the Crown, a Minister of the Crown or a government department or any other function which is of a public nature and is exercised in the public interest.

Journalism, literature and art

4.37   In Chapter 1, consideration was given to the definition of 'special purposes' in s 3 of the Act to mean the purposes of journalism, artistic purposes and literary purposes. Section 32 provides that processing of personal data for these special purposes will be exempt from all the data protection principles except the seventh principle (taking adequate security measures etc), and also from ss 7, 10, 12 and 14(1)–(3) (right of access, right to stop processing likely to cause damage or distress, rights in relation to automated decision-taking and the right to rectification, respectively), but only where:

- the processing is undertaken with a view to the publication by any person of any journalistic, literary or artistic material;
- the data controller reasonably believes that, having regard in particular to the special importance of freedom of expression, publication would be in the public interest; and
- the data controller reasonably believes that, in all the circumstances, compliance with the provision in question is incompatible with the special purposes.

4.38 Public interest is very hard to define and it is likely that the Human Rights Act 1998 implementing the European Convention on Human Rights may modify this area of the law. Section 32 does provide some assistance in interpretation by stating that regard must be had to the compliance of the data controller with any code of practice which is relevant to the publication in question and is designated by the Secretary of State by order under the section.

4.39 If a data subject begins legal proceedings for breach of the Act, as specified in s 32(4), and the data controller claims that the data are used only for special purposes and 'with a view to the publication by any person of any journalistic, literary or artistic material which, at the time 24 hours immediately before the relevant time, had not previously been published by the data controller', the court will stay the proceedings until the claim is withdrawn or the Commissioner makes a determination under s 45 with respect to the data in question and this takes effect.

'Publish' is defined under s 32 to mean making material available to the public or any section of the public, and thus may include putting the information in a newspaper or on the internet.

Research, history and statistics

4.40 This exemption applies to data processed for 'research purposes', which are deemed to include statistical or historical purposes. Under s 33, it is provided that when applying the second data protection principle (ie that data should be obtained and used for the specified purposes), further processing for research purposes only is not to be treated as incompatible with the purposes for which the data were obtained provided that the processing is in compliance with 'the relevant conditions'. The relevant conditions in relation to processing of personal data are:

(a) that the data are not processed to support measures or decisions with respect to particular individuals; and
(b) that the data are not processed in such a way that substantial damage or substantial distress is, or is likely to be, caused to any data subject.

The first condition helps greatly in deciding whether the data is in fact being used for research purposes. The second condition is to ensure that even if the use of the data is clearly for research purposes, the data is not used in a way which will cause damage to the data subject.

4.41 There is also an exemption from the fifth principle which states that data must not be kept for longer than is necessary. Where the data is processed only for research purposes, as defined above, and in compliance with the relevant conditions, it can be kept indefinitely under s 33(3).

4.42   In addition, there is an exemption from s 7 (the right of access to personal data) where the data are processed only for research purposes, provided they are processed in compliance with the relevant conditions, and the results of the research or any resulting statistics are not made available in a form which identifies the data subjects or any of them.

4.43   Data are still treated as being processed for research purposes when they are disclosed to someone else also for research purposes only. If they are disclosed for any other reason then the exemption will no longer apply. Data will still come within the exemption where they are disclosed to the data subject or someone acting on his behalf, or with the consent or at the request of the data subject or a person acting on his behalf, or in circumstances in which the person making the disclosure has reasonable grounds for believing that the disclosure falls within the above provisions.

Information available to the public under the law

4.44   There is an exemption from the subject information provisions, the fourth data protection principle, s 14(1)–(3) and the non-disclosure provisions if the data consist of information which the data controller is obliged by an enactment to make available to the public, whether by publishing it, making it available for inspection or otherwise, and whether gratuitously or on payment of a fee (s 34).

Legal disclosures and legal proceedings

4.45   By s 35, nothing in the data protection principles is taken as restricting any disclosure required by a court order or a rule of law or enactment. There is a right to disclose where this is necessary for the purpose of or in connection with any legal proceedings including prospective legal proceedings or for the purposes of obtaining legal advice. Section 35(2) contains a catch-all provision permitting disclosure wherever this is necessary for the purposes of establishing, exercising or defending legal rights.

Domestic purposes

4.46   It is permissible for individuals to process data for the purposes of their own personal, family or household affairs, including recreational purposes (s 36). This personal data is exempt from the data protection principles and the provisions of Parts II and III of the Act. In the Data Protection Registrar's document on the EU Data Protection Directive *Questions to Answer* (April 1996) the definition of 'personal activity' is considered. Individuals who control personal data only about themselves have not been exempt under the 1984 Act if the data were held for business purposes, such as trading in stocks and shares. It is not yet clear what a 'personal activity' will comprise under the new Act.

Other exemptions

4.47   Other exemptions can be made by order, and Sch 7 contains the following miscellaneous additional exemptions.

Confidential references

4.48   Data are exempt from s 7 (right of access to personal data) where they consist of a reference given or to be given in confidence by the data controller for the purposes of the education or employment or prospective education or employment of the data subject or the provision or prospective provision by the data subject of any service. Therefore, if XYZ plc provides a reference to ABC Ltd about Mr X who used to work for XYZ and this is given in confidence (as is usual), Mr X has no right to see the reference. If Miss B's school provides a reference to her prospective university this is similarly confidential, as would be any reference in relation to Mr Y's business provided by company V to company U, which is thinking of using Mr Y's services.

4.49   Note that this paragaph does not explicitly include credit references, but only references relating to education or employment or provision of services, although it is arguable that the provision could apply to credit references for services since, for example, a reference as to a computer services company's financial standing comes within the clear wording of Sch 7, para 1(c). However, there would be no similar provision covering credit references for companies selling goods, rather than services, and it is doubtful that it was intended that this paragraph should give an exemption from s 7 for credit references of any type, given the debate over the issue in both Houses of Parliament.

Armed forces

4.50   There is an exemption in Sch 7 from the subject information provisions for information which is likely to prejudice the combat effectiveness of any of the armed forces of the Crown.

Judicial appointment and honours

4.51   Personal data processed to assess a person's suitability for judicial office or the office of Queen's Counsel or the conferring of honours by the Crown are exempt from the subject information provisions.

Crown employment

4.52   By order, the Secretary of State may exempt from the subject information provisions personal data processed to assess a person's suitability for employment by the Crown or any office to which appointments are made by the Queen or a Minister.

Management forecasts

4.53   If personal data are processed to assist management forecasting or management planning to help the data controller in the conduct of a business then the subject information provisions do not apply.

Corporate finance

4.54   The corporate finance exemption under Sch 7, para 6 was included as a late amendment to the Bill. It applies where a 'relevant person' (which is defined broadly to mean people regulated under the Financial Services Act 1986) processes data for certain purposes relating to a corporate finance service, which is defined as a service consisting of underwriting or issuing instruments (such as shares – see the definition in Sch 7, para 6(3)), advice on capital structure, industrial strategy and related matters, advice and service relating to mergers and the purchase of undertakings, or services relating to underwriting.

4.55   Where such a relevant person processes data for corporate finance services as defined above, the data are exempt from the subject information provisions of the Act where:

– the application of the subject information provisions could 'affect the price of any instrument which is already in existence or is to be or may be created'; or
– the data controller reasonably believes that the application of those provisions to the data could affect the price of such an instrument; or
– an exemption is required 'for the purpose of safeguarding an important economic or financial interest of the United Kingdom'.

The Secretary of State is given powers to specify by order matters of which account should be taken in determining whether exemption is required in the economic or financial interest of the UK.

Negotiations

4.56   Where the data controller has personal data consisting of a record of the data controller's intentions regarding negotiations with the data subject, these are exempt from the subject information provisions in any case in which the application of those provisions would be likely to prejudice the negotiations.

Examination marks

4.57   Data processed in relation to marks or other information about a data subject to determine results of an academic, professional or other examination or to allow the results of the examination to be ascertained, or in consequence of the determination of any such results, are dealt with in a special manner. Under s 7 of the Act, information must be supplied within a prescribed period after the date when a request is made (the 'relevant day'). Under Sch 7, para 8, in relation to such examination material the prescribed period is five months from the beginning of the relevant day under s 7, or 40 days, beginning with the date when the examination results are announced. If a longer period passes before the request is complied with then the data controller has to supply more information, including the information as it stood when the request was received and (if different) how it stands when the request is complied with. An examination result is treated as announced when the results are first published or first made available to the candidate in question.

4.58   An examination is any process for determining the knowledge, intelligence, skill or ability of a candidate by reference to his performance in any test or other activity.

Examination scripts

4.59   The information which candidates write or record in exams is exempt altogether from the provisions of s 7. This means that an individual does not have the right to see the script again once it has been submitted for marking.

Legal professional privilege

4.60   Personal data are exempt from the subject information provisions if the data consist of information in respect of which a claim to legal professional privilege could be maintained. This exemption would include advice from a solicitor to his or her client, perhaps naming a third party and revealing personal data about that person.

Self-incrimination

4.61   Finally, a person need not comply with a s 7 request if compliance would expose that person to proceedings for an offence by revealing evidence of the commission of an offence other than under the 1998 Act. Information which a person discloses in response to a s 7 request or order is not admissible against him in proceedings for an offence under the 1998 Act.

Loss of exemptions under the 1998 Act

4.62   Those familiar with the 1984 Act will see that several important categories of information exempted under that Act are no longer exempt under the 1998 Act. For example, exemptions for payroll, pensions, and accounts purposes, for the processing of simple mailing lists and for unincorporated members' clubs no longer exist. (The members' clubs exemption was considered in an article at p 483 of the *New Law Journal* in April 1998.) The exemption for those who are simply processing text has also been dropped. This was raised in Parliament but no special amendments were agreed (see HL Deb, 16 March 1998, p 466). Nor is there any exemption for back-up data in the Directive or the Act.

Transitional relief for lost exemptions

4.63   Schedule 8, Part II contains transitional relief for the exemptions no longer available under the new Act. These are:

(i)   manual data;
(ii)   processing otherwise than by reference to the data subject;
(iii)   payroll and accounts;
(iv)   unincorporated members' clubs and mailing lists;
(v)   back-up data.

The transitional provisions are not covered in detail here, but readers who currently benefit from such exemptions must study these provisions carefully to ascertain the impact on them of the withdrawal of these exemptions.

Exemptions under proposed regulations

4.64   In the summer of 1998 the Government began consulting on reguolations under the 1998 Act, part of which exercise covered exemptions. As well as the exemptions in the Act for manual data, processing to maintain a public register and to safeguard national security, and processing for individuals' personal, family or household affairs, the Government is also proposing an exemption for four standard business operations, together with more specific processing by particular organisations. These would include:

–   payroll, some personnel and work planning;
–   purchase and sales administration;
–   advertising, marketing and public relations (to exempt data controller's own marketing but not independent direct marketing);
–   general administrations (including any word processing not covered by a more specific exempted purpose);
–   unincorporated members' clubs as under the 1984 Act;
–   non-profit making bodies with a political, philosophical, religious or trade union aim; and
–   small voluntary organisations.

It will be interesting to see if these proposed exemptions will be put in place. This is an example of how readers should not rely on the detailed text in the 1998 Act as the 'sum total' of the new data protection law because extra exemptions and much of the important detail will be contained in regulations yet to be drafted.

Chapter 5

ENFORCEMENT, APPEALS AND POWERS OF ENTRY

INTRODUCTION

5.1 This chapter examines enforcement. In some ways, this is the most important issue of all. Many companies which should have registered under the Data Protection Act 1984 have not done so, and most have not been found out. Whilst the acknowledgement of this is not helpful to the data protection regime and no lawyer would encourage a client to break the law, the reality remains that a 'softly softly' approach has been taken by the Registrar. It remains to be seen whether this will change under the 1998 Act, but there is no doubt that the enforcement provisions under the new law are much stricter than under the old.

THE ENFORCEMENT NOTICE

5.2 Part V of the Act sets out the provisions on enforcement and the consequences of non-compliance. By s 40, if a data controller has contravened any of the data protection principles considered in Chapter 2, an 'enforcement notice' can be served. Such notice will require the data controller either to take steps to comply within a time period set out in the notice or to refrain after that time from taking certain steps, or to refrain from processing any personal data at all or from processing data of a type described in the notice, or to refrain from processing once a specified period has passed, or any combination of the above.

5.3 This gives the Commissioner a number of alternatives when issuing a notice and the nature of the breach of the Act will determine the form of the enforcement notice issued. However, the Commissioner must have regard to whether the contravention of the Act has caused 'any person damage or distress' or is likely to do so (s 40(2)). The Act does not provide that a notice may not be issued if no damage is caused, but clearly the Commissioner must bear the damage or distress caused in mind in deciding when to issue a notice.

Contravention of the fourth principle

5.4 The fourth principle requires that data be accurate and up to date. If this principle is contravened then the notice may require the data controller:

—   to rectify, block, erase or destroy any inaccurate data and any other data held by him and containing an expression of opinion which appears to be based on the inaccurate data; or

–   where data accurately record information received from the data subject or a
    third party, to take steps specified in the notice for securing compliance with the
    requirements of Sch 1, Part II, para 7, which provides that the fourth principle is
    not regarded as contravened where the data come from the data subject or a third
    party and the data controller has taken reasonable steps to ensure accuracy, and
    the data indicate that the data subject believes the data are inaccurate.

A notice in relation to contravention of the fourth principle may also include a
requirement that third parties to whom the data has been disclosed must be notified of
the rectification, etc. In deciding if it is reasonably practicable to require such
notification, regard must be had to the number of people who would have to be so
notified.

Enforcement notices were introduced under the 1984 Act, and in the Guidelines the
Registrar said:

> 'The decision to serve an enforcement notice is at the discretion of the Registrar who must
> consider, in making that decision, whether the breach of Principle has caused, or is likely
> to cause, anyone damage or distress. However, the fact that there is no evidence of this
> does not prevent the Registrar from serving an enforcement notice. Usually the Registrar
> will have had some contact with the data user or computer bureau before a notice is served
> and, in many cases, it should be possible to resolve problems by informal discussions and
> negotiations without serving a notice. In these circumstances, where the Registrar has
> grounds for serving a notice, the data user or computer bureau may be required to give the
> Registrar a formal undertaking as to its future conduct and practice, so that there should be
> no repetition of the breach of Principle in future. If this should occur then the Registrar
> would immediately serve an enforcement notice.' (Registrar's Guidelines, November
> 1994, p 113.)

5.5   Although the terminology in the 1998 Act is different, the principles in
relation to enforcement notices are much the same, and it is likely that the same
policies will be followed.

Contents of the enforcement notice and time-limits

5.6   The notice must contain:

(a) a statement of the principle(s) contravened and the Commissioner's reasons why
     she has reached that conclusion;
(b) particulars of the rights of appeal under s 48.

The notice will give a period for compliance and this normally must not expire before
the end of the period within which an appeal can be brought. If an appeal is brought
then there is no requirement to comply with the notice during the appeal period.
However, in special circumstances, the Commissioner can require as a matter of
urgency compliance within a shorter period, but no shorter than seven days beginning
with the day when the notice is served. There will be notification regulations drafted in
due course which will deal with such matters as the means of effecting service of a
notice. The Commissioner is given the right under s 41 to cancel an enforcement
notice where the principles would otherwise be complied with in any event. It is also
permissible as a data controller to apply to the Commissioner for a cancellation or
variation of the notice because of a change of circumstances. .

REQUESTS FOR ASSESSMENT

5.7   Individuals who are directly affected by the processing of personal data may request the Commissioner to carry out an assessment as to whether it is likely or unlikely that the processing has not been carried out in accordance with the Act. The Commissioner must be supplied with enough information to convince herself of the identity of the person requesting the assessment and to enable her to identify the processing in question. If a request is made and these details are clear, then she must make an assessment in such manner as appears to her appropriate. This does not mean that every case must be taken up. There will be cases, for example, where an individual believes that the Act has been breached where it does not in fact apply. In such a case the assessment could be to the effect that the Act does not apply, and the individual will be duly informed.

5.8   In determining an assessment the Commissioner may have regard to whether the matter is one of substance, whether there has been undue delay in making the request (for example, if the data subject has waited 12 months before complaining) and whether or not the person making the request is entitled to make a s 7 application for access to the data held about him. A person who makes a request for an assessment must be told whether an assessment has been made and, to the extent which the Commissioner considers appropriate, having regard to any exemption from s 7 applying, of any view formed or action taken as a result of the request.

5.9   This suggests that the Commissioner must tell the data subject whether or not an assessment has been made. In fact, the earlier provisions of this Part appear to require that an assessment be made whenever a request is received. Section 42(2) provides that where a request is made the 'Commissioner shall make an assessment …'. This is a very important point as individuals are not always able to persuade official bodies to investigate matters on their behalf, and many do not have the funds to take companies to court over breach of data protection rights. However, even if the Commissioner is obliged to make an assessment, this obligation could be fulfilled by a simple letter from the Commissioner stating that the matter is not of sufficient interest to merit further consideration. The more evidence a data subject can provide and perhaps the more examples of the same principle being breached in relation to other data subjects, the more likely it will be that a proper investigation will be undertaken by the Commissioner.

INFORMATION NOTICES

5.10   Where a request is made for an assessment under s 42 or the Commissioner has reasonable grounds for suspecting that a data controller has contravened the data protection principles, an 'information notice' may be served on the data controller requiring him within the time specified on the notice to supply information to the Commissioner. The notice has to state either that the Commissioner has received a request for an assessment under s 42 or that the Commissioner believes that the data protection principles have been contravened and her reasons for so believing. It should also contain particulars of the rights of appeal given in s 46. The period to respond must not expire before the end of the period within which an appeal may be made. If an appeal is brought before the information is supplied then an application for a warrant cannot be made until the appeal has been concluded.

5.11   As with enforcement notices, in special circumstances of urgency the Commissioner can require information to be supplied within shorter periods although such periods should be of at least seven days beginning with the day when the notice is served.

Exceptions to the obligation to provide information

5.12   There is no obligation to supply information under s 43 where:

–   it would involve furnishing information on a communication 'between a professional legal adviser and his client in connection with the giving of legal advice to the client with respect to his obligations, liability or rights under this Act'; or
–   the information would relate to a communication between a legal adviser and his client or someone else made in connection with or in contemplation of proceedings under the Act, including proceedings before the Tribunal.

The Commissioner is also given the right to cancel information notices.

SPECIAL INFORMATION NOTICES

5.13   A special information notice can be served when a request for an assessment under s 42 has been received or where there are reasonable grounds for suspecting that personal data are not being processed only for the special purposes defined in s 3 of the Act (the purposes of journalism, artistic purposes and literary purposes). The special information notice can be issued where the Commissioner has reasonable grounds for suspecting that the data are not being processed with a view to the publication by any person of any journalistic, literary or artistic material which has not previously been published by the data controller.

5.14   When such a special notice is served it must include a notice requiring the data controller within the time specified in the notice to furnish the Commissioner in a specified form with the information that is required in order to ascertain whether the personal data are indeed being processed only for the special purposes or whether they are being processed with a view to the publication by any person of any journalistic, literary or artistic material which has not previously been published by the data controller.

5.15   The special information notice must contain a statement that the Commissioner has received a request under s 42 in relation to specified processing or, where there are grounds to believe the data are not being processed only for special purposes, the notice must state the Commissioner's grounds for suspecting this. Details of the rights of appeal must also be given on the notice, and the time given for complying with the notice must not expire before the period within which an appeal may be made. Where an appeal is made against the notice, the information does not have to be sent until the appeal is either held or withdrawn. The exception for cases of urgency where special circumstances exist applies as for information notices. There are also similar exceptions for communications with legal advisers in s 44(7). There is no obligation to furnish information if so doing would reveal evidence that someone had committed an offence, although this does not include offences under the 1998 Act. Special information notices may be cancelled by the Commissioner by written notice.

DETERMINATIONS AS TO SPECIAL PURPOSES

5.16   Separately from the right to issue special information notices described above, the Commissioner has the right to make a determination that personal data are not being processed only for special purposes or are not being processed with a view to publication by any person of any journalistic, literary or artistic material which has not previously been published. Such a determination may be made after a person has submitted information in response to a special information notice. By s 45, notice of such a determination must be given to the data controller who must also be given notice of the rights of appeal under s 48.

No enforcement notice can be served on a person in relation to processing personal data for special purposes unless a determination under s 45 has been made and has taken effect, and the court has given leave. The court will grant leave only where it is satisfied that the Commissioner has reason to suspect a contravention of the data protection principles which is of substantial public importance and, unless it is an urgent case, the data controller has been given notice of the application for leave (s 46). This notice must comply with the rules of court.

Thus, it can be seen that the normal procedure where a breach in relation to special purposes is suspected might be for an application to be made by an aggrieved member of the public for an assessment, an initial informal letter to be sent to the data controller by the Commissioner, a special information notice issued and only after this, with leave of the court, for an enforcement notice to be served. As under the 1984 Act, it is likely that few enforcement notices will be served. Most companies will be willing to co-operate and change their practices to comply with the law before matters proceed to such a stage.

FAILURE TO COMPLY

5.17   If a person fails to comply with an enforcement notice, an information notice or a special information notice he will be guilty of an offence (s 47). If a person who replies to an information or special information notice makes statements which he knows to be false in a material respect or recklessly makes a statement which is false in a material respect, then he will be guilty of an offence. It is a defence under s 47(3), however, to prove that the person concerned exercised all due diligence to comply with the notice.

APPEALS

5.18   Section 48 sets out the procedures for appeals. This should be read in conjunction with Sch 6 which provides more detail. If an enforcement notice, information notice or special information notice is served then there is a right of appeal to the Tribunal against the notice. As seen above, all of these notices have to mention the right of appeal and there must be time to make an appeal within any time periods specified for compliance with the notice. There are also rights of appeal where the Commissioner has refused an application to cancel or vary a notice.

5.19   Where a case has been considered urgent, there are rights under s 48 to appeal against the requirement that in special circumstances due to the urgency of the case the data controller act immediately to right a wrong under the Act rather than allowing the period for an appeal to be made to pass first. A written determination by the Commissioner under s 45 in relation to special purposes can also be appealed.

Schedule 6 procedures

5.20   The chairman or deputy chairman of the Tribunal may decide when appeals will be held. The Tribunal may sit in two or more divisions. There will be a specially constituted panel in national security cases. Further detail on the constitution of appeals panels is given in Sch 6. There will normally be a chairman and deputy chairman, and appeal will be decided by majority. In certain cases, such as cases of urgency, the Tribunal can act ex parte. Schedule 6 also provides that the Secretary of State can make rules for regulating the exercise of rights of appeal. Such rules will make provision for:

–   the period within which an appeal can be brought and the burden of proof on an appeal;
–   the summoning of witnesses and administration of oaths;
–   securing the production of documents and materials used in processing personal data;
–   the inspection, examination, operating and testing of any equipment or material used in connection with processing personal data;
–   the hearing of appeals wholly or partly in camera (secret);
–   the hearing of appeals in the absence of the appellant or the determination of appeals without a hearing;
–   enabling appeals to be dealt with by the chairman or deputy chairman against information notices or matters which are preliminary or incidental to an appeal;
–   the awarding of costs (or, in Scotland, expenses);
–   publication of reports of the Tribunal's decisions;
–   giving the Tribunal such ancillary powers as the Secretary of State thinks necessary for the proper discharge of its functions.

The rules will in particular have regard to ensuring that information is not disclosed where this might be contrary to the public interest.

5.21   If anyone is guilty of an act or omission in relation to proceedings before the Tribunal, then this is contempt of court (Sch 6, para 8).

Determining appeals

5.22   If an appeal is brought in relation to a notice and the Tribunal decides the notice was against the law or that the Commissioner exercised her discretion incorrectly then the Tribunal will allow the appeal (s 49). It may also substitute a correct notice in place of an incorrect one. The Tribunal has a right to review any determination of fact on which a notice is based. The Tribunal also has powers to order that an enforcement notice be cancelled or varied. It can also order that certain statements be removed from notices, and that determinations of the Commissioner be cancelled. Where there has been an appeal to the Tribunal under s 48, there is also a right to appeal under s 47(6) 'on a point of law' to the court. In England and Wales, the relevant court will be the High Court of Justice, in Scotland, it will be the Court of Session, and in Northern Ireland, the High Court of Justice.

POWERS OF ENTRY AND INSPECTION

5.23   Schedule 9 deals with the important issue of powers of entry and inspection. When can the Commissioner enter premises and what authority is required in advance? For the grant of a warrant, a circuit judge must be satisfied by information on oath that there are reasons for suspecting that the data controller has contravened or is contravening any of the data protection principles or that an offence under the Act has been or is being committed. He must also be satisfied that there is information that evidence on the contravention is at the premises specified. Note that this provision applies where an offence has already been committed or is in the process of being committed; it does not apply when it is expected that an offence will be committed in the future. No warrant may be issued in relation to data for special purposes unless a s 45 determination by the Commissioner has already been made.

Rights of search

5.24   A warrant lasts for seven days and allows the Commissioner or any of his officers or staff at any time:

> '... to enter the premises, to search them, to inspect, examine, operate and test any equipment found there which is used or intended to be used for the processing of personal data and to inspect and seize any documents or other material found there which may be such evidence as is mentioned in [sub-paragraph (1)].' (Sch 9, para 1(3))

5.25   The warrant will not be issued unless the judge is satisfied that the Commissioner has given seven days' notice. Premises other than the data controller's premises may be searched. For example, data may have been given to a facilities management company or may be located off-site for some other reason and in such circumstances the warrant could relate to search of another person's premises. The judge has power to issue a warrant where seven days' notice was given to the occupier of the premises and either:

(a)   access was demanded at a reasonable hour and unreasonably refused; or

(b)   although entry to the premises was granted, the occupier unreasonably refused to comply with a request by the Commissioner to permit her to exercise any of the rights covered by the warrant (for example, the right of inspection).

The occupier of the premises must be told that a warrant is being applied for so that he has a chance to be heard before the judge. The person executing the warrant may use such reasonable force as may be necessary, such as for the purposes of gaining entry to the premises. The warrant should be executed at a reasonable hour. However, if it appears that the evidence would not be found at a reasonable hour then another time can be chosen to execute the warrant.

5.26   When the Commissioner's officers arrive, the warrant should be shown to the people at the premises, and if the occupier is not there, then a copy of the warrant should be left in a prominent place at the premises.

Seizure

5.27   If property is seized then a receipt should be given if it is requested. It would be advisable for those whose property is seized to request a receipt so that they are able to tell their legal advisers exactly what the Commissioner has. If documents or computer software are taken, a duplicate copy should be kept. In fact, Sch 9, para 7(2) requires that where anything is seized and the occupier so requests, he should be given a copy of anything seized without undue delay. Property which is seized can be retained for as long as is necessary in all the circumstances.

Exemption from inspection and seizure

5.28   There are no powers of inspection and seizure in relation to personal data which are exempt. (The exemptions were considered in Chapter 4 above.) Nor can information be inspected or seized which is:

–   any communication between a professional legal adviser and client in connection with giving legal advice of the client in relation to obligations, liability or rights under the Act (note it does not apply to legal advice under any other Act);

–   any communication between a professional legal adviser and his client or any other person made in connection with or in contemplation of proceedings under or arising out of the Act.

5.29   In practice, those giving legal advice to clients under the Act should mark letters as privileged or protected under the provisions of the Act so that such documents can be easily identified when an inspection visit is taking place. The exemption does not apply to any document in the possession of anyone other than the professional legal adviser or his client (for example, legal advice which the client has given to a third party or perhaps even a sister company within the same corporate group would not be exempt) nor does it apply to information held with the intention of furthering a criminal purpose. A professional legal adviser includes 'any person representing such a client'. This might include a 'next friend' or someone with knowledge of the law but without qualifications who is assisting a legal adviser, as well as counsel and solicitors. The advice given to the board of directors by a data protection officer employed by a company might be exempted under Sch 9, para 9(4) if it were intended that the officer would 'represent' the client. However, this does not happen in practice.

5.30   Where the occupier of premises claims that part of the information intended to be seized consists of matters in relation to which the seizure powers do not operate, then that person may hand over only material which is not so exempt.

5.31   Once a warrant has been issued it is returned to the court after execution. It must also be returned where it is not executed within the authorised time. The person who has executed the warrant endorses on it to what use it has been put.

5.32   Anyone who obstructs the execution of a warrant commits an offence. It is also an offence to fail without reasonable excuse to give a person executing a warrant such assistance as he may reasonably require.

Entry without warrant

5.33   There is no need to give any notice to the occupier if the judge is satisfied that the case is one of urgency (which appears to be very broad wording) or that compliance with the notice provisions 'would defeat the object of the entry'. This might be the case where it is believed that if notice were given the data controller would immediately destroy incriminating evidence.

What can be searched?

5.34   The Act allows 'premises' to be searched. Under Sch 9, para 13, 'premises' is defined as including:

– vessels;
– vehicles;
– aircraft; and
– hovercraft.

5.35   There is no requirement that the premises be business premises, so that people's homes may be searched nor does the Act state that the premises must be in the UK although that may be implied. Does this give the Commissioner the right, for example, to 'hack into' a computer located abroad and gain access to data in that way? However, data held on a computer abroad is not held in the UK, and the Act may not apply (see Chapter 1). There are certain provisions in relation to Scotland and Northern Ireland in Sch 10 which simply make reference to the different judicial systems in those jurisdictions but are not material to the powers and rights described above.

GENERAL

5.36   This chapter has examined the enforcement provisions under the Act. When the Act obtained its second reading, the Government stated that there would be a twin-track approach on enforcement in the Act for individuals seeking a remedy:

> 'In the same way that they may now go to the Registrar, under [the Bill] they will be able to seek the help of the Commissioner. They will also be able to go direct to the court where they believe that any of their rights under the Bill have been contravened. This is an important strengthening of individuals' rights. The 1984 Act provides only a very limited right to go direct to court: where subject access has been refused or to seek the correction

of inaccurate data. The enforcement notice, which is the main instrument for enforcing the data protection principles under the 1984 Act is retained in clause [ ]. But because of the restructuring of the data protection principles, it has wider scope under this Bill.'

5.37   This is a useful summary of how the Act is intended to operate in this respect. The Government went on to say that the Bill:

'... puts the onus for taking enforcement action on the individuals concerned rather than the Commissioner; but in clause [ ] it gives the Commissioner a power to assist individuals in going to court, but only in cases involving matters of substantial public importance.' (*Hansard*, 2 February 1998)

5.38   Whether it has struck the right balance remains to be seen. There have been very few cases reaching the courts under the 1984 Act and it will be interesting to note whether the situation changes under the 1998 Act.

Chapter 6

MISCELLANEOUS

INTRODUCTION

6.1   This chapter looks at Part VI of the Data Protection Act 1998 and other miscellaneous matters not covered elsewhere in the book.

DUTIES OF COMMISSIONER

General duties

6.2   As well as having a duty to ensure compliance with the legislation, the Commissioner also has to promote the following of good practice (see **6.6** below) and the observance of the requirements of the Act by data controllers. As under the 1984 Act, her duties will therefore continue to include the provision of education in the data protection field by issuing booklets and giving advice via her own internet web site. She is also expressly allowed to give advice to any person about data protection matters. Section 51 gives the Commissioner a wide discretion to determine the form in which information should be made available to the public and the ways in which to ensure best practice is encouraged. Section 51 gives the following examples of how she may fulfil these functions:

–   by preparing codes of practice and guidance;
–   by encouraging trade associations to prepare codes of practice and disseminate these to their members;
–   by considering codes of practice sent to her by trade associations and, after consultation with data subjects or those representing them, notifying the association whether the code promotes the following of good practice or not;
–   by disseminating EC decisions made under the Data Protection Directive and other matters relevant to the processing of personal data in and outside the EU/EEA.

6.3   If a data controller consents, the Commissioner may assess whether processing of personal data observes good practice and inform the data controller accordingly.

6.4   The Commissioner may charge such sums as the Secretary of State agrees in providing advice under this Part of the Act. Under the 1984 Act, advice provided was free of charge.

6.5   As under the 1984 Act, an annual report will be produced on the Commissioner's performance of her functions under the Act and laid before the

Houses of Parliament. Other reports may also be laid before the Houses of Parliament in due course if she so wishes.

6.6   Under s 51(9), 'good practice' for the purposes of the section means what is desirable having regard to the interests of data subjects and others, and includes compliance with the Act. 'Trade association' includes any body representing data controllers.

Assistance to data subjects – processing for special purposes

6.7   Individuals who bring proceedings under certain provisions of the Act relating to the processing of personal data for special purposes can apply to the Commissioner for assistance under s 53. The Commissioner will only grant assistance, however, upon a matter of substantial public importance. In other cases, the individual must bring the proceedings himself. Reasons must be given for any refusal to assist. Schedule 10 sets out more detail on these provisions. The type of assistance it describes includes the giving of advice or assistance and even representation by a solicitor or counsel. Obviously, the Commissioner will not want to do so in every case and the intention of the new legislation is that in most cases individuals will bring proceedings themselves.

6.8   If assistance is provided then it shall include an agreement by the Commissioner to indemnify the applicant in respect of any liability to pay costs or expenses arising by virtue of a judgment. This means that if the individual loses his case, the costs awarded against him by the court will be paid by the Commissioner. Similarly, the Commissioner may agree to pay costs arising following a settlement and liability for damages although she is not likely to exercise her discretion to do so frequently because of the financial burden. The party who is being sued must be told that assistance is being provided by the Commissioner. As is the case with legal aid, where damages are recovered, the money goes by way of a first charge to pay the costs of the Commissioner (Sch 10, para 5). In some cases, the costs may exceed the damages. Of course, if the plaintiff wins then the defendant may be ordered to pay most of the costs as well as damages so that the charge will not arise. The charge also applies to any sum recovered by way of a settlement. There are special provisions for Scotland.

International co-operation

6.9   Data and its processing is an international business. In particular, e-mail has made it easier for data to be sent abroad for processing. The issues relating to transferring data abroad and the restrictions on such transfer imposed under the eighth principle were considered in Chapter 2. Section 54 of the Act deals with international matters of a different kind. The Commissioner remains the designated authority in the UK in respect of Art 13 of the Convention for the Protection of Individuals with regard to Automatic Processing of Personal Data, which was opened for signature on 28 January 1981. She is also the supervisory authority in the UK for the purposes of the Data Protection Directive.

6.10   The Secretary of State is given powers to make orders dealing with co-operation between the Commissioner and other EC bodies. The Commissioner also carries out any general functions of the Government to enable the UK to carry out its international obligations in the data protection field. The Commissioner will also report to the European Commission where approvals are given for the export of data under Sch 4, paras 8 and 9.

UNLAWFUL OBTAINING OF PERSONAL DATA

6.11   Section 55 makes it an offence knowingly or recklessly without the consent of the data controller to obtain or disclose personal data or information contained in personal data or to procure the disclosure to another person of the information contained in the data. It was the Criminal Justice and Public Order Act 1994 which originally established three new criminal offences along these lines, including the offence of procuring disclosure of personal data.

6.12   No offence is committed where:

–   the obtaining, etc, was necessary to prevent or detect crime or was required by law or by a court order;
–   the individual acted in the reasonable belief that he had a right in law to obtain or disclose or procure disclosure of the data;
–   the person shows that he acted in the reasonable belief that the data controller would have given his consent if asked; or
–   his actions were justified in the public interest.

6.13   It is also an offence to sell personal data if it is obtained in breach of s 55(1). It is expressly provided that an advertisement indicating that data are for sale is an offer to sell them. In her December 1995 guidelines on the equivalent provisions of the 1994 Act, the Registrar said:

> 'For organisations which intend to employ third parties to trace individuals, it is recommended that they use the services only of agents who can guarantee that they comply with the Act in their attempts to obtain information. It may be of interest in this context, that both the Association of British Investigators (ABI) and the Institute of Professional Investigators (IPI) are putting in place Data Protection Codes of Practice. Members will be required to comply with these Codes which should be in force by Autumn 1995 and will have the approval of the Data Protection Registrar and may have their membership revoked if they fail to do so.'

REQUIREMENTS TO SUPPLY INFORMATION UNDER DATA SUBJECT'S ACCESS RIGHT

No compulsory access to information concerning convictions or cautions

6.14   Section 56 prohibits anyone in connection with the recruitment or continued employment of employees or with any contract for the provision of services from requiring that employee, prospective employee or contractor or a third party to supply him with a relevant record or produce a relevant record to him. Section 56(2) states that no person concerned with the provision of goods, facilities or services to the public, or a section of public, shall make it a condition of such provision that the recipient or a third party supplies a relevant record.

6.15   A 'relevant record' is defined as a record obtained by a data subject from a data controller where the data subject's right under s 7 is exercised (his subject access right) as specified on a table in s 56(6). This effectively covers data held by the police or the Secretary of State relating to convictions and cautions. The table can be amended by order. Section 56 provides that a person 'must not' require the production of such relevant records. However, under s 56(3), these provisions do not apply if a person shows that the imposition of the requirement is required by a court order or rule of law or if, in the particular circumstances, the imposition is justified as being in the public interest.

Example 1
Mandy Jones is returning to work after maternity leave. She is recruiting a nanny, and requires applicants to produce a Data Protection Act subject access request and result from the police. It is very likely that this is in the public interest and would be allowed, as a similar check is made by local authorities under the law when childminders are compulsorily registered.

Example 2
Mr Smith wants to hire young Nick from the council estate. He is a keen boy but comes from a very dubious family and Mr Smith knows that the rest of his family have been in and out of prison over the years. Nick says he has never been in trouble. Mr Smith requires Nick to produce the results of a subject access request under s 7 from the police. Is it in the public interest that this be produced? The life of a child is not at stake but Mr Smith may be concerned about potential damage to property or to the safety of other employees if Nick were to have a criminal record for physical damage. It is likely that Mr Smith is not allowed to require that Nick produce such a record and that to do so would not be in the public interest although the Commissioner is likely to issue guidance notes in due course to determine this matter.

6.16   Section 56(4) provides that forcing employees and others to exercise rights of subject access in relation to certificates of criminal records etc is not in the public interest 'on the ground that it would assist in the prevention or detection of crime'. Does this mean that forcing the nanny in Example 1 to exercise her rights is not allowed because it is designed to prevent a crime occurring? That is one possible interpretation.

6.17   Anyone contravening this section commits an offence. However, it is the imposition of a *requirement* to produce a relevant record as a condition of employment or supply which constitutes an offence. If, instead, the employer says that he prefers to hire people who are able to produce such a record but that it is not a requirement or condition, then it can hardly be said to have been 'required'. If one applicant chooses not to produce such a record but every other applicant does so, the employer can draw his own conclusions. If this interpretation is possible, it is likely to cause employers to feel that they are walking a difficult tightrope.

Contract terms and health records

6.18 Section 57 renders void terms in contracts which require an individual to supply anyone with a health record or to produce to anyone a copy of such a record or part of it. This applies to records obtained by the individual under s 7 which constitute a 'health record', defined in s 68(2) as any record which consists of information relating to the physical or mental health or condition of an individual and has been made by or on behalf of a health professional in connection with the care of that individual. Thus, it is submitted that if a potential employee has in the past taken an HIV test for the purpose of obtaining life insurance, this is not a health record as it is not made 'in connection with the care of that individual'. The individual is not being cared for at all but is simply applying for a financial product. However, if, instead, he had been sent by his doctor for an HIV test because he felt unwell then this would be a 'health record' and the employer could not require him to produce it.

6.19 Similarly, if an employee moves from Employer A to Employer B and Employer B knows that Employer A required employees to have, say, a chest X-ray before starting work there, then, again, the result of this X-ray would not be a record produced by a health professional in connection with the care of that individual unless 'care' is given a very broad interpretation. There is a long list in s 69 of those who are regarded as health professionals for the purposes of the Act, and they include doctors, dentists, opticians, nurses and psychologists.

6.20 Notwithstanding the exceptions mentioned above, most health tests and records of individuals will fall within s 57, and potential and existing employers cannot require their production by a term in a contract. There is nothing in either s 56 or s 57, however, which precludes a potential employer or purchaser of the services of an individual from requiring that person to undergo medical tests of any kind as a pre-condition to an offer of employment.

DISCLOSURE OF INFORMATION TO THE COMMISSIONER OR TRIBUNAL

6.21 Section 58 states that no law which prohibits disclosure of information will preclude a person from furnishing the Commissioner or the Tribunal with information. However, it does not expressly refer to a confidentiality agreement which may preclude certain people from disclosing information requested by the Commissioner. It is uncertain whether compliance with a confidentiality agreement or an obligation of confidence imposed by common law could be regarded as a rule of law.

6.22 Section 59 provides that no member of staff or agent of the Data Protection Commissioner shall disclose any information which has been furnished to the Commissioner, which relates to an identifiable individual or business and is not at the time of disclosure or has not previously been available to the public from other sources, unless the disclosure is made with lawful authority (such as where the data subject agrees, where the information is made available under a provision of the Act or where it is made to discharge a function under the Act, for the purposes of proceedings or in the public interest).

6.23 This restriction on disclosure by the Commissioner has been criticised by the current Registrar's office because it precludes her from disclosing information about an identified or identifiable individual or business without consent. This could make it very difficult for the Commissioner to issue press releases and describe cases in annual reports. However, it is likely that most of the publicity currently given to individual cases can be justified as in the public interest. The Registrar is concerned that there will be a threat of prosecution from those offending under the Act who are often unhappy in any event because of the prosecution or investigation. In many cases, the meagre fine meted out to them is insignificant compared with the adverse publicity a press release or inclusion as a case study in the Commissioner's annual report can bring.

6.24 Anyone who breaches this provision commits an offence, and that could include the Commissioner herself.

PROSECUTIONS AND PENALTIES

6.25 The Commissioner and the Director of Public Prosecutions are the only people able to bring proceedings for an offence under the Act (s 60(1)). There are provisions for fines for breaches of the Act in s 60(2). Under s 60(4), certain documents can be ordered, forfeited, destroyed or erased under the Act.

Directors' liability

6.26 Where an offence by a company is proved to have been committed 'with the consent or connivance of or to be attributable to any neglect on the part of any director, manager, secretary or similar officer of the body corporate or any person who was purporting to act in any such capacity, he as well as the body corporate shall be guilty of that offence' (s 61(1)). In almost every case, an individual employed by a limited company will be responsible for the company breaching the Act, so this section is particularly important. If a body corporate is managed by its members (who may be shareholders), then a member can commit an offence as if he were a director. There are special provisions for Scottish partnerships in s 61(3).

AMENDMENTS TO THE CONSUMER CREDIT ACT 1974

6.27 Section 62 makes various amendments to the Consumer Credit Act 1974 including the right to have inaccurate data corrected.

APPLICATION OF THE ACT TO THE CROWN

6.28 One of the biggest holders of personal data in the UK is the Government, which holds tax and social security records in addition to many other records.

Section 63 provides that the Act binds the Crown and that each Government department is treated as a separate person under the Act. There are special provisions in relation to processing by the Royal Household, the Duchy of Lancaster and the Duchy of Cornwall.

6.29 Government departments or people within the royal provisions shall be liable to prosecution under the Act. Section 55, which prohibits the unlawful obtaining of personal data, and Sch 9, para 12, which makes it an offence intentionally to obstruct execution of a warrant, shall apply to a person in service of the Crown. Note that the Act does still apply to Government departments. It is simply that offences cannot in many cases be committed by them.

OTHER PROVISIONS

6.30 There are provisions in Part VI which cover the service of notices (ss 64 and 65), and the making of regulations by statutory instrument (s 67), and a helpful set of supplementary definitions is given in ss 68–71. This includes definitions of terms such as 'recipient of data', 'registered company', 'third party', 'health professional' and 'a business'.

6.31 Section 75 provides that certain provisions of the Act (relating to definitions and the powers of the Secretary of State to make regulations) apply with immediate effect from the date on which the Act was passed (16 July 1998). The other provisions will come into force later by regulations.

Consequential amendments

6.32 Readers are referred to Sch 15 for various minor and consequential amendments to legislation such as the Public Records Act 1958, the Access to Personal Files Act 1987, the Access to Medical Reports Act 1988, the Football Spectators Act 1989, the Education (Student Loans) Act 1990, and the Access to Health Records Act 1990, and Sch 16 contains a schedule of repeals and revocations.

Transitional provisions

6.33 Finally, some consideration should be given to the important transitional provisions. It is difficult to cover these at length when the regulations for implementation have not been drafted. However, there is considerable detail given in Sch 8 to the Act, to which reference should be made. Chapter 1 mentioned the exemptions available before 24 October 2001 (the date three years from the date by which the UK and all other EU States have a duty to implement the Directive into national law) and transitional provisions for manual data. The exemptions for this period also apply to:

- processing otherwise than by reference to the data subject;
- payrolls and accounts;
- unincorporated members' clubs and mailing lists;
- back-up data; and
- eligible automated data (from some requirements only).

6.34   Part III of Sch 8 lists the exemptions available after 23 October 2001 but before 24 October 2007. This is known as the second transitional period and applies principally to certain eligible manual data and certain accessible records (s 68).

Finally, there is an exemption after 23 October 2001 for historical research.

6.35   Note the following points:

(1) The exemptions are not general exemptions and some relate to particular obligations under the Act only.
(2) The provisions relating to each type of data differ and it is, therefore, necessary to read Sch 8 very carefully.
(3) The provisions are likely to be expanded upon by regulations which have not yet been issued.
(4) Under Sch 8, para 19, there is an exemption for processing already under way immediately before 24 October 1998. This is not assessable processing for the purposes of s 22.

DRAFT REGULATIONS

6.36   The Government began consulting on regulations under the Data Protection Act 1998 during the summer of 1998. The consultation papers may be obtained from:

Colin McGrath
Home Office
Data Protection Section
Room 1173
50 Queen Anne's Gate
London SW1H 9AT
tel: 0171 273 3386
fax: 0171 273 3205.

The paper may be freely copied and is also to be found on the Home Office internet website at:

http://www.homeoffice.gov.uk/index.htm

The paper sets out what regulations there will be under the Act.

Subject access fees and time-limits (s 7)

6.37   There is a right of access for individuals to personal data which is held about them under the Act (as there is under the current 1984 Act). There will be regulations setting out what can be charged for those exercising this right of access. According to the draft regulations, the Government does not currently intend to change the existing £10 fee and 40-day response period but the final regulations will need to be studied when they are available.

Information provided in response to subject access request (ss 7(7) and 8(1))

6.38   Regulations will deal with information to be provided in response to a subject access request.

Consumer credit – statement of individuals' rights (s 9(3))

6.39 Section 9(3) of the 1998 Act requires credit reference agencies' responses to subject access requests to include a statement of individuals' rights under s 159 of the Consumer Credit Act 1974 and under the 1998 Act. Regulations may set out the form of this statement. The Government is taking the opportunity to revise the form of that statement generally.

Copy of register entry (s 19(7))

6.40 Those who hold personal data have to register under the 1998 Act (as under the 1984 Act). They therefore have a register entry setting out certain details which members of the public can access. This is not the information that the data controller holds about a data subject, but instead certain statutory information such as the name and address of the data controller. The Government proposes that the same £2 fee as under the old Act should be charged to those seeking copies of the register entry.

Preliminary assessment (s 22(1))

6.41 Certain processing of data can only be undertaken under the Act once it has been assessed by the Commissioner for compliance with the provisions of the Act. This is processing which may cause substantial damage or substantial distress to data subjects or which otherwise significantly prejudices the rights and freedoms of data subjects. The areas to which the Government will apply this are:

- data matching;
- processing involving genetic data;
- processing by private investigators.

It may also apply this requirement to other areas. The data controller will be obliged to notify the Commissioner before the processing occurs if it proposes to engage in processing in any of the areas covered in the regulations to be drafted under this section.

Subject information exemptions (ss 30 and 38 and Sch 10)

6.42 The subject information exemptions which apply to personal data consisting of health, education or social work information may be modified by regulations. The Orders made will be similar to the Data Protection (Subject Access Modification) (Health) Order 1987 (SI 1987/1903) and the Data Protection (Subject Access Modification) (Social Work) Order 1987 (SI 1987/1904). Regulations will also be made broadly preserving the effect of certain rights in relation to school records.

Special purposes codes of practice (s 32(3))

6.43 Data which is processed for journalistic, artistic or literary purposes is subject to special provisions in the Act. Greater rights to publish are given and there will be regulations dealing with this area.

International co-operation (s 54)

6.44 Section 54 of the 1998 Act allows the Secretary of State to make regulations designating the Commissioner as the authority in the UK under the Council of Europe Convention on Data Protection 1981. This will continue under new regulations.

Informing data subjects (Sch 1, Part II, para 3)

6.45 Data subjects have to be informed about certain matters in relation to the data held about them. There are exemptions where this would involve disproportionate effort or where recording or disclosure is required by law. The EU Directive (95/46/EC) on which the 1998 Act is based requires Member States to ensure that there are appropriate safeguards in this area. The Government in its original White Paper on the Directive suggested that one safeguard might be a requirement on the data controller to provide the information when he first makes contact with the data subject, but further comments on this proposal are sought.

General identifiers (Sch 1, Part II, para 4)

6.46 Regulations made under the 1998 Act may prescribe descriptions of general identifiers which may be processed only in accordance with specified conditions. The latest consultation paper does not say what they will be but simply that the Government is considering the issue.

Processing of sensitive data (Sch 3, para 10)

6.47 There are restrictions in the 1998 Act on processing data which is 'sensitive' (under s 2), ie which relates to racial or ethnic origin, political opinions, religious or similar beliefs, trade union membership, health, sexual life, involvement in criminal offences and criminal convictions, etc. The Act allows further regulations in this area to be made. The Directive requires that suitable safeguards be put in place, and the Government proposes:

(1) to allow financial institutions such as banks and some voluntary bodies to process information about criminal offences and convictions to prevent or detect fraud and other offences;

(2) to permit political parties to process information about political opinions in connection with canvassing;

(3) to allow the police or other investigatory organisations to process various categories of sensitive data in connection with functions wider than in Sch 7, para 7.

Tribunal rules (Sch 6)

6.48 Schedule 6 sets out the arrangements for appeals to the data protection tribunal. Regulations will be made on the subject of these appeals as permitted under the Schedule. The Government intends that these new rules be based on the Data Protection Tribunal Rules 1985 (SI 1985/1568) but reflecting changes to appeal arrangements under the 1998 Act.

Notification regulations

6.49 The Government has produced a separate consultation document, 'Notification Regulations'. It intends that there will be about 30 pre-defined purposes in total under which companies may be registered, such as 'education', 'credit reference', 'health administration', etc. Large organisations need only have one register entery under the Act, and the Registrar is considering how those enties could be subdivided for clarity. There may, for example, be division by business subdivision.

Notification procedures would be similar to those for registration. Most enquiries are likely to be made by telephone in the first place. The data controller would be sent a set of personalised forms which he would endorse or complete and send to the Commissioner. Only once an entry is on the register can processing begin. It is hoped that, in due course, it will be possible for those who so wish to file the forms electronically.

The proposed regulations setting out further exemptions are described at **4.64**.

Chapter 7

THE ISDN DIRECTIVE – TELECOMMUNICATIONS AND DATA PROTECTION

INTRODUCTION

7.1   This chapter moves away from the Data Protection Act 1998 to examine the related EC Directive on telecommunications and data protection. At the end of January 1998, the European Commission published a new Directive 97/66 (OJ 1998 L24/1) concerning the processing of personal data and the protection of privacy in the telecommunications sector. (This Directive is reproduced in Appendix 3.) The new Directive relates to privacy and telecommunications and the date for its implementation is exactly the same as for the Data Protection Directive 1995, ie 24 October 1998. Both Directives will be implemented in early 1999.

7.2   The new telecommunications Directive is sometimes known by lawyers as 'the ISDN Directive', as it partially relates to the Integrated Services Digital Network and digital mobile networks, which are referred to in its lengthy recitals. It is a privacy measure which harmonises the law in this field throughout the EU.

CONFIDENTIALITY

7.3   The first requirement of the Directive is that those providing telephone services must ensure the security of those services. However, they may have regard to the state of technology at the time (for example, not every system will be impregnable against telephone tapping) and cost. If there is a particular risk to security, then subscribers (which includes individuals and limited companies who use the service) must be told as soon as possible and also notified of the remedies that can be undertaken to remove the risk and the costs involved.

7.4   The Directive requires all Member States to prohibit:

–   listening;
–   tapping;
–   storage; and
–   other kinds of interception or surveillance of communications.

These activities are, however, allowed if the user consents, and there are certain other exceptions. The recording of telephone calls is allowed in the course of lawful business practice for the purpose of providing evidence of a commercial transaction or any other business communication. Many businesses do record telephone calls as a matter of course, and in some industries, it is a legal requirement. Buyers of shares will routinely have their calls monitored in case there is a dispute later about the number of shares ordered. This will continue to be permitted under the Directive as it is carried out in order to provide evidence of a commercial transaction.

7.5   It does, however, appear that recording calls for staff monitoring purposes may be banned under the Directive. Companies running very large customer service departments often record staff calls to monitor their staff's dealings with customers and to ensure they are carrying out their job properly. Staff do not know when they are being recorded otherwise the whole purpose of the exercise would be undermined. Such recordings are not 'recordings to provide evidence of a transaction', but it is hoped that the national regulations implementing the Directive will allow some latitude of interpretation and continue to allow such recording.

BILLING OF CUSTOMERS

Data on billing

7.6   Telecommunications companies hold much personal information about individuals. The Directive allows them to keep data relevant to billing. However, they cannot keep such data for ever. Data protection laws commonly require those using personal data to keep it no longer than is necessary. The requirement here is to retain the data only for so long as a bill could lawfully be challenged or payment pursued.

Itemised billing

7.7   Not everyone wants their telephone calls to be itemised on the bill. For example, one spouse may not wish the other to know what calls he or she is making. The Directive provides that all subscribers must have the right *not* to receive itemised bills. A telephone company therefore cannot insist that all subscribers receive bills on which all calls are itemised. The Directive does not give subscribers a right to receive itemised bills if they do want them, however.

IDENTIFICATION OF CALLER

Calling line identification

7.8   Calling line identification (CLI) allows the recipient of the call to see the number of the person who is calling. Readers in the UK will know that they can dial a code to ascertain the number of the last caller, unless the caller has disabled such function before calling. Under the ISDN Directive, callers must be allowed by a simple means which is free of charge to stop calling line identification on a per call and a per-line basis.

Malicious calls

7.9   Member States must allow for the tracing of malicious or nuisance calls. In such cases, the data about the calling subscriber can be stored and can be made available by the provider of a public telecommunications network or publicly available telecommunications service.

Emergency services

7.10 There is also a right to identify callers, whether or not they want to be identified, where the emergency services are involved, including law enforcement agencies, ambulance services and the fire brigade. In other words, all '999' callers in the UK may have the number from which they are calling identified.

Preventing forwarding of calls

7.11 There is also a right for subscribers, free of charge and by a simple means, to stop automatic call forwarding by a third party to their telephone. If this were not the case, then a stranger could arrange for all his or her calls to be forwarded to the subscriber.

DIRECTORIES

7.12 Directories must not contain too much private information. Telephone directories or the information obtainable through directory enquiries should only provide what is necessary to identify a particular subscriber unless the subscriber has given an unambiguous consent to more details being released.

7.13 Subscribers may indicate that they will not allow their data to be used for direct marketing.They may also have their address omitted in part and may insist that there is no reference to their sex if this is possible. In the UK, for example, an entry for 'S. Singleton' does not reveal the sex of the telephone subscriber, whereas 'Susan Singleton' or 'Mrs Singleton' would do so. In some languages, it may be impossible to disguise the sex of someone by using a different form of their name. Women, in particular, may want to disguise their sex because, for example, they may think that, as women, they are more likely to get nuisance calls.

7.14 The Directive does allow telephone companies to charge subscribers to keep their name out of a directory as long as the charge is not excessive. The rights outlined above apply to individuals. Subscribers which are companies are not given the same rights: the Directive merely states that their rights must be sufficiently protected (whatever that might mean).

UNSOLICITED CALLS

7.15 Most readers will have received unsolicited calls, such as from people selling double glazing. The Directive provides that using automated calling systems and fax machines for direct marketing is allowed only if subscribers have given prior consent. Other unsolicited calls will not be allowed unless the subscriber consents. The provision states:

'Member states shall take appropriate measures to ensure that, free of charge, unsolicited calls for purposes of direct marketing by means other than those referred to in paragraph 1, [automatic calling machines and faxes] are not allowed either without the consent of the subscribers concerned or in respect of subscribers who do not wish to receive these calls, the choice between these options to be determined by national legislation.'

Direct mail companies will need to examine carefully these provisions and the local implementing legislation which should be passed this year.

7.16   Other provisions in the Directive relate to technical features and standardisation of telephones and systems. There are also rights for Member States to restrict certain obligations in the Directive in the interests of national security; defence; public security; prevention, investigation, detection and prosecution of criminal offences or of unauthorised use of the telecommunications system as provided under the general Data Protection Directive 95/46. Liability and sanctions and remedies under the ISDN Directive will be the same as for Directive 95/46.

TIMING OF IMPLEMENTATION

7.17   Although Member States have until 24 October 1998 to implement the Directive, the provisions in Art 5 relating to the recording of calls do not have to be brought in until 24 October 2000. Editions of telephone directories already published do not need to be withdrawn and replaced, although it is unclear how the provisions will affect on-line directories which are updated regularly.

IMPLEMENTATION OF THE DIRECTIVE IN THE UK

7.18   The Department of Trade and Industry (DTI) is responsible for handling the implementation of the Directive in the UK. Draft UK legislation to implement the Directive was issued for consultation in August 1998.

7.19   In late April 1998, the DTI issued its first consultation on the Directive. The DTI stated that the ISDN Directive applies to the processing of personal data in connection with the provision of publicly available telecoms services, for example voice, data, fax and electronic mail, in public telecommunications networks, whereas those using non-publicly available telecoms services will be subject to the general Data Protection Directive. The DTI has usefully summarised the issues in the Directive on which it would welcome comments. In particular, unlike some EU Directives, this one gives Member States some options as to how the provisions are implemented.

THE DRAFT TELECOMMUNICATIONS (DATA PROTECTION AND PRIVACY) REGULATIONS 1998

7.20   The draft regulations were published for consultation by the DTI in the summer of 1998 and, at the date of writing, have not been finalised. Appendix 4 reproduces these draft regulations as published at 31 July 1998; however, readers should always check the latest position.

Application of the regulations

7.21   The regulations apply to publicly available telecommunications services. For most people, this means their telephone and fax machine. They apply to publicly available voice, data, fax and electronic mail. Some provisions of the Directive apply only to telephone voice services, such as those relating to unsolicited calls or calling line identification and, therefore, readers need to read the regulations carefully in each case to ascertain whether their particular form of communication falls within the relevant provision. Some provisions apply to e-mail and others do not. Provisions relating to directories, for example, apply equally to voice and e-mail directories.

If a service is not publicly available, the Directive and regulations do not apply. This would be the case with a private network, for example. In such a case, the general Data Protection Directive 95/46 and the Data Protection Act 1998 would apply.

There are provisions in the Directive which just apply to natural persons and the draft regulations use the term 'individuals' for this. This does not just mean individuals in their private capacity, but also sole traders and those trading in partnerships, although these provisions do not apply to companies. As will be seen below, some of the other provisions in the regulations do, however, apply to companies.

Penalties

7.22   Enforcement of the regulations is the responsibility of the Data Protection Commissioner (previously known as the Registrar). One of the problems with the old data protection legislation was the lack of effective enforcement. Under the new regulations, when agreed, those who fail to comply with an enforcement notice can be fined up to £5,000 and, where convicted on indictment, an unlimited fine can be imposed. In addition, anyone who suffers damage through a breach of the regulations can sue for damages under reg 33.

Traffic data and billing data

7.23   Telecommunications companies hold important information about individuals which they could easily abuse. The regulations require that once a telephone call is made, certain data must be erased or depersonalised. This is called 'traffic data'. Other data are called 'billing data'. Schedule 1 of the regulations lists the data which telecommunications network providers or service providers may process in relation to billing or interconnection charges, as follows:

(a) the number or other identification of the subscriber's station;
(b) the subscriber's address and the type of station;
(c) the total number of units of use by reference to which the sum payable in respect of an accounting period is calculated;
(d) the type, date, starting time and duration of calls and the volume of data transmissions in respect of which sums are payable by the subscriber and the numbers or other identification of the stations to which they were made;
(e) the date of the provision of any service not falling within sub-paragraph (d); and

(f)   other matters concerning payments including, in particular, advance payments, payments by instalments, reminders and disconnections.

These types of data may only be processed for billing and charges until the end of the period during which legal proceedings may be brought. Under the Limitation Act 1980, this is normally six years for contract claims (although such periods differ under Scottish law). The aim is to ensure that data are not kept longer than is necessary, as under general data protection legislation.

Further processing of data

7.24   Where subscribers consent, the data listed above can be used by the telecommunications provider to market its own telecommunications services to subscribers. There is no definition of this 'consent' and the Data Protection Commissioner believes that the consent should be freely given and that there should be a specific and informed indication of the wishes of the data subject. Recital 17 of the ISDN Directive provides that further processing is only allowed if the subscriber has agreed on the basis of accurate and full information. The DTI says:

> 'There is clearly a difference between re-ordering and consolidating itemised billing information in order to advise a customer of his or her most frequently called numbers and analysing a customer's calling patterns in order to target special offers to those who make overseas calls in the night. Even more intrusive would be analysing customer bills to identify those using particular services in order to offer similar competing services or contacting those whose numbers appear on a particular subscriber's bill to offer a special tariff for returning such calls.'

The DTI believes that consent can be given in contractual terms and can also be given orally.

Processing of traffic and billing data is also allowed in order to manage billing, deal with customer enquiries, detect fraud and to market telecommunications services.

Connected and calling line identification

7.25   Calling line identification (CLI) enables subscribers to see who is calling them either on a display or by calling back later. British Telecom subscribers can do this by calling 1471. OFTEL's existing rules in the *Code of Practice for Network Operators in relation to Customer Line Identification Display Services and other Related Services* (2nd edn, June 1998) will continue to apply in this field to UK operators and this Code includes more detailed practical guidance than is the case with the regulations.

Those making calls must, under the regulations, be able to disable (or 'call block') CLI. This is already the case in the UK. Users must be able to disable identification on a per-line basis for all calls if they wish, and there must be no charge for such blocking. There should also be provisions which apply the other way round so that someone receiving a call should have the right not to receive CLI on incoming calls.

The Directive provides that callers should be entitled to refuse to accept calls from people whose numbers are not identified (someone may want to do this if he is worried about calls from strangers). This provision applies to caller display rather than caller return services (ie only to those telephones which display the caller's number). Charges may be levied for users exercising such rights. There are other details on CLI given in the regulations which are not described here.

Directories

7.26 Part IV of the draft regulations deals with directories. Individuals' details in directories should be limited to the number and information necessary to identify that person unless the subscriber agrees otherwise. Individuals whose numbers appear in public directories have the right to request that entries relating to a particular number, a reference to their sex and such part of their address as they request are excluded. This is different from being ex-directory and represents a compromise between a full listing and an ex-directory status. Telecommunications companies will have to ask people in future whether they want their address or part of it omitted and they can obviously, if they wish, seek to persuade people that directories are a lot less useful if addresses are omitted.

Direct marketing

7.27 Individuals are given a right to indicate that they do not want their data used for direct marketing purposes. Initially, the DTI wondered if this could be indicated by an asterisk against an entry but they have now dropped this idea. Some individuals thought it gave them even less privacy – it tells the world they do not want their details used and directory owners thought it may be difficult to incorporate the relevant field. The regulations therefore give all subscribers the right to opt out of unsolicited direct marketing.

Ex-directory

7.28 Subscribers are given a right to go ex-directory free of charge. Member States can vary this provision in the Directive. At present, in most areas there is currently no charge for this and this will continue to be a free service.

Companies

7.29 Corporate subscribers do not have as many privacy concerns as individuals. However the regulations will give corporate subscribers the right to tell telecommunications companies that they wish to be omitted from a directory.

Unsolicited faxes and calls for direct marketing purposes

7.30 The provisions which have received the most publicity concern unsolicited faxes and calls for the purposes of direct marketing and these are set out in Part V of the regulations. Regulation 21 will say that no one can use a publicly available telecommunications service to send a direct marketing fax to an individual subscriber (which includes partnerships and sole traders) unless that subscriber has given prior consent.

Automated calling systems

7.31   Some machines can send direct marketing material to individuals without human intervention. This will henceforth be allowed only where the individual has consented.

Unsolicited calls

7.32   The Directive requires Member States to establish a system so that subscribers can protect themselves against direct marketing calls. After some consideration, the Government has chosen an 'opt-out' arrangement, rather than an 'opting-in' alternative as favoured by consumer groups. The Government does reserve the right to alter the regulations where necessary in future on this issue. No direct marketing calls will be allowed where the individual has told that caller he does not want such calls or where he puts himself on a record of individuals not wanting such calls.

Unsolicited faxes to companies

7.33   The draft regulations do not regulate unsolicited direct marketing calls to companies. However, there will be an opt-out scheme enabling companies to opt out of receiving unsolicited faxes where they so choose.

Caller details

7.34   All unsolicited faxes and calls must include a name and address or freephone number so the recipient knows from whom they have come.

Security

7.35   Those providing publicly available telecommunications services are required to take appropriate measures to safeguard the security of their services.

Itemised billing

7.36   All subscribers are given the right to receive non-itemised bills where they make such a request. Those who do not want their number to appear on someone else's itemised bills could call from a pay phone paying cash or using a pre-paid phone card.

Automatic call forwarding

7.37   Regulation 28 will say that service providers, on request, must ensure that any automatic call forwarding ceases without any avoidable delay.

Further information

7.38   A hard copy of the consultation paper and the latest version of the draft regulations can be obtained from the DTI by contacting:

Mrs Jane Duck
Bay 202
151 Buckingham Palace Road
London SW1W 9SS
Fax: 0171 215 4161
e-mail: tdpd@ciid.dti.gov.uk.

However, for those with internet access, a full copy of the regulations is on the DTI website at:

http://www.dti.gov.uk/cii/tdpd/condoc2.htm.

The earlier consultation paper is at condoc.htm.

Appendix 1

DATA PROTECTION ACT 1998
(1998 c 29)

ARRANGEMENT OF SECTIONS

Part I
Preliminary

Part II
Rights of data subjects and others

Part III
Notification by data controllers

Part IV
Exemptions

Part V
Enforcement

Part VI
Miscellaneous and General

Functions of Commissioner

An Act to make new provision for the regulation of the processing of information relating to individuals, including the obtaining, holding, use or disclosure of such information.

[16th July 1998]

Part I
Preliminary

1 Basic interpretative provisions

(1) In this Act, unless the context otherwise requires –

'data' means information which –

(a) is being processed by means of equipment operating automatically in response to instructions given for that purpose,

(b) is recorded with the intention that it should be processed by means of such equipment,

(c) is recorded as part of a relevant filing system or with the intention that it should form part of a relevant filing system, or

(d) does not fall within paragraph (a), (b) or (c) but forms part of an accessible record as defined by section 68;

'data controller' means, subject to subsection (4), a person who (either alone or jointly or in common with other persons) determines the purposes for which and the manner in which any personal data are, or are to be, processed;

'data processor', in relation to personal data, means any person (other than an employee of the data controller) who processes the data on behalf of the data controller;

'data subject' means an individual who is the subject of personal data;

'personal data' means data which relate to a living individual who can be identified –

(a) from those data, or
(b) from those data and other information which is in the possession of, or is likely to come into the possession of, the data controller,

and includes any expression of opinion about the individual and any indication of the intentions of the data controller or any other person in respect of the individual;

'processing', in relation to information or data, means obtaining, recording or holding the information or data or carrying out any operation or set of operations on the information or data, including –

(a) organisation, adaptation or alteration of the information or data,
(b) retrieval, consultation or use of the information or data,
(c) disclosure of the information or data by transmission, dissemination or otherwise making available, or
(d) alignment, combination, blocking, erasure or destruction of the information or data;

'relevant filing system' means any set of information relating to individuals to the extent that, although the information is not processed by means of equipment operating automatically in response to instructions given for that purpose, the set is structured, either by reference to individuals or by reference to criteria relating to individuals, in such a way that specific information relating to a particular individual is readily accessible.

(2) In this Act, unless the context otherwise requires –

(a) 'obtaining' or 'recording', in relation to personal data, includes obtaining or recording the information to be contained in the data, and
(b) 'using' or 'disclosing', in relation to personal data, includes using or disclosing the information contained in the data.

(3) In determining for the purposes of this Act whether any information is recorded with the intention –

(a) that it should be processed by means of equipment operating automatically in response to instructions given for that purpose, or
(b) that it should form part of a relevant filing system,

it is immaterial that it is intended to be so processed or to form part of such a system only after being transferred to a country or territory outside the European Economic Area.

(4) Where personal data are processed only for purposes for which they are required by or under any enactment to be processed, the person on whom the obligation to process the data is imposed by or under that enactment is for the purposes of this Act the data controller.

2 Sensitive personal data

In this Act 'sensitive personal data' means personal data consisting of information as to –

(a) the racial or ethnic origin of the data subject,
(b) his political opinions,
(c) his religious beliefs or other beliefs of a similar nature,
(d) whether he is a member of a trade union (within the meaning of the Trade Union and Labour Relations (Consolidation) Act 1992),

(e) his physical or mental health or condition,

(f) his sexual life,

(g) the commission or alleged commission by him of any offence, or

(h) any proceedings for any offence committed or alleged to have been committed by him, the disposal of such proceedings or the sentence of any court in such proceedings.

3 The special purposes

In this Act 'the special purposes' means any one or more of the following –

(a) the purposes of journalism,

(b) artistic purposes, and

(c) literary purposes.

4 The data protection principles

(1) References in this Act to the data protection principles are to the principles set out in Part I of Schedule 1.

(2) Those principles are to be interpreted in accordance with Part II of Schedule 1.

(3) Schedule 2 (which applies to all personal data) and Schedule 3 (which applies only to sensitive personal data) set out conditions applying for the purposes of the first principle; and Schedule 4 sets out cases in which the eighth principle does not apply.

(4) Subject to section 27(1), it shall be the duty of a data controller to comply with the data protection principles in relation to all personal data with respect to which he is the data controller.

5 Application of Act

(1) Except as otherwise provided by or under section 54, this Act applies to a data controller in respect of any data only if –

(a) the data controller is established in the United Kingdom and the data are processed in the context of that establishment, or

(b) the data controller is established neither in the United Kingdom nor in any other EEA State but uses equipment in the United Kingdom for processing the data otherwise than for the purposes of transit through the United Kingdom.

(2) A data controller falling within subsection (1)(b) must nominate for the purposes of this Act a representative established in the United Kingdom.

(3) For the purposes of subsections (1) and (2), each of the following is to be treated as established in the United Kingdom –

(a) an individual who is ordinarily resident in the United Kingdom,

(b) a body incorporated under the law of, or of any part of, the United Kingdom,

(c) a partnership or other unincorporated association formed under the law of any part of the United Kingdom, and

(d) any person who does not fall within paragraph (a), (b) or (c) but maintains in the United Kingdom –

    (i) an office, branch or agency through which he carries on any activity, or

    (ii) a regular practice;

and the reference to establishment in any other EEA State has a corresponding meaning.

6 The Commissioner and the Tribunal

(1) The office originally established by section 3(1)(a) of the Data Protection Act 1984 as the office of Data Protection Registrar shall continue to exist for the purposes of this Act but shall be known as the office of Data Protection Commissioner; and in this Act the Data Protection Commissioner is referred to as 'the Commissioner'.

(2) The Commissioner shall be appointed by Her Majesty by Letters Patent.

(3) For the purposes of this Act there shall continue to be a Data Protection Tribunal (in this Act referred to as 'the Tribunal').

(4) The Tribunal shall consist of –

(a) a chairman appointed by the Lord Chancellor after consultation with the Lord Advocate,
(b) such number of deputy chairmen so appointed as the Lord Chancellor may determine, and
(c) such number of other members appointed by the Secretary of State as he may determine.

(5) The members of the Tribunal appointed under subsection (4)(a) and (b) shall be –

(a) persons who have a 7 year general qualification, within the meaning of section 71 of the Courts and Legal Services Act 1990,
(b) advocates or solicitors in Scotland of at least 7 years' standing, or
(c) members of the bar of Northern Ireland or solicitors of the Supreme Court of Northern Ireland of at least 7 years' standing.

(6) The members of the Tribunal appointed under subsection (4)(c) shall be –

(a) persons to represent the interests of data subjects, and
(b) persons to represent the interests of data controllers.

(7) Schedule 5 has effect in relation to the Commissioner and the Tribunal.

Part II
Rights of data subjects and others

7 Right of access to personal data

(1) Subject to the following provisions of this section and to sections 8 and 9, an individual is entitled –

(a) to be informed by any data controller whether personal data of which that individual is the data subject are being processed by or on behalf of that data controller,
(b) if that is the case, to be given by the data controller a description of –
  (i) the personal data of which that individual is the data subject,
  (ii) the purposes for which they are being or are to be processed, and
  (iii) the recipients or classes of recipients to whom they are or may be disclosed,
(c) to have communicated to him in an intelligible form –
  (i) the information constituting any personal data of which that individual is the data subject, and
  (ii) any information available to the data controller as to the source of those data, and
(d) where the processing by automatic means of personal data of which that individual is the data subject for the purpose of evaluating matters relating to him such as, for example, his performance at work, his creditworthiness, his reliability or his conduct,

has constituted or is likely to constitute the sole basis for any decision significantly affecting him, to be informed by the data controller of the logic involved in that decision-taking.

(2) A data controller is not obliged to supply any information under subsection (1) unless he has received –

    (a) a request in writing, and

    (b) except in prescribed cases, such fee (not exceeding the prescribed maximum) as he may require.

(3) A data controller is not obliged to comply with a request under this section unless he is supplied with such information as he may reasonably require in order to satisfy himself as to the identity of the person making the request and to locate the information which that person seeks.

(4) Where a data controller cannot comply with the request without disclosing information relating to another individual who can be identified from that information, he is not obliged to comply with the request unless –

    (a) the other individual has consented to the disclosure of the information to the person making the request, or

    (b) it is reasonable in all the circumstances to comply with the request without the consent of the other individual.

(5) In subsection (4) the reference to information relating to another individual includes a reference to information identifying that individual as the source of the information sought by the request; and that subsection is not to be construed as excusing a data controller from communicating so much of the information sought by the request as can be communicated without disclosing the identity of the other individual concerned, whether by the omission of names or other identifying particulars or otherwise.

(6) In determining for the purposes of subsection (4)(b) whether it is reasonable in all the circumstances to comply with the request without the consent of the other individual concerned, regard shall be had, in particular, to –

    (a) any duty of confidentiality owed to the other individual,

    (b) any steps taken by the data controller with a view to seeking the consent of the other individual,

    (c) whether the other individual is capable of giving consent, and

    (d) any express refusal of consent by the other individual.

(7) An individual making a request under this section may, in such cases as may be prescribed, specify that his request is limited to personal data of any prescribed description.

(8) Subject to subsection (4), a data controller shall comply with a request under this section promptly and in any event before the end of the prescribed period beginning with the relevant day.

(9) If a court is satisfied on the application of any person who has made a request under the foregoing provisions of this section that the data controller in question has failed to comply with the request in contravention of those provisions, the court may order him to comply with the request.

(10) In this section –

    'prescribed' means prescribed by the Secretary of State by regulations;

    'the prescribed maximum' means such amount as may be prescribed;

'the prescribed period' means forty days or such other period as may be prescribed;

'the relevant day', in relation to a request under this section, means the day on which the data controller receives the request or, if later, the first day on which the data controller has both the required fee and the information referred to in subsection (3).

(11) Different amounts or periods may be prescribed under this section in relation to different cases.

8 Provisions supplementary to section 7

(1) The Secretary of State may by regulations provide that, in such cases as may be prescribed, a request for information under any provision of subsection (1) of section 7 is to be treated as extending also to information under other provisions of that subsection.

(2) The obligation imposed by section 7(1)(c)(i) must be complied with by supplying the data subject with a copy of the information in permanent form unless –

(a) the supply of such a copy is not possible or would involve disproportionate effort, or
(b) the data subject agrees otherwise;

and where any of the information referred to in section 7(1)(c)(i) is expressed in terms which are not intelligible without explanation the copy must be accompanied by an explanation of those terms.

(3) Where a data controller has previously complied with a request made under section 7 by an individual, the data controller is not obliged to comply with a subsequent identical or similar request under that section by that individual unless a reasonable interval has elapsed between compliance with the previous request and the making of the current request.

(4) In determining for the purposes of subsection (3) whether requests under section 7 are made at reasonable intervals, regard shall be had to the nature of the data, the purpose for which the data are processed and the frequency with which the data are altered.

(5) Section 7(1)(d) is not to be regarded as requiring the provision of information as to the logic involved in any decision-taking if, and to the extent that, the information constitutes a trade secret.

(6) The information to be supplied pursuant to a request under section 7 must be supplied by reference to the data in question at the time when the request is received, except that it may take account of any amendment or deletion made between that time and the time when the information is supplied, being an amendment or deletion that would have been made regardless of the receipt of the request.

(7) For the purposes of section 7(4) and (5) another individual can be identified from the information being disclosed if he can be identified from that information, or from that and any other information which, in the reasonable belief of the data controller, is likely to be in, or to come into, the possession of the data subject making the request.

9 Application of section 7 where data controller is credit reference agency

(1) Where the data controller is a credit reference agency, section 7 has effect subject to the provisions of this section.

(2) An individual making a request under section 7 may limit his request to personal data relevant to his financial standing, and shall be taken to have so limited his request unless the request shows a contrary intention.

(3) Where the data controller receives a request under section 7 in a case where personal data of which the individual making the request is the data subject are being processed by or on behalf of the data controller, the obligation to supply information under that section includes an obligation to give the individual making the request a statement, in such form as may be prescribed by the Secretary of State by regulations, of the individual's rights –

(a) under section 159 of the Consumer Credit Act 1974, and
(b) to the extent required by the prescribed form, under this Act.

10 Right to prevent processing likely to cause damage or distress

(1) Subject to subsection (2), an individual is entitled at any time by notice in writing to a data controller to require the data controller at the end of such period as is reasonable in the circumstances to cease, or not to begin, processing, or processing for a specified purpose or in a specified manner, any personal data in respect of which he is the data subject, on the ground that, for specified reasons –

(a) the processing of those data or their processing for that purpose or in that manner is causing or is likely to cause substantial damage or substantial distress to him or to another, and
(b) that damage or distress is or would be unwarranted.

(2) Subsection (1) does not apply –

(a) in a case where any of the conditions in paragraphs 1 to 4 of Schedule 2 is met, or
(b) in such other cases as may be prescribed by the Secretary of State by order.

(3) The data controller must within twenty-one days of receiving a notice under subsection (1) ('the data subject notice') give the individual who gave it a written notice –

(a) stating that he has complied or intends to comply with the data subject notice, or
(b) stating his reasons for regarding the data subject notice as to any extent unjustified and the extent (if any) to which he has complied or intends to comply with it.

(4) If a court is satisfied, on the application of any person who has given a notice under subsection (1) which appears to the court to be justified (or to be justified to any extent), that the data controller in question has failed to comply with the notice, the court may order him to take such steps for complying with the notice (or for complying with it to that extent) as the court thinks fit.

(5) The failure by a data subject to exercise the right conferred by subsection (1) or section 11(1) does not affect any other right conferred on him by this Part.

11 Right to prevent processing for purpose of direct marketing

(1) An individual is entitled at any time by notice in writing to a data controller to require the data controller at the end of such period as is reasonable in the circumstances to cease, or not to begin, processing for the purposes of direct marketing personal data in respect of which he is the data subject.

(2) If the court is satisfied, on the application of any person who has given a notice under subsection (1), that the data controller has failed to comply with the notice, the court may order him to take such steps for complying with the notice as the court thinks fit.

(3) In this section 'direct marketing' means the communication (by whatever means) of any advertising or marketing material which is directed to particular individuals.

12 Rights in relation to automated decision-taking

(1) An individual is entitled at any time, by notice in writing to any data controller, to require the data controller to ensure that no decision taken by or on behalf of the data controller which significantly affects that individual is based solely on the processing by automatic means of personal data in respect of which that individual is the data subject for the purpose of evaluating matters relating to him such as, for example, his performance at work, his creditworthiness, his reliability or his conduct.

(2) Where, in a case where no notice under subsection (1) has effect, a decision which significantly affects an individual is based solely on such processing as is mentioned in subsection (1) –

(a) the data controller must as soon as reasonably practicable notify the individual that the decision was taken on that basis, and

(b) the individual is entitled, within twenty-one days of receiving that notification from the data controller, by notice in writing to require the data controller to reconsider the decision or to take a new decision otherwise than on that basis.

(3) The data controller must, within twenty-one days of receiving a notice under subsection (2)(b) ('the data subject notice') give the individual a written notice specifying the steps that he intends to take to comply with the data subject notice.

(4) A notice under subsection (1) does not have effect in relation to an exempt decision; and nothing in subsection (2) applies to an exempt decision.

(5) In subsection (4) 'exempt decision' means any decision –

(a) in respect of which the condition in subsection (6) and the condition in subsection (7) are met, or

(b) which is made in such other circumstances as may be prescribed by the Secretary of State by order.

(6) The condition in this subsection is that the decision –

(a) is taken in the course of steps taken –
   (i) for the purpose of considering whether to enter into a contract with the data subject,
   (ii) with a view to entering into such a contract, or
   (iii) in the course of performing such a contract, or

(b) is authorised or required by or under any enactment.

(7) The condition in this subsection is that either –

(a) the effect of the decision is to grant a request of the data subject, or

(b) steps have been taken to safeguard the legitimate interests of the data subject (for example, by allowing him to make representations).

(8) If a court is satisfied on the application of a data subject that a person taking a decision in respect of him ('the responsible person') has failed to comply with subsection (1) or (2)(b), the court may order the responsible person to reconsider the decision, or to take a new decision which is not based solely on such processing as is mentioned in subsection (1).

(9) An order under subsection (8) shall not affect the rights of any person other than the data subject and the responsible person.

13 Compensation for failure to comply with certain requirements

(1) An individual who suffers damage by reason of any contravention by a data controller of any of the requirements of this Act is entitled to compensation from the data controller for that damage.

(2) An individual who suffers distress by reason of any contravention by a data controller of any of the requirements of this Act is entitled to compensation from the data controller for that distress if –

(a) the individual also suffers damage by reason of the contravention, or
(b) the contravention relates to the processing of personal data for the special purposes.

(3) In proceedings brought against a person by virtue of this section it is a defence to prove that he had taken such care as in all the circumstances was reasonably required to comply with the requirement concerned.

14 Rectification, blocking, erasure and destruction

(1) If a court is satisfied on the application of a data subject that personal data of which the applicant is the subject are inaccurate, the court may order the data controller to rectify, block, erase or destroy those data and any other personal data in respect of which he is the data controller and which contain an expression of opinion which appears to the court to be based on the inaccurate data.

(2) Subsection (1) applies whether or not the data accurately record information received or obtained by the data controller from the data subject or a third party but where the data accurately record such information, then –

(a) if the requirements mentioned in paragraph 7 of Part II of Schedule 1 have been complied with, the court may, instead of making an order under subsection (1), make an order requiring the data to be supplemented by such statement of the true facts relating to the matters dealt with by the data as the court may approve, and
(b) if all or any of those requirements have not been complied with, the court may, instead of making an order under that subsection, make such order as it thinks fit for securing compliance with those requirements with or without a further order requiring the data to be supplemented by such a statement as is mentioned in paragraph (a).

(3) Where the court –

(a) makes an order under subsection (1), or
(b) is satisfied on the application of a data subject that personal data of which he was the data subject and which have been rectified, blocked, erased or destroyed were inaccurate,

it may, where it considers it reasonably practicable, order the data controller to notify third parties to whom the data have been disclosed of the rectification, blocking, erasure or destruction.

(4) If a court is satisfied on the application of a data subject –

(a) that he has suffered damage by reason of any contravention by a data controller of any of the requirements of this Act in respect of any personal data, in circumstances entitling him to compensation under section 13, and
(b) that there is a substantial risk of further contravention in respect of those data in such circumstances,

the court may order the rectification, blocking, erasure or destruction of any of those data.

(5) Where the court makes an order under subsection (4) it may, where it considers it reasonably practicable, order the data controller to notify third parties to whom the data have been disclosed of the rectification, blocking, erasure or destruction.

(6) In determining whether it is reasonably practicable to require such notification as is mentioned in subsection (3) or (5) the court shall have regard, in particular, to the number of persons who would have to be notified.

15 Jurisdiction and procedure

(1) The jurisdiction conferred by sections 7 to 14 is exercisable by the High Court or a county court or, in Scotland, by the Court of Session or the sheriff.

(2) For the purpose of determining any question whether an applicant under subsection (9) of section 7 is entitled to the information which he seeks (including any question whether any relevant data are exempt from that section by virtue of Part IV) a court may require the information constituting any data processed by or on behalf of the data controller and any information as to the logic involved in any decision-taking as mentioned in section 7(1)(d) to be made available for its own inspection but shall not, pending the determination of that question in the applicant's favour, require the information sought by the applicant to be disclosed to him or his representatives whether by discovery (or, in Scotland, recovery) or otherwise.

Part III
Notification by data controllers

16 Preliminary

(1) In this Part 'the registrable particulars', in relation to a data controller, means –

   (a) his name and address,
   (b) if he has nominated a representative for the purposes of this Act, the name and address of the representative,
   (c) a description of the personal data being or to be processed by or on behalf of the data controller and of the category or categories of data subject to which they relate,
   (d) a description of the purpose or purposes for which the data are being or are to be processed,
   (e) a description of any recipient or recipients to whom the data controller intends or may wish to disclose the data,
   (f) the names, or a description of, any countries or territories outside the European Economic Area to which the data controller directly or indirectly transfers, or intends or may wish directly or indirectly to transfer, the data, and
   (g) in any case where –
       (i) personal data are being, or are intended to be, processed in circumstances in which the prohibition in subsection (1) of section 17 is excluded by subsection (2) or (3) of that section, and
       (ii) the notification does not extend to those data,
       a statement of that fact.

(2) In this Part –

   'fees regulations' means regulations made by the Secretary of State under section 18(5) or 19(4) or (7);

   'notification regulations' means regulations made by the Secretary of State under the other provisions of this Part;

'prescribed', except where used in relation to fees regulations, means prescribed by notification regulations.

(3) For the purposes of this Part, so far as it relates to the addresses of data controllers –

  (a) the address of a registered company is that of its registered office, and
  (b) the address of a person (other than a registered company) carrying on a business is that of his principal place of business in the United Kingdom.

17 Prohibition on processing without registration

(1) Subject to the following provisions of this section, personal data must not be processed unless an entry in respect of the data controller is included in the register maintained by the Commissioner under section 19 (or is treated by notification regulations made by virtue of section 19(3) as being so included).

(2) Except where the processing is assessable processing for the purposes of section 22, subsection (1) does not apply in relation to personal data consisting of information which falls neither within paragraph (a) of the definition of 'data' in section 1(1) nor within paragraph (b) of that definition.

(3) If it appears to the Secretary of State that processing of a particular description is unlikely to prejudice the rights and freedoms of data subjects, notification regulations may provide that, in such cases as may be prescribed, subsection (1) is not to apply in relation to processing of that description.

(4) Subsection (1) does not apply in relation to any processing whose sole purpose is the maintenance of a public register.

18 Notification by data controllers

(1) Any data controller who wishes to be included in the register maintained under section 19 shall give a notification to the Commissioner under this section.

(2) A notification under this section must specify in accordance with notification regulations –

  (a) the registrable particulars, and
  (b) a general description of measures to be taken for the purpose of complying with the seventh data protection principle.

(3) Notification regulations made by virtue of subsection (2) may provide for the determination by the Commissioner, in accordance with any requirements of the regulations, of the form in which the registrable particulars and the description mentioned in subsection (2)(b) are to be specified, including in particular the detail required for the purposes of section 16(1)(c), (d), (e) and (f) and subsection (2)(b).

(4) Notification regulations may make provision as to the giving of notification –

  (a) by partnerships, or
  (b) in other cases where two or more persons are the data controllers in respect of any personal data.

(5) The notification must be accompanied by such fee as may be prescribed by fees regulations.

(6) Notification regulations may provide for any fee paid under subsection (5) or section 19(4) to be refunded in prescribed circumstances.

19 Register of notifications

(1) The Commissioner shall –

(a) maintain a register of persons who have given notification under section 18, and
(b) make an entry in the register in pursuance of each notification received by him under that section from a person in respect of whom no entry as data controller was for the time being included in the register.

(2) Each entry in the register shall consist of –

(a) the registrable particulars notified under section 18 or, as the case requires, those particulars as amended in pursuance of section 20(4), and
(b) such other information as the Commissioner may be authorised or required by notification regulations to include in the register.

(3) Notification regulations may make provision as to the time as from which any entry in respect of a data controller is to be treated for the purposes of section 17 as having been made in the register.

(4) No entry shall be retained in the register for more than the relevant time except on payment of such fee as may be prescribed by fees regulations.

(5) In subsection (4) 'the relevant time' means twelve months or such other period as may be prescribed by notification regulations; and different periods may be prescribed in relation to different cases.

(6) The Commissioner –

(a) shall provide facilities for making the information contained in the entries in the register available for inspection (in visible and legible form) by members of the public at all reasonable hours and free of charge, and
(b) may provide such other facilities for making the information contained in those entries available to the public free of charge as he considers appropriate.

(7) The Commissioner shall, on payment of such fee, if any, as may be prescribed by fees regulations, supply any member of the public with a duly certified copy in writing of the particulars contained in any entry made in the register.

20 Duty to notify changes

(1) For the purpose specified in subsection (2), notification regulations shall include provision imposing on every person in respect of whom an entry as a data controller is for the time being included in the register maintained under section 19 a duty to notify to the Commissioner, in such circumstances and at such time or times and in such form as may be prescribed, such matters relating to the registrable particulars and measures taken as mentioned in section 18(2)(b) as may be prescribed.

(2) The purpose referred to in subsection (1) is that of ensuring, so far as practicable, that at any time –

(a) the entries in the register maintained under section 19 contain current names and addresses and describe the current practice or intentions of the data controller with respect to the processing of personal data, and
(b) the Commissioner is provided with a general description of measures currently being taken as mentioned in section 18(2)(b).

(3) Subsection (3) of section 18 has effect in relation to notification regulations made by virtue of subsection (1) as it has effect in relation to notification regulations made by virtue of subsection (2) of that section.

(4) On receiving any notification under notification regulations made by virtue of subsection (1), the Commissioner shall make such amendments of the relevant entry in the register maintained under section 19 as are necessary to take account of the notification.

21 Offences

(1) If section 17(1) is contravened, the data controller is guilty of an offence.

(2) Any person who fails to comply with the duty imposed by notification regulations made by virtue of section 20(1) is guilty of an offence.

(3) It shall be a defence for a person charged with an offence under subsection (2) to show that he exercised all due diligence to comply with the duty.

22 Preliminary assessment by Commissioner

(1) In this section 'assessable processing' means processing which is of a description specified in an order made by the Secretary of State as appearing to him to be particularly likely –

    (a) to cause substantial damage or substantial distress to data subjects, or
    (b) otherwise significantly to prejudice the rights and freedoms of data subjects.

(2) On receiving notification from any data controller under section 18 or under notification regulations made by virtue of section 20 the Commissioner shall consider –

    (a) whether any of the processing to which the notification relates is assessable processing, and
    (b) if so, whether the assessable processing is likely to comply with the provisions of this Act.

(3) Subject to subsection (4), the Commissioner shall, within the period of twenty-eight days beginning with the day on which he receives a notification which relates to assessable processing, give a notice to the data controller stating the extent to which the Commissioner is of the opinion that the processing is likely or unlikely to comply with the provisions of this Act.

(4) Before the end of the period referred to in subsection (3) the Commissioner may, by reason of special circumstances, extend that period on one occasion only by notice to the data controller by such further period not exceeding fourteen days as the Commissioner may specify in the notice.

(5) No assessable processing in respect of which a notification has been given to the Commissioner as mentioned in subsection (2) shall be carried on unless either –

    (a) the period of twenty-eight days beginning with the day on which the notification is received by the Commissioner (or, in a case falling within subsection (4), that period as extended under that subsection) has elapsed, or
    (b) before the end of that period (or that period as so extended) the data controller has received a notice from the Commissioner under subsection (3) in respect of the processing.

(6) Where subsection (5) is contravened, the data controller is guilty of an offence.

(7) The Secretary of State may by order amend subsections (3), (4) and (5) by substituting for the number of days for the time being specified there a different number specified in the order.

23 Power to make provision for appointment of data protection supervisors

(1) The Secretary of State may by order –

   (a) make provision under which a data controller may appoint a person to act as a data protection supervisor responsible in particular for monitoring in an independent manner the data controller's compliance with the provisions of this Act, and

   (b) provide that, in relation to any data controller who has appointed a data protection supervisor in accordance with the provisions of the order and who complies with such conditions as may be specified in the order, the provisions of this Part are to have effect subject to such exemptions or other modifications as may be specified in the order.

(2) An order under this section may –

   (a) impose duties on data protection supervisors in relation to the Commissioner, and

   (b) confer functions on the Commissioner in relation to data protection supervisors.

24 Duty of certain data controllers to make certain information available

(1) Subject to subsection (3), where personal data are processed in a case where –

   (a) by virtue of subsection (2) or (3) of section 17, subsection (1) of that section does not apply to the processing, and

   (b) the data controller has not notified the relevant particulars in respect of that processing under section 18,

the data controller must, within twenty-one days of receiving a written request from any person, make the relevant particulars available to that person in writing free of charge.

(2) In this section 'the relevant particulars' means the particulars referred to in paragraphs (a) to (f) of section 16(1).

(3) This section has effect subject to any exemption conferred for the purposes of this section by notification regulations.

(4) Any data controller who fails to comply with the duty imposed by subsection (1) is guilty of an offence.

(5) It shall be a defence for a person charged with an offence under subsection (4) to show that he exercised all due diligence to comply with the duty.

25 Functions of Commissioner in relation to making of notification regulations

(1) As soon as practicable after the passing of this Act, the Commissioner shall submit to the Secretary of State proposals as to the provisions to be included in the first notification regulations.

(2) The Commissioner shall keep under review the working of notification regulations and may from time to time submit to the Secretary of State proposals as to amendments to be made to the regulations.

(3) The Secretary of State may from time to time require the Commissioner to consider any matter relating to notification regulations and to submit to him proposals as to amendments to be made to the regulations in connection with that matter.

(4) Before making any notification regulations, the Secretary of State shall –

(a) consider any proposals made to him by the Commissioner under subsection (1), (2) or (3), and

(b) consult the Commissioner.

26 Fees regulations

(1) Fees regulations prescribing fees for the purposes of any provision of this Part may provide for different fees to be payable in different cases.

(2) In making any fees regulations, the Secretary of State shall have regard to the desirability of securing that the fees payable to the Commissioner are sufficient to offset –

(a) the expenses incurred by the Commissioner and the Tribunal in discharging their functions and any expenses of the Secretary of State in respect of the Commissioner or the Tribunal, and

(b) to the extent that the Secretary of State considers appropriate –
  (i)   any deficit previously incurred (whether before or after the passing of this Act) in respect of the expenses mentioned in paragraph (a), and
  (ii) expenses incurred or to be incurred by the Secretary of State in respect of the inclusion of any officers or staff of the Commissioner in any scheme under section 1 of the Superannuation Act 1972.

Part IV
Exemptions

27 Preliminary

(1) References in any of the data protection principles or any provision of Parts II and III to personal data or to the processing of personal data do not include references to data or processing which by virtue of this Part are exempt from that principle or other provision.

(2) In this Part 'the subject information provisions' means –

(a) the first data protection principle to the extent to which it requires compliance with paragraph 2 of Part II of Schedule 1, and

(b) section 7.

(3) In this Part 'the non-disclosure provisions' means the provisions specified in subsection (4) to the extent to which they are inconsistent with the disclosure in question.

(4) The provisions referred to in subsection (3) are –

(a) the first data protection principle, except to the extent to which it requires compliance with the conditions in Schedules 2 and 3,

(b) the second, third, fourth and fifth data protection principles, and

(c) sections 10 and 14(1) to (3).

(5) Except as provided by this Part, the subject information provisions shall have effect notwithstanding any enactment or rule of law prohibiting or restricting the disclosure, or authorising the withholding, of information.

28 National security

(1) Personal data are exempt from any of the provisions of –

(a) the data protection principles,

(b)   Parts II, III and V, and

(c)   section 55,

if the exemption from that provision is required for the purpose of safeguarding national security.

(2)   Subject to subsection (4), a certificate signed by a Minister of the Crown certifying that exemption from all or any of the provisions mentioned in subsection (1) is or at any time was required for the purpose there mentioned in respect of any personal data shall be conclusive evidence of that fact.

(3)   A certificate under subsection (2) may identify the personal data to which it applies by means of a general description and may be expressed to have prospective effect.

(4)   Any person directly affected by the issuing of a certificate under subsection (2) may appeal to the Tribunal against the certificate.

(5)   If on an appeal under subsection (4), the Tribunal finds that, applying the principles applied by the court on an application for judicial review, the Minister did not have reasonable grounds for issuing the certificate, the Tribunal may allow the appeal and quash the certificate.

(6)   Where in any proceedings under or by virtue of this Act it is claimed by a data controller that a certificate under subsection (2) which identifies the personal data to which it applies by means of a general description applies to any personal data, any other party to the proceedings may appeal to the Tribunal on the ground that the certificate does not apply to the personal data in question and, subject to any determination under subsection (7), the certificate shall be conclusively presumed so to apply.

(7)   On any appeal under subsection (6), the Tribunal may determine that the certificate does not so apply.

(8)   A document purporting to be a certificate under subsection (2) shall be received in evidence and deemed to be such a certificate unless the contrary is proved.

(9)   A document which purports to be certified by or on behalf of a Minister of the Crown as a true copy of a certificate issued by that Minister under subsection (2) shall in any legal proceedings be evidence (or, in Scotland, sufficient evidence) of that certificate.

(10)   The power conferred by subsection (2) on a Minister of the Crown shall not be exercisable except by a Minister who is a member of the Cabinet or by the Attorney General or the Lord Advocate.

(11)   No power conferred by any provision of Part V may be exercised in relation to personal data which by virtue of this section are exempt from that provision.

(12)   Schedule 6 shall have effect in relation to appeals under subsection (4) or (6) and the proceedings of the Tribunal in respect of any such appeal.

29   Crime and taxation

(1)   Personal data processed for any of the following purposes –

(a)   the prevention or detection of crime,

(b)   the apprehension or prosecution of offenders, or

(c)   the assessment or collection of any tax or duty or of any imposition of a similar nature,

are exempt from the first data protection principle (except to the extent to which it requires compliance with the conditions in Schedules 2 and 3) and section 7 in any case to the extent to which the application of those provisions to the data would be likely to prejudice any of the matters mentioned in this subsection.

(2) Personal data which –

(a) are processed for the purpose of discharging statutory functions, and
(b) consist of information obtained for such a purpose from a person who had it in his possession for any of the purposes mentioned in subsection (1),

are exempt from the subject information provisions to the same extent as personal data processed for any of the purposes mentioned in that subsection.

(3) Personal data are exempt from the non-disclosure provisions in any case in which –

(a) the disclosure is for any of the purposes mentioned in subsection (1), and
(b) the application of those provisions in relation to the disclosure would be likely to prejudice any of the matters mentioned in that subsection.

(4) Personal data in respect of which the data controller is a relevant authority and which –

(a) consist of a classification applied to the data subject as part of a system of risk assessment which is operated by that authority for either of the following purposes –
    (i) the assessment or collection of any tax or duty or any imposition of a similar nature, or
    (ii) the prevention or detection of crime, or apprehension or prosecution of offenders, where the offence concerned involves any unlawful claim for any payment out of, or any unlawful application of, public funds, and
(b) are processed for either of those purposes,

are exempt from section 7 to the extent to which the exemption is required in the interests of the operation of the system.

(5) In subsection (4) –

'public funds' includes funds provided by any Community institution;

'relevant authority' means –

(a) a government department,
(b) a local authority, or
(c) any other authority administering housing benefit or council tax benefit.

30 Health, education and social work

(1) The Secretary of State may by order exempt from the subject information provisions, or modify those provisions in relation to, personal data consisting of information as to the physical or mental health or condition of the data subject.

(2) The Secretary of State may by order exempt from the subject information provisions, or modify those provisions in relation to –

(a) personal data in respect of which the data controller is the proprietor of, or a teacher at, a school, and which consist of information relating to persons who are or have been pupils at the school, or
(b) personal data in respect of which the data controller is an education authority in Scotland, and which consist of information relating to persons who are receiving, or have received, further education provided by the authority.

(3) The Secretary of State may by order exempt from the subject information provisions, or modify those provisions in relation to, personal data of such other descriptions as may be specified in the order, being information –

(a) processed by government departments or local authorities or by voluntary organisations or other bodies designated by or under the order, and

(b) appearing to him to be processed in the course of, or for the purposes of, carrying out social work in relation to the data subject or other individuals;

but the Secretary of State shall not under this subsection confer any exemption or make any modification except so far as he considers that the application to the data of those provisions (or of those provisions without modification) would be likely to prejudice the carrying out of social work.

(4) An order under this section may make different provision in relation to data consisting of information of different descriptions.

(5) In this section –

'education authority' and 'further education' have the same meaning as in the Education (Scotland) Act 1980 ('the 1980 Act'), and

'proprietor' –

(a) in relation to a school in England or Wales, has the same meaning as in the Education Act 1996,

(b) in relation to a school in Scotland, means –

(i) in the case of a self-governing school, the board of management within the meaning of the Self-Governing Schools etc. (Scotland) Act 1989,

(ii) in the case of an independent school, the proprietor within the meaning of the 1980 Act,

(iii) in the case of a grant-aided school, the managers within the meaning of the 1980 Act, and

(iv) in the case of a public school, the education authority within the meaning of the 1980 Act, and

(c) in relation to a school in Northern Ireland, has the same meaning as in the Education and Libraries (Northern Ireland) Order 1986 and includes, in the case of a controlled school, the Board of Governors of the school.

31 Regulatory activity

(1) Personal data processed for the purposes of discharging functions to which this subsection applies are exempt from the subject information provisions in any case to the extent to which the application of those provisions to the data would be likely to prejudice the proper discharge of those functions.

(2) Subsection (1) applies to any relevant function which is designed –

(a) for protecting members of the public against –

(i) financial loss due to dishonesty, malpractice or other seriously improper conduct by, or the unfitness or incompetence of, persons concerned in the provision of banking, insurance, investment or other financial services or in the management of bodies corporate,

(ii) financial loss due to the conduct of discharged or undischarged bankrupts, or

(iii) dishonesty, malpractice or other seriously improper conduct by, or the unfitness or incompetence of, persons authorised to carry on any profession or other activity,

(b) for protecting charities against misconduct or mismanagement (whether by trustees or other persons) in their administration,

(c) for protecting the property of charities from loss or misapplication,

(d) for the recovery of the property of charities,

(e) for securing the health, safety and welfare of persons at work, or

(f) for protecting persons other than persons at work against risk to health or safety arising out of or in connection with the actions of persons at work.

(3) In subsection (2) 'relevant function' means –

(a) any function conferred on any person by or under any enactment,

(b) any function of the Crown, a Minister of the Crown or a government department, or

(c) any other function which is of a public nature and is exercised in the public interest.

(4) Personal data processed for the purpose of discharging any function which –

(a) is conferred by or under any enactment on –
   (i)   the Parliamentary Commissioner for Administration,
   (ii) the Commission for Local Administration in England, the Commission for Local Administration in Wales or the Commissioner for Local Administration in Scotland,
   (iii) the Health Service Commissioner for England, the Health Service Commissioner for Wales or the Health Service Commissioner for Scotland,
   (iv) the Welsh Administration Ombudsman,
   (v)   the Assembly Ombudsman for Northern Ireland, or
   (vi) the Northern Ireland Commissioner for Complaints, and

(b) is designed for protecting members of the public against –
   (i)   maladministration by public bodies,
   (ii) failures in services provided by public bodies, or
   (iii) a failure of a public body to provide a service which it was a function of the body to provide,

are exempt from the subject information provisions in any case to the extent to which the application of those provisions to the data would be likely to prejudice the proper discharge of that function.

(5) Personal data processed for the purpose of discharging any function which –

(a) is conferred by or under any enactment on the Director General of Fair Trading, and

(b) is designed –
   (i)   for protecting members of the public against conduct which may adversely affect their interests by persons carrying on a business,
   (ii) for regulating agreements or conduct which have as their object or effect the prevention, restriction or distortion of competition in connection with any commercial activity, or
   (iii) for regulating conduct on the part of one or more undertakings which amounts to the abuse of a dominant position in a market,

are exempt from the subject information provisions in any case to the extent to which the application of those provisions to the data would be likely to prejudice the proper discharge of that function.

32 Journalism, literature and art

(1) Personal data which are processed only for the special purposes are exempt from any provision to which this subsection relates if –

(a) the processing is undertaken with a view to the publication by any person of any journalistic, literary or artistic material,

(b) the data controller reasonably believes that, having regard in particular to the special importance of the public interest in freedom of expression, publication would be in the public interest, and

(c) the data controller reasonably believes that, in all the circumstances, compliance with that provision is incompatible with the special purposes.

(2) Subsection (1) relates to the provisions of –

(a) the data protection principles except the seventh data protection principle,

(b) section 7,

(c) section 10,

(d) section 12, and

(e) section 14(1) to (3).

(3) In considering for the purposes of subsection (1)(b) whether the belief of a data controller that publication would be in the public interest was or is a reasonable one, regard may be had to his compliance with any code of practice which –

(a) is relevant to the publication in question, and

(b) is designated by the Secretary of State by order for the purposes of this subsection.

(4) Where at any time ('the relevant time') in any proceedings against a data controller under section 7(9), 10(4), 12(8) or 14 or by virtue of section 13 the data controller claims, or it appears to the court, that any personal data to which the proceedings relate are being processed –

(a) only for the special purposes, and

(b) with a view to the publication by any person of any journalistic, literary or artistic material which, at the time twenty-four hours immediately before the relevant time, had not previously been published by the data controller,

the court shall stay the proceedings until either of the conditions in subsection (5) is met.

(5) Those conditions are –

(a) that a determination of the Commissioner under section 45 with respect to the data in question takes effect, or

(b) in a case where the proceedings were stayed on the making of a claim, that the claim is withdrawn.

(6) For the purposes of this Act 'publish', in relation to journalistic, literary or artistic material, means make available to the public or any section of the public.

33 Research, history and statistics

(1) In this section –

'research purposes' includes statistical or historical purposes;

'the relevant conditions', in relation to any processing of personal data, means the conditions –

(a) that the data are not processed to support measures or decisions with respect to particular individuals, and

(b) that the data are not processed in such a way that substantial damage or substantial distress is, or is likely to be, caused to any data subject.

(2) For the purposes of the second data protection principle, the further processing of personal data only for research purposes in compliance with the relevant conditions is not to be regarded as incompatible with the purposes for which they were obtained.

(3) Personal data which are processed only for research purposes in compliance with the relevant conditions may, notwithstanding the fifth data protection principle, be kept indefinitely.

(4) Personal data which are processed only for research purposes are exempt from section 7 if –

    (a) they are processed in compliance with the relevant conditions, and

    (b) the results of the research or any resulting statistics are not made available in a form which identifies data subjects or any of them.

(5) For the purposes of subsections (2) to (4) personal data are not to be treated as processed otherwise than for research purposes merely because the data are disclosed –

    (a) to any person, for research purposes only,

    (b) to the data subject or a person acting on his behalf,

    (c) at the request, or with the consent, of the data subject or a person acting on his behalf, or

    (d) in circumstances in which the person making the disclosure has reasonable grounds for believing that the disclosure falls within paragraph (a), (b) or (c).

34 Information available to the public by or under enactment

Personal data are exempt from –

    (a) the subject information provisions,

    (b) the fourth data protection principle and section 14(1) to (3), and

    (c) the non-disclosure provisions,

if the data consist of information which the data controller is obliged by or under any enactment to make available to the public, whether by publishing it, by making it available for inspection, or otherwise and whether gratuitously or on payment of a fee.

35 Disclosures required by law or made in connection with legal proceedings etc

(1) Personal data are exempt from the non-disclosure provisions where the disclosure is required by or under any enactment, by any rule of law or by the order of a court.

(2) Personal data are exempt from the non-disclosure provisions where the disclosure is necessary –

    (a) for the purpose of, or in connection with, any legal proceedings (including prospective legal proceedings), or

    (b) for the purpose of obtaining legal advice,

or is otherwise necessary for the purposes of establishing, exercising or defending legal rights.

36 Domestic purposes

Personal data processed by an individual only for the purposes of that individual's personal, family or household affairs (including recreational purposes) are exempt from the data protection principles and the provisions of Parts II and III.

37 Miscellaneous exemptions

Schedule 7 (which confers further miscellaneous exemptions) has effect.

38 Powers to make further exemptions by order

(1) The Secretary of State may by order exempt from the subject information provisions personal data consisting of information the disclosure of which is prohibited or restricted by or under any enactment if and to the extent that he considers it necessary for the safeguarding of the interests of the data subject or the rights and freedoms of any other individual that the prohibition or restriction ought to prevail over those provisions.

(2) The Secretary of State may by order exempt from the non-disclosure provisions any disclosures of personal data made in circumstances specified in the order, if he considers the exemption is necessary for the safeguarding of the interests of the data subject or the rights and freedoms of any other individual.

39 Transitional relief

Schedule 8 (which confers transitional exemptions) has effect.

Part V
Enforcement

40 Enforcement notices

(1) If the Commissioner is satisfied that a data controller has contravened or is contravening any of the data protection principles, the Commissioner may serve him with a notice (in this Act referred to as 'an enforcement notice') requiring him, for complying with the principle or principles in question, to do either or both of the following –

(a) to take within such time as may be specified in the notice, or to refrain from taking after such time as may be so specified, such steps as are so specified, or

(b) to refrain from processing any personal data, or any personal data of a description specified in the notice, or to refrain from processing them for a purpose so specified or in a manner so specified, after such time as may be so specified.

(2) In deciding whether to serve an enforcement notice, the Commissioner shall consider whether the contravention has caused or is likely to cause any person damage or distress.

(3) An enforcement notice in respect of a contravention of the fourth data protection principle which requires the data controller to rectify, block, erase or destroy any inaccurate data may also require the data controller to rectify, block, erase or destroy any other data held by him and containing an expression of opinion which appears to the Commissioner to be based on the inaccurate data.

(4) An enforcement notice in respect of a contravention of the fourth data protection principle, in the case of data which accurately record information received or obtained by the data controller from the data subject or a third party, may require the data controller either –

(a) to rectify, block, erase or destroy any inaccurate data and any other data held by him and containing an expression of opinion as mentioned in subsection (3), or

(b) to take such steps as are specified in the notice for securing compliance with the requirements specified in paragraph 7 of Part II of Schedule 1 and, if the Commissioner thinks fit, for supplementing the data with such statement of the true facts relating to the matters dealt with by the data as the Commissioner may approve.

(5) Where –

(a) an enforcement notice requires the data controller to rectify, block, erase or destroy any personal data, or

(b) the Commissioner is satisfied that personal data which have been rectified, blocked, erased or destroyed had been processed in contravention of any of the data protection principles,

an enforcement notice may, if reasonably practicable, require the data controller to notify third parties to whom the data have been disclosed of the rectification, blocking, erasure or destruction; and in determining whether it is reasonably practicable to require such notification regard shall be had, in particular, to the number of persons who would have to be notified.

(6) An enforcement notice must contain –

(a) a statement of the data protection principle or principles which the Commissioner is satisfied have been or are being contravened and his reasons for reaching that conclusion, and

(b) particulars of the rights of appeal conferred by section 48.

(7) Subject to subsection (8), an enforcement notice must not require any of the provisions of the notice to be complied with before the end of the period within which an appeal can be brought against the notice and, if such an appeal is brought, the notice need not be complied with pending the determination or withdrawal of the appeal.

(8) If by reason of special circumstances the Commissioner considers that an enforcement notice should be complied with as a matter of urgency he may include in the notice a statement to that effect and a statement of his reasons for reaching that conclusion; and in that event subsection (7) shall not apply but the notice must not require the provisions of the notice to be complied with before the end of the period of seven days beginning with the day on which the notice is served.

(9) Notification regulations (as defined by section 16(2)) may make provision as to the effect of the service of an enforcement notice on any entry in the register maintained under section 19 which relates to the person on whom the notice is served.

(10) This section has effect subject to section 46(1).

41 Cancellation of enforcement notice

(1) If the Commissioner considers that all or any of the provisions of an enforcement notice need not be complied with in order to ensure compliance with the data protection principle or principles to which it relates, he may cancel or vary the notice by written notice to the person on whom it was served.

(2) A person on whom an enforcement notice has been served may, at any time after the expiry of the period during which an appeal can be brought against that notice, apply in writing to the Commissioner for the cancellation or variation of that notice on the ground that, by reason of a change of circumstances, all or any of the provisions of that notice need not be complied with in order to ensure compliance with the data protection principle or principles to which that notice relates.

42 Request for assessment

(1) A request may be made to the Commissioner by or on behalf of any person who is, or believes himself to be, directly affected by any processing of personal data for an assessment as to whether it is likely or unlikely that the processing has been or is being carried out in compliance with the provisions of this Act.

(2) On receiving a request under this section, the Commissioner shall make an assessment in such manner as appears to him to be appropriate, unless he has not been supplied with such information as he may reasonably require in order to –

(a) satisfy himself as to the identity of the person making the request, and
(b) enable him to identify the processing in question.

(3) The matters to which the Commissioner may have regard in determining in what manner it is appropriate to make an assessment include –

(a) the extent to which the request appears to him to raise a matter of substance,
(b) any undue delay in making the request, and
(c) whether or not the person making the request is entitled to make an application under section 7 in respect of the personal data in question.

(4) Where the Commissioner has received a request under this section he shall notify the person who made the request –

(a) whether he has made an assessment as a result of the request, and
(b) to the extent that he considers appropriate, having regard in particular to any exemption from section 7 applying in relation to the personal data concerned, of any view formed or action taken as a result of the request.

43 Information notices

(1) If the Commissioner –

(a) has received a request under section 42 in respect of any processing of personal data, or
(b) reasonably requires any information for the purpose of determining whether the data controller has complied or is complying with the data protection principles,

he may serve the data controller with a notice (in this Act referred to as 'an information notice') requiring the data controller, within such time as is specified in the notice, to furnish the Commissioner, in such form as may be so specified, with such information relating to the request or to compliance with the principles as is so specified.

(2) An information notice must contain –

(a) in a case falling within subsection (1)(a), a statement that the Commissioner has received a request under section 42 in relation to the specified processing, or
(b) in a case falling within subsection (1)(b), a statement that the Commissioner regards the specified information as relevant for the purpose of determining whether the data controller has complied, or is complying, with the data protection principles and his reasons for regarding it as relevant for that purpose.

(3) An information notice must also contain particulars of the rights of appeal conferred by section 48.

(4) Subject to subsection (5), the time specified in an information notice shall not expire before the end of the period within which an appeal can be brought against the notice and, if such an

appeal is brought, the information need not be furnished pending the determination or withdrawal of the appeal.

(5) If by reason of special circumstances the Commissioner considers that the information is required as a matter of urgency, he may include in the notice a statement to that effect and a statement of his reasons for reaching that conclusion; and in that event subsection (4) shall not apply, but the notice shall not require the information to be furnished before the end of the period of seven days beginning with the day on which the notice is served.

(6) A person shall not be required by virtue of this section to furnish the Commissioner with any information in respect of –

(a) any communication between a professional legal adviser and his client in connection with the giving of legal advice to the client with respect to his obligations, liabilities or rights under this Act, or

(b) any communication between a professional legal adviser and his client, or between such an adviser or his client and any other person, made in connection with or in contemplation of proceedings under or arising out of this Act (including proceedings before the Tribunal) and for the purposes of such proceedings.

(7) In subsection (6) references to the client of a professional legal adviser include references to any person representing such a client.

(8) A person shall not be required by virtue of this section to furnish the Commissioner with any information if the furnishing of that information would, by revealing evidence of the commission of any offence other than an offence under this Act, expose him to proceedings for that offence.

(9) The Commissioner may cancel an information notice by written notice to the person on whom it was served.

(10) This section has effect subject to section 46(3).

44 Special information notices

(1) If the Commissioner –

(a) has received a request under section 42 in respect of any processing of personal data, or
(b) has reasonable grounds for suspecting that, in a case in which proceedings have been stayed under section 32, the personal data to which the proceedings relate –
  (i) are not being processed only for the special purposes, or
  (ii) are not being processed with a view to the publication by any person of any journalistic, literary or artistic material which has not previously been published by the data controller,

he may serve the data controller with a notice (in this Act referred to as a 'special information notice') requiring the data controller, within such time as is specified in the notice, to furnish the Commissioner, in such form as may be so specified, with such information as is so specified for the purpose specified in subsection (2).

(2) That purpose is the purpose of ascertaining –

(a) whether the personal data are being processed only for the special purposes, or
(b) whether they are being processed with a view to the publication by any person of any journalistic, literary or artistic material which has not previously been published by the data controller.

(3) A special information notice must contain –

(a) in a case falling within paragraph (a) of subsection (1), a statement that the Commissioner has received a request under section 42 in relation to the specified processing, or

(b) in a case falling within paragraph (b) of that subsection, a statement of the Commissioner's grounds for suspecting that the personal data are not being processed as mentioned in that paragraph.

(4) A special information notice must also contain particulars of the rights of appeal conferred by section 48.

(5) Subject to subsection (6), the time specified in a special information notice shall not expire before the end of the period within which an appeal can be brought against the notice and, if such an appeal is brought, the information need not be furnished pending the determination or withdrawal of the appeal.

(6) If by reason of special circumstances the Commissioner considers that the information is required as a matter of urgency, he may include in the notice a statement to that effect and a statement of his reasons for reaching that conclusion; and in that event subsection (5) shall not apply, but the notice shall not require the information to be furnished before the end of the period of seven days beginning with the day on which the notice is served.

(7) A person shall not be required by virtue of this section to furnish the Commissioner with any information in respect of –

(a) any communication between a professional legal adviser and his client in connection with the giving of legal advice to the client with respect to his obligations, liabilities or rights under this Act, or

(b) any communication between a professional legal adviser and his client, or between such an adviser or his client and any other person, made in connection with or in contemplation of proceedings under or arising out of this Act (including proceedings before the Tribunal) and for the purposes of such proceedings.

(8) In subsection (7) references to the client of a professional legal adviser include references to any person representing such a client.

(9) A person shall not be required by virtue of this section to furnish the Commissioner with any information if the furnishing of that information would, by revealing evidence of the commission of any offence other than an offence under this Act, expose him to proceedings for that offence.

(10) The Commissioner may cancel a special information notice by written notice to the person on whom it was served.

45 Determination by Commissioner as to the special purposes

(1) Where at any time it appears to the Commissioner (whether as a result of the service of a special information notice or otherwise) that any personal data –

(a) are not being processed only for the special purposes, or

(b) are not being processed with a view to the publication by any person of any journalistic, literary or artistic material which has not previously been published by the data controller,

he may make a determination in writing to that effect.

(2) Notice of the determination shall be given to the data controller; and the notice must contain particulars of the right of appeal conferred by section 48.

(3) A determination under subsection (1) shall not take effect until the end of the period within which an appeal can be brought and, where an appeal is brought, shall not take effect pending the determination or withdrawal of the appeal.

46 Restriction on enforcement in case of processing for the special purposes

(1) The Commissioner may not at any time serve an enforcement notice on a data controller with respect to the processing of personal data for the special purposes unless –

    (a) a determination under section 45(1) with respect to those data has taken effect, and

    (b) the court has granted leave for the notice to be served.

(2) The court shall not grant leave for the purposes of subsection (1)(b) unless it is satisfied –

    (a) that the Commissioner has reason to suspect a contravention of the data protection principles which is of substantial public importance, and

    (b) except where the case is one of urgency, that the data controller has been given notice, in accordance with rules of court, of the application for leave.

(3) The Commissioner may not serve an information notice on a data controller with respect to the processing of personal data for the special purposes unless a determination under section 45(1) with respect to those data has taken effect.

47 Failure to comply with notice

(1) A person who fails to comply with an enforcement notice, an information notice or a special information notice is guilty of an offence.

(2) A person who, in purported compliance with an information notice or a special information notice –

    (a) makes a statement which he knows to be false in a material respect, or

    (b) recklessly makes a statement which is false in a material respect, is guilty of an offence.

(3) It is a defence for a person charged with an offence under subsection (1) to prove that he exercised all due diligence to comply with the notice in question.

48 Rights of appeal

(1) A person on whom an enforcement notice, an information notice or a special information notice has been served may appeal to the Tribunal against the notice.

(2) A person on whom an enforcement notice has been served may appeal to the Tribunal against the refusal of an application under section 41(2) for cancellation or variation of the notice.

(3) Where an enforcement notice, an information notice or a special information notice contains a statement by the Commissioner in accordance with section 40(8), 43(5) or 44(6) then, whether or not the person appeals against the notice, he may appeal against –

    (a) the Commissioner's decision to include the statement in the notice, or

    (b) the effect of the inclusion of the statement as respects any part of the notice.

(4) A data controller in respect of whom a determination has been made under section 45 may appeal to the Tribunal against the determination.

(5) Schedule 6 has effect in relation to appeals under this section and the proceedings of the Tribunal in respect of any such appeal.

49 Determination of appeals

(1) If on an appeal under section 48(1) the Tribunal considers –

  (a) that the notice against which the appeal is brought is not in accordance with the law, or
  (b) to the extent that the notice involved an exercise of discretion by the Commissioner, that he ought to have exercised his discretion differently,

the Tribunal shall allow the appeal or substitute such other notice or decision as could have been served or made by the Commissioner; and in any other case the Tribunal shall dismiss the appeal.

(2) On such an appeal, the Tribunal may review any determination of fact on which the notice in question was based.

(3) If on an appeal under section 48(2) the Tribunal considers that the enforcement notice ought to be cancelled or varied by reason of a change in circumstances, the Tribunal shall cancel or vary the notice.

(4) On an appeal under subsection (3) of section 48 the Tribunal may direct –

  (a) that the notice in question shall have effect as if it did not contain any such statement as is mentioned in that subsection, or
  (b) that the inclusion of the statement shall not have effect in relation to any part of the notice,

and may make such modifications in the notice as may be required for giving effect to the direction.

(5) On an appeal under section 48(4), the Tribunal may cancel the determination of the Commissioner.

(6) Any party to an appeal to the Tribunal under section 48 may appeal from the decision of the Tribunal on a point of law to the appropriate court; and that court shall be –

  (a) the High Court of Justice in England if the address of the person who was the appellant before the Tribunal is in England or Wales,
  (b) the Court of Session if that address is in Scotland, and
  (c) the High Court of Justice in Northern Ireland if that address is in Northern Ireland.

(7) For the purposes of subsection (6) –

  (a) the address of a registered company is that of its registered office, and
  (b) the address of a person (other than a registered company) carrying on a business is that of his principal place of business in the United Kingdom.

50 Powers of entry and inspection

Schedule 9 (powers of entry and inspection) has effect.

Part VI
Miscellaneous and General

Functions of Commissioner

51 General duties of Commissioner

(1) It shall be the duty of the Commissioner to promote the following of good practice by data controllers and, in particular, so to perform his functions under this Act as to promote the observance of the requirements of this Act by data controllers.

(2) The Commissioner shall arrange for the dissemination in such form and manner as he considers appropriate of such information as it may appear to him expedient to give to the public about the operation of this Act, about good practice, and about other matters within the scope of his functions under this Act, and may give advice to any person as to any of those matters.

(3) Where –

(a)   the Secretary of State so directs by order, or
(b)   the Commissioner considers it appropriate to do so,

the Commissioner shall, after such consultation with trade associations, data subjects or persons representing data subjects as appears to him to be appropriate, prepare and disseminate to such persons as he considers appropriate codes of practice for guidance as to good practice.

(4) The Commissioner shall also –

(a)   where he considers it appropriate to do so, encourage trade associations to prepare, and to disseminate to their members, such codes of practice, and
(b)   where any trade association submits a code of practice to him for his consideration, consider the code and, after such consultation with data subjects or persons representing data subjects as appears to him to be appropriate, notify the trade association whether in his opinion the code promotes the following of good practice.

(5) An order under subsection (3) shall describe the personal data or processing to which the code of practice is to relate, and may also describe the persons or classes of persons to whom it is to relate.

(6) The Commissioner shall arrange for the dissemination in such form and manner as he considers appropriate of –

(a)   any Community finding as defined by paragraph 15(2) of Part II of Schedule 1,
(b)   any decision of the European Commission, under the procedure provided for in Article 31(2) of the Data Protection Directive, which is made for the purposes of Article 26(3) or (4) of the Directive, and
(c)   such other information as it may appear to him to be expedient to give to data controllers in relation to any personal data about the protection of the rights and freedoms of data subjects in relation to the processing of personal data in countries and territories outside the European Economic Area.

(7) The Commissioner may, with the consent of the data controller, assess any processing of personal data for the following of good practice and shall inform the data controller of the results of the assessment.

(8) The Commissioner may charge such sums as he may with the consent of the Secretary of State determine for any services provided by the Commissioner by virtue of this Part.

(9) In this section –

'good practice' means such practice in the processing of personal data as appears to the Commissioner to be desirable having regard to the interests of data subjects and others, and includes (but is not limited to) compliance with the requirements of this Act;

'trade association' includes any body representing data controllers.

52 Reports and codes of practice to be laid before Parliament

(1) The Commissioner shall lay annually before each House of Parliament a general report on the exercise of his functions under this Act.

(2) The Commissioner may from time to time lay before each House of Parliament such other reports with respect to those functions as he thinks fit.

(3) The Commissioner shall lay before each House of Parliament any code of practice prepared under section 51(3) for complying with a direction of the Secretary of State, unless the code is included in any report laid under subsection (1) or (2).

53 Assistance by Commissioner in cases involving processing for the special purposes

(1) An individual who is an actual or prospective party to any proceedings under section 7(9), 10(4), 12(8) or 14 or by virtue of section 13 which relate to personal data processed for the special purposes may apply to the Commissioner for assistance in relation to those proceedings.

(2) The Commissioner shall, as soon as reasonably practicable after receiving an application under subsection (1), consider it and decide whether and to what extent to grant it, but he shall not grant the application unless, in his opinion, the case involves a matter of substantial public importance.

(3) If the Commissioner decides to provide assistance, he shall, as soon as reasonably practicable after making the decision, notify the applicant, stating the extent of the assistance to be provided.

(4) If the Commissioner decides not to provide assistance, he shall, as soon as reasonably practicable after making the decision, notify the applicant of his decision and, if he thinks fit, the reasons for it.

(5) In this section –

    (a) references to 'proceedings' include references to prospective proceedings, and
    (b) 'applicant', in relation to assistance under this section, means an individual who applies for assistance.

(6) Schedule 10 has effect for supplementing this section.

54 International co-operation

(1) The Commissioner –

    (a) shall continue to be the designated authority in the United Kingdom for the purposes of Article 13 of the Convention, and
    (b) shall be the supervisory authority in the United Kingdom for the purposes of the Data Protection Directive.

(2) The Secretary of State may by order make provision as to the functions to be discharged by the Commissioner as the designated authority in the United Kingdom for the purposes of Article 13 of the Convention.

(3) The Secretary of State may by order make provision as to co-operation by the Commissioner with the European Commission and with supervisory authorities in other EEA States in connection with the performance of their respective duties and, in particular, as to –

(a) the exchange of information with supervisory authorities in other EEA States or with the European Commission, and
(b) the exercise within the United Kingdom at the request of a supervisory authority in another EEA State, in cases excluded by section 5 from the application of the other provisions of this Act, of functions of the Commissioner specified in the order.

(4) The Commissioner shall also carry out any data protection functions which the Secretary of State may by order direct him to carry out for the purpose of enabling Her Majesty's Government in the United Kingdom to give effect to any international obligations of the United Kingdom.

(5) The Commissioner shall, if so directed by the Secretary of State, provide any authority exercising data protection functions under the law of a colony specified in the direction with such assistance in connection with the discharge of those functions as the Secretary of State may direct or approve, on such terms (including terms as to payment) as the Secretary of State may direct or approve.

(6) Where the European Commission makes a decision for the purposes of Article 26(3) or (4) of the Data Protection Directive under the procedure provided for in Article 31(2) of the Directive, the Commissioner shall comply with that decision in exercising his functions under paragraph 9 of Schedule 4 or, as the case may be, paragraph 8 of that Schedule.

(7) The Commissioner shall inform the European Commission and the supervisory authorities in other EEA States –

(a) of any approvals granted for the purposes of paragraph 8 of Schedule 4, and
(b) of any authorisations granted for the purposes of paragraph 9 of that Schedule.

(8) In this section –

'the Convention' means the Convention for the Protection of Individuals with regard to Automatic Processing of Personal Data which was opened for signature on 28th January 1981;

'data protection functions' means functions relating to the protection of individuals with respect to the processing of personal information.

Unlawful obtaining etc of personal data

55 Unlawful obtaining etc of personal data

(1) A person must not knowingly or recklessly, without the consent of the data controller –

(a) obtain or disclose personal data or the information contained in personal data, or
(b) procure the disclosure to another person of the information contained in personal data.

(2) Subsection (1) does not apply to a person who shows –

(a) that the obtaining, disclosing or procuring –
    (i) was necessary for the purpose of preventing or detecting crime, or

     (ii)   was required or authorised by or under any enactment, by any rule of law or by the order of a court,

(b)   that he acted in the reasonable belief that he had in law the right to obtain or disclose the data or information or, as the case may be, to procure the disclosure of the information to the other person,

(c)   that he acted in the reasonable belief that he would have had the consent of the data controller if the data controller had known of the obtaining, disclosing or procuring and the circumstances of it, or

(d)   that in the particular circumstances the obtaining, disclosing or procuring was justified as being in the public interest.

(3) A person who contravenes subsection (1) is guilty of an offence.

(4) A person who sells personal data is guilty of an offence if he has obtained the data in contravention of subsection (1).

(5) A person who offers to sell personal data is guilty of an offence if –

(a)   he has obtained the data in contravention of subsection (1), or

(b)   he subsequently obtains the data in contravention of that subsection.

(6) For the purposes of subsection (5), an advertisement indicating that personal data are or may be for sale is an offer to sell the data.

(7) Section 1(2) does not apply for the purposes of this section; and for the purposes of subsections (4) to (6), 'personal data' includes information extracted from personal data.

(8) References in this section to personal data do not include references to personal data which by virtue of section 28 are exempt from this section.

Records obtained under data subject's right of access

56 Prohibition of requirement as to production of certain records

(1) A person must not, in connection with –

(a)   the recruitment of another person as an employee,

(b)   the continued employment of another person, or

(c)   any contract for the provision of services to him by another person,

require that other person or a third party to supply him with a relevant record or to produce a relevant record to him.

(2) A person concerned with the provision (for payment or not) of goods, facilities or services to the public or a section of the public must not, as a condition of providing or offering to provide any goods, facilities or services to another person, require that other person or a third party to supply him with a relevant record or to produce a relevant record to him.

(3) Subsections (1) and (2) do not apply to a person who shows –

(a)   that the imposition of the requirement was required or authorised by or under any enactment, by any rule of law or by the order of a court, or

(b)   that in the particular circumstances the imposition of the requirement was justified as being in the public interest.

(4) Having regard to the provisions of Part V of the Police Act 1997 (certificates of criminal records etc.), the imposition of the requirement referred to in subsection (1) or (2) is not to be

regarded as being justified as being in the public interest on the ground that it would assist in the prevention or detection of crime.

(5) A person who contravenes subsection (1) or (2) is guilty of an offence.

(6) In this section 'a relevant record' means any record which –

    (a) has been or is to be obtained by a data subject from any data controller specified in the first column of the Table below in the exercise of the right conferred by section 7, and

    (b) contains information relating to any matter specified in relation to that data controller in the second column,

and includes a copy of such a record or a part of such a record.

TABLE

Data controller	Subject-matter
1. Any of the following persons – (a) a chief officer of police of a police force in England and Wales. (b) a chief constable of a police force in Scotland. (c) the Chief Constable of the Royal Ulster Constabulary. (d) the Director General of the National Criminal Intelligence Service. (e) the Director General of the National Crime Squad.	(a) Convictions. (b) Cautions.
2. The Secretary of State.	(a) Convictions. (b) Cautions. (c) His functions under section 53 of the Children and Young Persons Act 1933, section 205(2) or 208 of the Criminal Procedure (Scotland) Act 1995 or section 73 of the Children and Young Persons Act (Northern Ireland) 1968 in relation to any person sentenced to detention. (d) His functions under the Prison Act 1952, the Prisons (Scotland) Act 1989 or the Prison Act (Northern Ireland) 1953 in relation to any person imprisoned or detained. (e) His functions under the Social Security Contributions and Benefits Act 1992, the Social Security Administration Act 1992 or the Jobseekers Act 1995. (f) His functions under Part V of the Police Act 1997.

Data controller	*Subject-matter*
3. The Department of Health and Social Services for Northern Ireland.	Its functions under the Social Security Contributions and Benefits (Northern Ireland) Act 1992, the Social Security Administration (Northern Ireland) Act 1992 or the Jobseekers (Northern Ireland) Order 1995.

(7) In the Table in subsection (6) –

'caution' means a caution given to any person in England and Wales or Northern Ireland in respect of an offence which, at the time when the caution is given, is admitted;

'conviction' has the same meaning as in the Rehabilitation of Offenders Act 1974 or the Rehabilitation of Offenders (Northern Ireland) Order 1978.

(8) The Secretary of State may by order amend –

(a) the Table in subsection (6), and
(b) subsection (7).

(9) For the purposes of this section a record which states that a data controller is not processing any personal data relating to a particular matter shall be taken to be a record containing information relating to that matter.

(10) In this section 'employee' means an individual who –

(a) works under a contract of employment, as defined by section 230(2) of the Employment Rights Act 1996, or
(b) holds any office,

whether or not he is entitled to remuneration; and 'employment' shall be construed accordingly.

57 Avoidance of certain contractual terms relating to health records

(1) Any term or condition of a contract is void in so far as it purports to require an individual –

(a) to supply any other person with a record to which this section applies, or with a copy of such a record or a part of such a record, or
(b) to produce to any other person such a record, copy or part.

(2) This section applies to any record which –

(a) has been or is to be obtained by a data subject in the exercise of the right conferred by section 7, and
(b) consists of the information contained in any health record as defined by section 68(2).

Information provided to Commissioner or Tribunal

58 Disclosure of information

No enactment or rule of law prohibiting or restricting the disclosure of information shall preclude a person from furnishing the Commissioner or the Tribunal with any information necessary for the discharge of their functions under this Act.

59 Confidentiality of information

(1) No person who is or has been the Commissioner, a member of the Commissioner's staff or an agent of the Commissioner shall disclose any information which –

    (a) has been obtained by, or furnished to, the Commissioner under or for the purposes of this Act,

    (b) relates to an identified or identifiable individual or business, and

    (c) is not at the time of the disclosure, and has not previously been, available to the public from other sources,

unless the disclosure is made with lawful authority.

(2) For the purposes of subsection (1) a disclosure of information is made with lawful authority only if, and to the extent that –

    (a) the disclosure is made with the consent of the individual or of the person for the time being carrying on the business,

    (b) the information was provided for the purpose of its being made available to the public (in whatever manner) under any provision of this Act,

    (c) the disclosure is made for the purposes of, and is necessary for, the discharge of –

        (i) any functions under this Act, or

        (ii) any Community obligation,

    (d) the disclosure is made for the purposes of any proceedings, whether criminal or civil and whether arising under, or by virtue of, this Act or otherwise, or

    (e) having regard to the rights and freedoms or legitimate interests of any person, the disclosure is necessary in the public interest.

(3) Any person who knowingly or recklessly discloses information in contravention of subsection (1) is guilty of an offence.

General provisions relating to offences

60 Prosecutions and penalties

(1) No proceedings for an offence under this Act shall be instituted –

    (a) in England or Wales, except by the Commissioner or by or with the consent of the Director of Public Prosecutions;

    (b) in Northern Ireland, except by the Commissioner or by or with the consent of the Director of Public Prosecutions for Northern Ireland.

(2) A person guilty of an offence under any provision of this Act other than paragraph 12 of Schedule 9 is liable –

    (a) on summary conviction, to a fine not exceeding the statutory maximum, or

    (b) on conviction on indictment, to a fine.

(3) A person guilty of an offence under paragraph 12 of Schedule 9 is liable on summary conviction to a fine not exceeding level 5 on the standard scale.

(4) Subject to subsection (5), the court by or before which a person is convicted of –

    (a) an offence under section 21(1), 22(6), 55 or 56,

    (b) an offence under section 21(2) relating to processing which is assessable processing for the purposes of section 22, or

    (c) an offence under section 47(1) relating to an enforcement notice, may order any document or other material used in connection with the processing of personal data and appearing to the court to be connected with the commission of the offence to be forfeited, destroyed or erased.

(5) The court shall not make an order under subsection (4) in relation to any material where a person (other than the offender) claiming to be the owner of or otherwise interested in the material applies to be heard by the court, unless an opportunity is given to him to show cause why the order should not be made.

61 Liability of directors etc

(1) Where an offence under this Act has been committed by a body corporate and is proved to have been committed with the consent or connivance of or to be attributable to any neglect on the part of any director, manager, secretary or similar officer of the body corporate or any person who was purporting to act in any such capacity, he as well as the body corporate shall be guilty of that offence and be liable to be proceeded against and punished accordingly.

(2) Where the affairs of a body corporate are managed by its members subsection (1) shall apply in relation to the acts and defaults of a member in connection with his functions of management as if he were a director of the body corporate.

(3) Where an offence under this Act has been committed by a Scottish partnership and the contravention in question is proved to have occurred with the consent or connivance of, or to be attributable to any neglect on the part of, a partner, he as well as the partnership shall be guilty of that offence and shall be liable to be proceeded against and punished accordingly.

Amendments of Consumer Credit Act 1974

62 Amendments of Consumer Credit Act 1974

(1) In section 158 of the Consumer Credit Act 1974 (duty of agency to disclose filed information) –

  (a) in subsection (1) –
     (i) in paragraph (a) for 'individual' there is substituted 'partnership or other unincorporated body of persons not consisting entirely of bodies corporate', and
     (ii) for 'him' there is substituted 'it',
  (b) in subsection (2), for 'his' there is substituted 'the consumer's', and
  (c) in subsection (3), for 'him' there is substituted 'the consumer'.

(2) In section 159 of that Act (correction of wrong information) for subsection (1) there is substituted –

'(1) Any individual (the 'objector') given –

  (a) information under section 7 of the Data Protection Act 1998 by a credit reference agency, or
  (b) information under section 158,

who considers that an entry in his file is incorrect, and that if it is not corrected he is likely to be prejudiced, may give notice to the agency requiring it either to remove the entry from the file or amend it.'

(3) In subsections (2) to (6) of that section –

  (a) for 'consumer', wherever occurring, there is substituted 'objector', and
  (b) for 'Director', wherever occurring, there is substituted 'the relevant authority'.

(4) After subsection (6) of that section there is inserted –

'(7) The Data Protection Commissioner may vary or revoke any order made by him under this section.

(8) In this section "the relevant authority" means –

   (a) where the objector is a partnership or other unincorporated body of persons, the Director, and
   (b) in any other case, the Data Protection Commissioner.'

(5) In section 160 of that Act (alternative procedure for business consumers) –

   (a) in subsection (4) –
      (i)   for 'him' there is substituted 'to the consumer', and
      (ii) in paragraphs (a) and (b) for 'he' there is substituted 'the consumer' and for 'his' there is substituted 'the consumer's', and
   (b) after subsection (6) there is inserted –

   '(7) In this section "consumer" has the same meaning as in section 158.'

General

63 Application to Crown

(1) This Act binds the Crown.

(2) For the purposes of this Act each government department shall be treated as a person separate from any other government department.

(3) Where the purposes for which and the manner in which any personal data are, or are to be, processed are determined by any person acting on behalf of the Royal Household, the Duchy of Lancaster or the Duchy of Cornwall, the data controller in respect of those data for the purposes of this Act shall be –

   (a) in relation to the Royal Household, the Keeper of the Privy Purse,
   (b) in relation to the Duchy of Lancaster, such person as the Chancellor of the Duchy appoints, and
   (c) in relation to the Duchy of Cornwall, such person as the Duke of Cornwall, or the possessor for the time being of the Duchy of Cornwall, appoints.

(4) Different persons may be appointed under subsection (3)(b) or (c) for different purposes.

(5) Neither a government department nor a person who is a data controller by virtue of subsection (3) shall be liable to prosecution under this Act, but section 55 and paragraph 12 of Schedule 9 shall apply to a person in the service of the Crown as they apply to any other person.

64 Transmission of notices etc by electronic or other means

(1) This section applies to –

   (a) a notice or request under any provision of Part II,
   (b) a notice under subsection (1) of section 24 or particulars made available under that subsection, or
   (c) an application under section 41(2),

but does not apply to anything which is required to be served in accordance with rules of court.

(2) The requirement that any notice, request, particulars or application to which this section applies should be in writing is satisfied where the text of the notice, request, particulars or application –

    (a) is transmitted by electronic means,

    (b) is received in legible form, and

    (c) is capable of being used for subsequent reference.

(3) The Secretary of State may by regulations provide that any requirement that any notice, request, particulars or application to which this section applies should be in writing is not to apply in such circumstances as may be prescribed by the regulations.

65 Service of notices by Commissioner

(1) Any notice authorised or required by this Act to be served on or given to any person by the Commissioner may –

    (a) if that person is an individual, be served on him –
        (i)   by delivering it to him, or
        (ii) by sending it to him by post addressed to him at his usual or last-known place of residence or business, or
        (iii) by leaving it for him at that place;

    (b) if that person is a body corporate or unincorporate, be served on that body –
        (i)   by sending it by post to the proper officer of the body at its principal office, or
        (ii) by addressing it to the proper officer of the body and leaving it at that office;

    (c) if that person is a partnership in Scotland, be served on that partnership –
        (i)   by sending it by post to the principal office of the partnership, or
        (ii) by addressing it to that partnership and leaving it at that office.

(2) In subsection (1)(b) 'principal office', in relation to a registered company, means its registered office and 'proper officer', in relation to any body, means the secretary or other executive officer charged with the conduct of its general affairs.

(3) This section is without prejudice to any other lawful method of serving or giving a notice.

66 Exercise of rights in Scotland by children

(1) Where a question falls to be determined in Scotland as to the legal capacity of a person under the age of sixteen years to exercise any right conferred by any provision of this Act, that person shall be taken to have that capacity where he has a general understanding of what it means to exercise that right.

(2) Without prejudice to the generality of subsection (1), a person or twelve years of age or more shall be presumed to be of sufficient age and maturity to have such understanding as is mentioned in that subsection.

67 Orders, regulations and rules

(1) Any power conferred by this Act on the Secretary of State to make an order, regulations or rules shall be exercisable by statutory instrument.

(2) Any order, regulations or rules made by the Secretary of State under this Act may –

    (a) make different provision for different cases, and

(b) make such supplemental, incidental, consequential or transitional provision or savings as the Secretary of State considers appropriate;

and nothing in section 7(11), 19(5), 26(1) or 30(4) limits the generality of paragraph (a).

(3) Before making –

(a) an order under any provision of this Act other than section 75(3),
(b) any regulations under this Act other than notification regulations (as defined by section 16(2)),

the Secretary of State shall consult the Commissioner.

(4) A statutory instrument containing (whether alone or with other provisions) an order under –

section 10(2)(b),
section 12(5)(b),
section 22(1),
section 30,
section 32(3),
section 38,
section 56(8),
paragraph 10 of Schedule 3, or
paragraph 4 of Schedule 7,

shall not be made unless a draft of the instrument has been laid before and approved by a resolution of each House of Parliament.

(5) A statutory instrument which contains (whether alone or with other provisions) –

(a) an order under –
section 22(7),
section 23,
section 51(3),
section 54(2), (3) or (4),
paragraph 3, 4 or 14 of Part II of Schedule 1,
paragraph 6 of Schedule 2,
paragraph 2, 7 or 9 of Schedule 3,
paragraph 4 of Schedule 4,
paragraph 6 of Schedule 7,
(b) regulations under section 7 which –
(i) prescribe cases for the purposes of subsection (2)(b),
(ii) are made by virtue of subsection (7), or
(iii) relate to the definition of 'the prescribed period',
(c) regulations under section 8(1) or 9(3),
(d) regulations under section 64,
(e) notification regulations (as defined by section 16(2)), or
(f) rules under paragraph 7 of Schedule 6,

and which is not subject to the requirement in subsection (4) that a draft of the instrument be laid before and approved by a resolution of each House of Parliament, shall be subject to annulment in pursuance of a resolution of either House of Parliament.

(6) A statutory instrument which contains only –

(a) regulations prescribing fees for the purposes of any provision of this Act, or
(b) regulations under section 7 prescribing fees for the purposes of any other enactment,

shall be laid before Parliament after being made.

68 Meaning of 'accessible record'

(1) In this Act 'accessible record' means –

    (a)   a health record as defined by subsection (2),

    (b)   an educational record as defined by Schedule 11, or

    (c)   an accessible public record as defined by Schedule 12.

(2) In subsection (1)(a) 'health record' means any record which –

    (a)   consists of information relating to the physical or mental health or condition of an individual, and

    (b)   has been made by or on behalf of a health professional in connection with the care of that individual.

69 Meaning of 'health professional'

(1) In this Act 'health professional' means any of the following –

    (a)   a registered medical practitioner,

    (b)   a registered dentist as defined by section 53(1) of the Dentists Act 1984,

    (c)   a registered optician as defined by section 36(1) of the Opticians Act 1989,

    (d)   a registered pharmaceutical chemist as defined by section 24(1) of the Pharmacy Act 1954 or a registered person as defined by Article 2(2) of the Pharmacy (Northern Ireland) Order 1976,

    (e)   a registered nurse, midwife or health visitor,

    (f)   a registered osteopath as defined by section 41 of the Osteopaths Act 1993,

    (g)   a registered chiropractor as defined by section 43 of the Chiropractors Act 1994,

    (h)   any person who is registered as a member of a profession to which the Professions Supplementary to Medicine Act 1960 for the time being extends,

    (i)   a clinical psychologist, child psychotherapist or speech therapist,

    (j)   a music therapist employed by a health service body, and

    (k)   a scientist employed by such a body as head of a department.

(2) In subsection (1)(a) 'registered medical practitioner' includes any person who is provisionally registered under section 15 or 21 of the Medical Act 1983 and is engaged in such employment as is mentioned in subsection (3) of that section.

(3) In subsection (1) 'health service body' means –

    (a)   a Health Authority established under section 8 of the National Health Service Act 1977,

    (b)   a Special Health Authority established under section 11 of that Act,

    (c)   a Health Board within the meaning of the National Health Service (Scotland) Act 1978,

    (d)   a Special Health Board within the meaning of that Act,

    (e)   the managers of a State Hospital provided under section 102 of that Act,

    (f)   a National Health Service trust first established under section 5 of the National Health Service and Community Care Act 1990 or section 12A of the National Health Service (Scotland) Act 1978,

    (g)   a Health and Social Services Board established under Article 16 of the Health and Personal Social Services (Northern Ireland) Order 1972,

    (h)   a special health and social services agency established under the Health and Personal Social Services (Special Agencies) (Northern Ireland) Order 1990, or

    (i)   a Health and Social Services trust established under Article 10 of the Health and Personal Social Services (Northern Ireland) Order 1991.

70 Supplementary definitions

(1) In this Act, unless the context otherwise requires –

'business' includes any trade or profession;

'the Commissioner' means the Data Protection Commissioner;

'credit reference agency' has the same meaning as in the Consumer Credit Act 1974;

'the Data Protection Directive' means Directive 95/46/EC on the protection of individuals with regard to the processing of personal data and on the free movement of such data;

'EEA State' means a State which is a contracting party to the Agreement on the European Economic Area signed at Oporto on 2nd May 1992 as adjusted by the Protocol signed at Brussels on 17th March 1993;

'enactment' includes an enactment passed after this Act;

'government department' includes a Northern Ireland department and any body or authority exercising statutory functions on behalf of the Crown;

'Minister of the Crown' has the same meaning as in the Ministers of the Crown Act 1975;

'public register' means any register which pursuant to a requirement imposed –

(a) by or under any enactment, or
(b) in pursuance of any international agreement,

is open to public inspection or open to inspection by any person having a legitimate interest;

'pupil' –

(a) in relation to a school in England and Wales, means a registered pupil within the meaning of the Education Act 1996,
(b) in relation to a school in Scotland, means a pupil within the meaning of the Education (Scotland) Act 1980, and
(c) in relation to a school in Northern Ireland, means a registered pupil within the meaning of the Education and Libraries (Northern Ireland) Order 1986;

'recipient', in relation to any personal data, means any person to whom the data are disclosed, including any person (such as an employee or agent of the data controller, a data processor or an employee or agent of a data processor) to whom they are disclosed in the course of processing the data for the data controller, but does not include any person to whom disclosure is or may be made as a result of, or with a view to, a particular inquiry by or on behalf of that person made in the exercise of any power conferred by law;

'registered company' means a company registered under the enactments relating to companies for the time being in force in the United Kingdom;

'school' –

(a) in relation to England and Wales, has the same meaning as in the Education Act 1996,
(b) in relation to Scotland, has the same meaning as in the Education (Scotland) Act 1980, and
(c) in relation to Northern Ireland, has the same meaning as in the Education and Libraries (Northern Ireland) Order 1986;

'teacher' includes –

(a) in Great Britain, head teacher, and
(b) in Northern Ireland, the principal of a school;

'third party', in relation to personal data, means any person other than –

(a) the data subject,

(b) the data controller, or

(c) any data processor or other person authorised to process data for the data controller or processor;

'the Tribunal' means the Data Protection Tribunal.

(2) For the purposes of this Act data are inaccurate if they are incorrect or misleading as to any matter of fact.

71 Index of defined expressions

The following Table shows provisions defining or otherwise explaining expressions used in this Act (other than provisions defining or explaining an expression only used in the same section or Schedule) –

accessible record	section 68
address (in Part III)	section 16(3)
business	section 70(1)
the Commissioner	section 70(1)
credit reference agency	section 70(1)
data	section 1(1)
data controller	sections 1(1) and (4) and 63(3)
data processor	section 1(1)
the Data Protection Directive	section 70(1)
data protection principles	section 4 and Schedule 1
data subject	section 1(1)
disclosing (of personal data)	section 1(2)(b)
EEA State	section 70(1)
enactment	section 70(1)
enforcement notice	section 40(1)
fees regulations (in Part III)	section 16(2)
government department	section 70(1)
health professional	section 69
inaccurate (in relation to data)	section 70(2)
information notice	section 43(1)
Minister of the Crown	section 70(1)
the non-disclosure provisions (in Part IV)	section 27(3)
notification regulations (in Part III)	section 16(2)
obtaining (of personal data)	section 1(2)(a)
personal data	section 1(1)
prescribed (in Part III)	section 16(2)
processing (of information or data)	section 1(1) and paragraph 5 of Schedule 8
public register	section 70(1)
publish (in relation to journalistic, literary or artistic material)	section 32(6)
pupil (in relation to a school)	section 70(1)
recipient (in relation to personal data)	section 70(1)
recording (of personal data)	section 1(2)(a)
registered company	section 70(1)
registrable particulars (in Part III)	section 16(1)
relevant filing system	section 1(1)

school	section 70(1)
sensitive personal data	section 2
special information notice	section 44(1)
the special purposes	section 3
the subject information provisions (in Part IV)	section 27(2)
teacher	section 70(1)
third party (in relation to processing of personal data)	section 70(1)
the Tribunal	section 70(1)
using (of personal data)	section 1(2)(b)

72 Modifications of Act

During the period beginning with the commencement of this section and ending with 23rd October 2007, the provisions of this Act shall have effect subject to the modifications set out in Schedule 13.

73 Transitional provisions and savings

Schedule 14 (which contains transitional provisions and savings) has effect.

74 Minor and consequential amendments and repeals and revocations

(1) Schedule 15 (which contains minor and consequential amendments) has effect.

(2) The enactments and instruments specified in Schedule 16 are repealed or revoked to the extent specified.

75 Short title, commencement and extent

(1) This Act may be cited as the Data Protection Act 1998.

(2) The following provisions of this Act –

   (a)   sections 1 to 3,
   (b)   section 25(1) and (4),
   (c)   section 26,
   (d)   sections 67 to 71,
   (e)   this section,
   (f)   paragraph 17 of Schedule 5,
   (g)   Schedule 11,
   (h)   Schedule 12, and
   (i)   so much of any other provision of this Act as confers any power to make subordinate legislation,

shall come into force on the day on which this Act is passed.

(3) The remaining provisions of this Act shall come into force on such day as the Secretary of State may by order appoint; and different days may be appointed for different purposes.

(4) The day appointed under subsection (3) for the coming into force of section 56 must not be earlier than the first day on which sections 112, 113 and 115 of the Police Act 1997 (which provide for the issue by the Secretary of State of criminal conviction certificates, criminal record certificates and enhanced criminal record certificates) are all in force.

(5) Subject to subsection (6), this Act extends to Northern Ireland.

(6) Any amendment, repeal or revocation made by Schedule 15 or 16 has the same extent as that of the enactment or instrument to which it relates.

SCHEDULES

SCHEDULE 1
The data protection principles

Part I
The principles

1 Personal data shall be processed fairly and lawfully and, in particular, shall not be processed unless –

(a) at least one of the conditions in Schedule 2 is met, and

(b) in the case of sensitive personal data, at least one of the conditions in Schedule 3 is also met.

2 Personal data shall be obtained only for one or more specified and lawful purposes, and shall not be further processed in any manner incompatible with that purpose or those purposes.

3 Personal data shall be adequate, relevant and not excessive in relation to the purpose or purposes for which they are processed.

4 Personal data shall be accurate and, where necessary, kept up to date.

5 Personal data processed for any purpose or purposes shall not be kept for longer than is necessary for that purpose or those purposes.

6 Personal data shall be processed in accordance with the rights of data subjects under this Act.

7 Appropriate technical and organisational measures shall be taken against unauthorised or unlawful processing of personal data and against accidental loss or destruction of, or damage to, personal data.

8 Personal data shall not be transferred to a country or territory outside the European Economic Area unless that country or territory ensures an adequate level of protection for the rights and freedoms of data subjects in relation to the processing of personal data.

Part II
Interpretation of the principles in Part I

The first principle

1—(1) In determining for the purposes of the first principle whether personal data are processed fairly, regard is to be had to the method by which they are obtained, including in particular whether any person from whom they are obtained is deceived or misled as to the purpose or purposes for which they are to be processed.

(2) Subject to paragraph 2, for the purposes of the first principle data are to be treated as obtained fairly if they consist of information obtained from a person who –

(a) is authorised by or under any enactment to supply it, or

(b) is required to supply it by or under any enactment or by any convention or other instrument imposing an international obligation on the United Kingdom.

2—(1) Subject to paragraph 3, for the purposes of the first principle personal data are not to be treated as processed fairly unless –

(a) in the case of data obtained from the data subject, the data controller ensures so far as practicable that the data subject has, is provided with, or has made readily available to him, the information specified in sub-paragraph (3), and

(b) in any other case, the data controller ensures so far as practicable that, before the relevant time or as soon as practicable after that time, the data subject has, is provided with, or has made readily available to him, the information specified in sub-paragraph (3).

(2) In sub-paragraph (1)(b) 'the relevant time' means –

(a) the time when the data controller first processes the data, or

(b) in a case where at that time disclosure to a third party within a reasonable period is envisaged –

    (i) if the data are in fact disclosed to such a person within that period, the time when the data are first disclosed,

    (ii) if within that period the data controller becomes, or ought to become, aware that the data are unlikely to be disclosed to such a person within that period, the time when the data controller does become, or ought to become, so aware, or

    (iii) in any other case, the end of that period.

(3) The information referred to in sub-paragraph (1) is as follows, namely –

(a) the identity of the data controller,

(b) if he has nominated a representative for the purposes of this Act, the identity of that representative,

(c) the purpose or purposes for which the data are intended to be processed, and

(d) any further information which is necessary, having regard to the specific circumstances in which the data are or are to be processed, to enable processing in respect of the data subject to be fair.

3—(1) Paragraph 2(1)(b) does not apply where either of the primary conditions in sub-paragraph (2), together with such further conditions as may be prescribed by the Secretary of State by order, are met.

(2) The primary conditions referred to in sub-paragraph (1) are –

(a) that the provision of that information would involve a disproportionate effort, or

(b) that the recording of the information to be contained in the data by, or the disclosure of the data by the data controller is necessary for compliance with any legal obligation to which the data controller is subject, other than an obligation imposed by contract.

4—(1) Personal data which contain a general identifier falling within a description prescribed by the Secretary of State by order are not to be treated as processed fairly and lawfully unless they are processed in compliance with any conditions so prescribed in relation to general identifiers of that description.

(2) In sub-paragraph (1) 'a general identifier' means any identifier (such as, for example, a number or code used for identification purposes) which –

(a) relates to an individual, and

(b) forms part of a set of similar identifiers which is of general application.

The second principle

5 The purpose or purposes for which personal data are obtained may in particular be specified –

(a) in a notice given for the purposes of paragraph 2 by the data controller to the data subject, or

(b) in a notification given to the Commissioner under Part III of this Act.

6 In determining whether any disclosure of personal data is compatible with the purpose or purposes for which the data were obtained, regard is to be had to the purpose or purposes for which the personal data are intended to be processed by any person to whom they are disclosed.

The fourth principle

7 The fourth principle is not to be regarded as being contravened by reason of any inaccuracy in personal data which accurately record information obtained by the data controller from the data subject or a third party in a case where –

(a) having regard to the purpose or purposes for which the data were obtained and further processed, the data controller has taken reasonable steps to ensure the accuracy of the data, and

(b) if the data subject has notified the data controller of the data subject's view that the data are inaccurate, the data indicate that fact.

The sixth principle

8 A person is to be regarded as contravening the sixth principle if, but only if –

(a) he contravenes section 7 by failing to supply information in accordance with that section,

(b) he contravenes section 10 by failing to comply with a notice given under subsection (1) of that section to the extent that the notice is justified or by failing to give a notice under subsection (3) of that section,

(c) he contravenes section 11 by failing to comply with a notice given under subsection (1) of that section, or

(d) he contravenes section 12 by failing to comply with a notice given under subsection (1) or (2)(b) of that section or by failing to give a notification under subsection (2)(a) of that section or a notice under subsection (3) of that section.

The seventh principle

9 Having regard to the state of technological development and the cost of implementing any measures, the measures must ensure a level of security appropriate to –

(a) the harm that might result from such unauthorised or unlawful processing or accidental loss, destruction or damage as are mentioned in the seventh principle, and

(b) the nature of the data to be protected.

10 The data controller must take reasonable steps to ensure the reliability of any employees of his who have access to the personal data.

11 Where processing of personal data is carried out by a data processor on behalf of a data controller, the data controller must in order to comply with the seventh principle –

(a) choose a data processor providing sufficient guarantees in respect of the technical and organisational security measures governing the processing to be carried out, and

(b) take reasonable steps to ensure compliance with those measures.

12 Where processing of personal data is carried out by a data processor on behalf of a data controller, the data controller is not to be regarded as complying with the seventh principle unless –

(a) the processing is carried out under a contract –
  (i)   which is made or evidenced in writing, and
  (ii) under which the data processor is to act only on instructions from the data controller, and
(b) the contract requires the data processor to comply with obligations equivalent to those imposed on a data controller by the seventh principle.

The eighth principle

13 An adequate level of protection is one which is adequate in all the circumstances of the case, having regard in particular to –

(a) the nature of the personal data,
(b) the country or territory of origin of the information contained in the data,
(c) the country or territory of final destination of that information,
(d) the purposes for which and period during which the data are intended to be processed,
(e) the law in force in the country or territory in question,
(f) the international obligations of that country or territory,
(g) any relevant codes of conduct or other rules which are enforceable in that country or territory (whether generally or by arrangement in particular cases), and
(h) any security measures taken in respect of the data in that country or territory.

14 The eighth principle does not apply to a transfer falling within any paragraph of Schedule 4, except in such circumstances and to such extent as the Secretary of State may by order provide.

15—(1) Where –

(a) in any proceedings under this Act any question arises as to whether the requirement of the eighth principle as to an adequate level of protection is met in relation to the transfer of any personal data to a country or territory outside the European Economic Area, and
(b) a Community finding has been made in relation to transfers of the kind in question,

that question is to be determined in accordance with that finding.

(2) In sub-paragraph (1) 'Community finding' means a finding of the European Commission, under the procedure provided for in Article 31(2) of the Data Protection Directive, that a country or territory outside the European Economic Area does, or does not, ensure an adequate level of protection within the meaning of Article 25(2) of the Directive.

SCHEDULE 2

Conditions relevant for purposes of the first principle: processing of any personal data

1 The data subject has given his consent to the processing.

2 The processing is necessary –

(a) for the performance of a contract to which the data subject is a party, or

(b) for the taking of steps at the request of the data subject with a view to entering into a contract.

3 The processing is necessary for compliance with any legal obligation to which the data controller is subject, other than an obligation imposed by contract.

4 The processing is necessary in order to protect the vital interests of the data subject.

5 The processing is necessary –

(a) for the administration of justice,

(b) for the exercise of any functions conferred on any person by or under any enactment,

(c) for the exercise of any functions of the Crown, a Minister of the Crown or a government department, or

(d) for the exercise of any other functions of a public nature exercised in the public interest by any person.

6—(1) The processing is necessary for the purposes of legitimate interests pursued by the data controller or by the third party or parties to whom the data are disclosed, except where the processing is unwarranted in any particular case by reason of prejudice to the rights and freedoms or legitimate interests of the data subject.

(2) The Secretary of State may by order specify particular circumstances in which this condition is, or is not, to be taken to be satisfied.

SCHEDULE 3

Conditions relevant for purposes of the first principle: processing of sensitive personal data

1 The data subject has given his explicit consent to the processing of the personal data.

2—(1) The processing is necessary for the purposes of exercising or performing any right or obligation which is conferred or imposed by law on the data controller in connection with employment.

(2) The Secretary of State may by order –

(a) exclude the application of sub-paragraph (1) in such cases as may be specified, or

(b) provide that, in such cases as may be specified, the condition in sub-paragraph (1) is not to be regarded as satisfied unless such further conditions as may be specified in the order are also satisfied.

3 The processing is necessary –

(a) in order to protect the vital interests of the data subject or another person, in a case where –

(i) consent cannot be given by or on behalf of the data subject, or

(ii) the data controller cannot reasonably be expected to obtain the consent of the data subject, or

(b) in order to protect the vital interests of another person, in a case where consent by or on behalf of the data subject has been unreasonably withheld.

4 The processing –

(a) is carried out in the course of its legitimate activities by any body or association which –

    (i)   is not established or conducted for profit, and

    (ii)   exists for political, philosophical, religious or trade-union purposes,

(b)   is carried out with appropriate safeguards for the rights and freedoms of data subjects,

(c)   relates only to individuals who either are members of the body or association or have regular contact with it in connection with its purposes, and

(d)   does not involve disclosure of the personal data to a third party without the consent of the data subject.

5 The information contained in the personal data has been made public as a result of steps deliberately taken by the data subject.

6 The processing –

(a)   is necessary for the purpose of, or in connection with, any legal proceedings (including prospective legal proceedings),

(b)   is necessary for the purpose of obtaining legal advice, or

(c)   is otherwise necessary for the purposes of establishing, exercising or defending legal rights.

7—(1) The processing is necessary –

(a)   for the administration of justice,

(b)   for the exercise of any functions conferred on any person by or under an enactment, or

(c)   for the exercise of any functions of the Crown, a Minister of the Crown or a government department.

(2) The Secretary of State may by order –

(a)   exclude the application of sub-paragraph (1) in such cases as may be specified, or

(b)   provide that, in such cases as may be specified, the condition in sub-paragraph (1) is not to be regarded as satisfied unless such further conditions as may be specified in the order are also satisfied.

8—(1) The processing is necessary for medical purposes and is undertaken by –

(a)   a health professional, or

(b)   a person who in the circumstances owes a duty of confidentiality which is equivalent to that which would arise if that person were a health professional.

(2) In this paragraph 'medical purposes' includes the purposes of preventative medicine, medical diagnosis, medical research, the provision of care and treatment and the management of healthcare services.

9—(1) The processing –

(a)   is of sensitive personal data consisting of information as to racial or ethnic origin,

(b)   is necessary for the purpose of identifying or keeping under review the existence or absence of equality of opportunity or treatment between persons of different racial or ethnic origins, with a view to enabling such equality to be promoted or maintained, and

(c)   is carried out with appropriate safeguards for the rights and freedoms of data subjects.

(2) The Secretary of State may by order specify circumstances in which processing falling within sub-paragraph (1)(a) and (b) is, or is not, to be taken for the purposes of sub-paragraph (1)(c) to be carried out with appropriate safeguards for the rights and freedoms of data subjects.

10 The personal data are processed in circumstances specified in an order made by the Secretary of State for the purposes of this paragraph.

SCHEDULE 4

Cases where the eighth principle does not apply

1 The data subject has given his consent to the transfer.

2 The transfer is necessary –

   (a) for the performance of a contract between the data subject and the data controller, or
   (b) for the taking of steps at the request of the data subject with a view to his entering into a contract with the data controller.

3 The transfer is necessary –

   (a) for the conclusion of a contract between the data controller and a person other than the data subject which –
       (i)   is entered into at the request of the data subject, or
       (ii) is in the interests of the data subject, or
   (b) for the performance of such a contract.

4—(1) The transfer is necessary for reasons of substantial public interest.

(2) The Secretary of State may by order specify –

   (a) circumstances in which a transfer is to be taken for the purposes of sub-paragraph (1) to be necessary for reasons of substantial public interest, and
   (b) circumstances in which a transfer which is not required by or under an enactment is not to be taken for the purpose of sub-paragraph (1) to be necessary for reasons of substantial public interest.

5 The transfer –

   (a) is necessary for the purpose of, or in connection with, any legal proceedings (including prospective legal proceedings),
   (b) is necessary for the purpose of obtaining legal advice, or
   (c) is otherwise necessary for the purposes of establishing, exercising or defending legal rights.

6 The transfer is necessary in order to protect the vital interests of the data subject.

7 The transfer is of part of the personal data on a public register and any conditions subject to which the register is open to inspection are complied with by any person to whom the data are or may be disclosed after the transfer.

8 The transfer is made on terms which are of a kind approved by the Commissioner as ensuring adequate safeguards for the rights and freedoms of data subjects.

9 The transfer has been authorised by the Commissioner as being made in such a manner as to ensure adequate safeguards for the rights and freedoms of data subjects.

SCHEDULE 5

The Data Protection Commissioner and the Data Protection Tribunal

Part I
The Commissioner

Status and capacity

1—(1) The corporation sole by the name of the Data Protection Registrar established by the Data Protection Act 1984 shall continue in existence by the name of the Data Protection Commissioner.

(2) The Commissioner and his officers and staff are not to be regarded as servants or agents of the Crown.

Tenure of office

2—(1) Subject to the provisions of this paragraph, the Commissioner shall hold office for such term not exceeding five years as may be determined at the time of his appointment.

(2) The Commissioner may be relieved of his office by Her Majesty at his own request.

(3) The Commissioner may be removed from office by Her Majesty in pursuance of an Address from both Houses of Parliament.

(4) The Commissioner shall in any case vacate his office –

    (a) on completing the year of service in which he attains the age of sixty-five years, or
    (b) if earlier, on completing his fifteenth year of service.

(5) Subject to sub-paragraph (4), a person who ceases to be Commissioner on the expiration of his term of office shall be eligible for re-appointment, but a person may not be re-appointed for a third or subsequent term as Commissioner unless, by reason of special circumstances, the person's re-appointment for such a term is desirable in the public interest.

Salary etc

3—(1) There shall be paid –

    (a) to the Commissioner such salary, and
    (b) to or in respect of the Commissioner such pension, as may be specified by a resolution of the House of Commons.

(2) A resolution for the purposes of this paragraph may –

    (a) specify the salary or pension,
    (b) provide that the salary or pension is to be the same as, or calculated on the same basis as, that payable to, or to or in respect of, a person employed in a specified office under, or in a specified capacity in the service of, the Crown, or
    (c) specify the salary or pension and provide for it to be increased by reference to such variables as may be specified in the resolution.

(3) A resolution for the purposes of this paragraph may take effect from the date on which it is passed or from any earlier or later date specified in the resolution.

(4) A resolution for the purposes of this paragraph may make different provision in relation to the pension payable to or in respect of different holders of the office of Commissioner.

(5) Any salary or pension payable under this paragraph shall be charged on and issued out of the Consolidated Fund.

(6) In this paragraph 'pension' includes an allowance or gratuity and any reference to the payment of a pension includes a reference to the making of payments towards the provision of a pension.

Officers and staff

4—(1) The Commissioner –

(a) shall appoint a deputy commissioner, and
(b) may appoint such number of other officers and staff as he may determine.

(2) The remuneration and other conditions of service of the persons appointed under this paragraph shall be determined by the Commissioner.

(3) The Commissioner may pay such pensions, allowances or gratuities to or in respect of the persons appointed under this paragraph, or make such payments towards the provision of such pensions, allowances or gratuities, as he may determine.

(4) The references in sub-paragraph (3) to pensions, allowances or gratuities to or in respect of the persons appointed under this paragraph include references to pensions, allowances or gratuities by way of compensation to or in respect of any of those persons who suffer loss of office or employment.

(5) Any determination under sub-paragraph (1)(b), (2) or (3) shall require the approval of the Secretary of State.

(6) The Employers' Liability (Compulsory Insurance) Act 1969 shall not require insurance to be effected by the Commissioner.

5—(1) The deputy commissioner shall perform the functions conferred by this Act on the Commissioner during any vacancy in that office or at any time when the Commissioner is for any reason unable to act.

(2) Without prejudice to sub-paragraph (1), any functions of the Commissioner under this Act may, to the extent authorised by him, be performed by any of his officers or staff.

Authentication of seal of the Commissioner

6 The application of the seal of the Commissioner shall be authenticated by his signature or by the signature of some other person authorised for the purpose.

Presumption of authenticity of documents issued by the Commissioner

7 Any document purporting to be an instrument issued by the Commissioner and to be duly executed under the Commissioner's seal or to be signed by or on behalf of the Commissioner shall be received in evidence and shall be deemed to be such an instrument unless the contrary is shown.

Money

8 The Secretary of State may make payments to the Commissioner out of money provided by Parliament.

9—(1) All fees and other sums received by the Commissioner in the exercise of his functions under this Act or section 159 of the Consumer Credit Act 1974 shall be paid by him to the Secretary of State.

(2) Sub-paragraph (1) shall not apply where the Secretary of State, with the consent of the Treasury, otherwise directs.

(3) Any sums received by the Secretary of State under sub-paragraph (1) shall be paid into the Consolidated Fund.

Accounts

10—(1) It shall be the duty of the Commissioner –

  (a) to keep proper accounts and other records in relation to the accounts,
  (b) to prepare in respect of each financial year a statement of account in such form as the Secretary of State may direct, and
  (c) to send copies of that statement to the Comptroller and Auditor General on or before 31st August next following the end of the year to which the statement relates or on or before such earlier date after the end of that year as the Treasury may direct.

(2) The Comptroller and Auditor General shall examine and certify any statement sent to him under this paragraph and lay copies of it together with his report thereon before each House of Parliament.

(3) In this paragraph 'financial year' means a period of twelve months beginning with 1st April.

Application of Part I in Scotland

11 Paragraphs 1(1), 6 and 7 do not extend to Scotland.

Part II
The Tribunal

Tenure of office

12—(1) Subject to the following provisions of this paragraph, a member of the Tribunal shall hold and vacate his office in accordance with the terms of his appointment and shall, on ceasing to hold office, be eligible for re-appointment.

(2) Any member of the Tribunal may at any time resign his office by notice in writing to the Lord Chancellor (in the case of the chairman or a deputy chairman) or to the Secretary of State (in the case of any other member).

(3) A person who is the chairman or deputy chairman of the Tribunal shall vacate his office on the day on which he attains the age of seventy years; but this sub-paragraph is subject to section 26(4) to (6) of the Judicial Pensions and Retirement Act 1993 (power to authorise continuance in office up to the age of seventy-five years).

Salary etc.

13 The Secretary of State shall pay to the members of the Tribunal out of money provided by Parliament such remuneration and allowances as he may determine.

Officers and staff

14 The Secretary of State may provide the Tribunal with such officers and staff as he thinks necessary for the proper discharge of its functions.

Expenses

15 Such expenses of the Tribunal as the Secretary of State may determine shall be defrayed by the Secretary of State out of money provided by Parliament.

Part III
Transitional provisions

16 Any reference in any enactment, instrument or other document to the Data Protection Registrar shall be construed, in relation to any time after the commencement of section 6(1), as a reference to the Commissioner.

17 Any reference in this Act or in any instrument under this Act to the Commissioner shall be construed, in relation to any time before the commencement of section 6(1), as a reference to the Data Protection Registrar.

SCHEDULE 6

Appeal proceedings

Hearing of appeals

1 For the purpose of hearing and determining appeals or any matter preliminary or incidental to an appeal the Tribunal shall sit at such times and in such places as the chairman or a deputy chairman may direct and may sit in two or more divisions.

Constitution of Tribunal in national security cases

2—(1) The Lord Chancellor shall from time to time designate, from among the chairman and deputy chairmen appointed by him under section 6(4)(a) and (b), those persons who are to be capable of hearing appeals under section 28(4) or (6).

(2) A designation under sub-paragraph (1) may at any time be revoked by the Lord Chancellor.

3 In any case where the application of paragraph 6(1) is excluded by rules under paragraph 7, the Tribunal shall be duly constituted for an appeal under section 28(4) or (6) if it consists of three of the persons designated under paragraph 2(1), of whom one shall be designated by the Lord Chancellor to preside.

Constitution of Tribunal in other cases

4—(1) Subject to any rules made under paragraph 7, the Tribunal shall be duly constituted for an appeal under section 48(1), (2) or (4) if it consists of –

   (a) the chairman or a deputy chairman (who shall preside), and
   (b) an equal number of the members appointed respectively in accordance with paragraphs (a) and (b) of section 6(6).

(2) The members who are to constitute the Tribunal in accordance with sub-paragraph (1) shall be nominated by the chairman or, if he is for any reason unable to act, by a deputy chairman.

Determination of questions by full Tribunal

5 The determination of any question before the Tribunal when constituted in accordance with paragraph 3 or 4 shall be according to the opinion of the majority of the members hearing the appeal.

Ex parte proceedings

6—(1) Subject to any rules made under paragraph 7, the jurisdiction of the Tribunal in respect of an appeal under section 28(4) or (6) shall be exercised ex parte by one or more persons designated under paragraph 2(1).

(2) Subject to any rules made under paragraph 7, the jurisdiction of the Tribunal in respect of an appeal under section 48(3) shall be exercised ex parte by the chairman or a deputy chairman sitting alone.

Rules of procedure

7—(1) The Secretary of State may make rules for regulating the exercise of the rights of appeal conferred by sections 28(4) or (6) and 48 and the practice and procedure of the Tribunal.

(2) Rules under this paragraph may in particular make provision –

    (a) with respect to the period within which an appeal can be brought and the burden of proof on an appeal,

    (b) for the summoning (or, in Scotland, citation) of witnesses and the administration of oaths,

    (c) for securing the production of documents and material used for the processing of personal data,

    (d) for the inspection, examination, operation and testing of any equipment or material used in connection with the processing of personal data,

    (e) for the hearing of an appeal wholly or partly in camera,

    (f) for hearing an appeal in the absence of the appellant or for determining an appeal without a hearing,

    (g) for enabling an appeal under section 48(1) against an information notice to be determined by the chairman or a deputy chairman,

    (h) for enabling any matter preliminary or incidental to an appeal to be dealt with by the chairman or a deputy chairman,

    (i) for the awarding of costs or, in Scotland, expenses,

    (j) for the publication of reports of the Tribunal's decisions, and

    (k) for conferring on the Tribunal such ancillary powers as the Secretary of State thinks necessary for the proper discharge of its functions.

(3) In making rules under this paragraph which relate to appeals under section 28(4) or (6) the Secretary of State shall have regard, in particular, to the need to secure that information is not disclosed contrary to the public interest.

Obstruction etc

8—(1) If any person is guilty of any act or omission in relation to proceedings before the Tribunal which, if those proceedings were proceedings before a court having power to commit for contempt, would constitute contempt of court, the Tribunal may certify the offence to the High Court or, in Scotland, the Court of Session.

(2) Where an offence is so certified, the court may inquire into the matter and, after hearing any witness who may be produced against or on behalf of the person charged with the offence, and after hearing any statement that may be offered in defence, deal with him in any manner in which it could deal with him if he had committed the like offence in relation to the court.

SCHEDULE 7

Miscellaneous exemptions

Confidential references given by the data controller

1 Personal data are exempt from section 7 if they consist of a reference given or to be given in confidence by the data controller for the purposes of –

 (a) the education, training or employment, or prospective education, training or employment, of the data subject,
 (b) the appointment, or prospective appointment, of the data subject to any office, or
 (c) the provision, or prospective provision, by the data subject of any service.

Armed forces

2 Personal data are exempt from the subject information provisions in any case to the extent to which the application of those provisions would be likely to prejudice the combat effectiveness of any of the armed forces of the Crown.

Judicial appointments and honours

3 Personal data processed for the purposes of –

 (a) assessing any person's suitability for judicial office or the office of Queen's Counsel, or
 (b) the conferring by the Crown of any honour,

are exempt from the subject information provisions.

Crown employment and Crown or Ministerial appointments

4 The Secretary of State may by order exempt from the subject information provisions personal data processed for the purposes of assessing any person's suitability for –

 (a) employment by or under the Crown, or
 (b) any office to which appointments are made by Her Majesty, by a Minister of the Crown or by a Northern Ireland department.

Management forecasts etc.

5 Personal data processed for the purposes of management forecasting or management planning to assist the data controller in the conduct of any business or other activity are exempt from the subject information provisions in any case to the extent to which the application of those provisions would be likely to prejudice the conduct of that business or other activity.

Corporate finance

6—(1) Where personal data are processed for the purposes of, or in connection with, a corporate finance service provided by a relevant person –

  (a) the data are exempt from the subject information provisions in any case to the extent to which either –
       (i)   the application of those provisions to the data could affect the price of any instrument which is already in existence or is to be or may be created, or
       (ii) the data controller reasonably believes that the application of those provisions to the data could affect the price of any such instrument, and
  (b) to the extent that the data are not exempt from the subject information provisions by virtue of paragraph (a), they are exempt from those provisions if the exemption is required for the purpose of safeguarding an important economic or financial interest of the United Kingdom.

(2) For the purposes of sub-paragraph (1)(b) the Secretary of State may by order specify –

  (a) matters to be taken into account in determining whether exemption from the subject information provisions is required for the purpose of safeguarding an important economic or financial interest of the United Kingdom, or
  (b) circumstances in which exemption from those provisions is, or is not, to be taken to be required for that purpose.

(3) In this paragraph –

'corporate finance service' means a service consisting in –

  (a) underwriting in respect of issues of, or the placing of issues of, any instrument,
  (b) advice to undertakings on capital structure, industrial strategy and related matters and advice and service relating to mergers and the purchase of undertakings, or
  (c) services relating to such underwriting as is mentioned in paragraph (a);

'instrument' means any instrument listed in section B of the Annex to the Council Directive on investment services in the securities field (93/22/EEC), as set out in Schedule 1 to the Investment Services Regulations 1995;

'price' includes value;

'relevant person' means –

  (a) any person who is authorised under Chapter III of Part I of the Financial Services Act 1986 or is an exempted person under Chapter IV of Part I of that Act,
  (b) any person who, but for Part III or IV of Schedule 1 to that Act, would require authorisation under that Act,
  (c) any European investment firm within the meaning given by Regulation 3 of the Investment Services Regulations 1995,
  (d) any person who, in the course of his employment, provides to his employer a service falling within paragraph (b) or (c) of the definition of 'corporate finance service', or
  (e) any partner who provides to other partners in the partnership a service falling within either of those paragraphs.

Negotiations

7 Personal data which consist of records of the intentions of the data controller in relation to any negotiations with the data subject are exempt from the subject information provisions in any case to the extent to which the application of those provisions would be likely to prejudice those negotiations.

Examination marks

8—(1) Section 7 shall have effect subject to the provisions of sub-paragraphs (2) to (4) in the case of personal data consisting of marks or other information processed by a data controller –

(a) for the purpose of determining the results of an academic, professional or other examination or of enabling the results of any such examination to be determined, or

(b) in consequence of the determination of any such results.

(2) Where the relevant day falls before the day on which the results of the examination are announced, the period mentioned in section 7(8) shall be extended until –

(a) the end of five months beginning with the relevant day, or

(b) the end of forty days beginning with the date of the announcement,

whichever is the earlier.

(3) Where by virtue of sub-paragraph (2) a period longer than the prescribed period elapses after the relevant day before the request is complied with, the information to be supplied pursuant to the request shall be supplied both by reference to the data in question at the time when the request is received and (if different) by reference to the data as from time to time held in the period beginning when the request is received and ending when it is complied with.

(4) For the purposes of this paragraph the results of an examination shall be treated as announced when they are first published or (if not published) when they are first made available or communicated to the candidate in question.

(5) In this paragraph –

'examination' includes any process for determining the knowledge, intelligence, skill or ability of a candidate by reference to his performance in any test, work or other activity;

'the prescribed period' means forty days or such other period as is for the time being prescribed under section 7 in relation to to the personal data in question;

'relevant day' has the same meaning as in section 7.

Examination scripts etc

9—(1) Personal data consisting of information recorded by candidates during an academic, professional or other examination are exempt from section 7.

(2) In this paragraph 'examination' has the same meaning as in paragraph 8.

Legal professional privilege

10 Personal data are exempt from the subject information provisions if the data consist of information in respect of which a claim to legal professional privilege or, in Scotland, to confidentiality as between client and professional legal adviser, could be maintained in legal proceedings.

Self-incrimination

11—(1) A person need not comply with any request or order under section 7 to the extent that compliance would, by revealing evidence of the commission of any offence other than an offence under this Act, expose him to proceedings for that offence.

(2) Information disclosed by any person in compliance with any request or order under section 7 shall not be admissible against him in proceedings for an offence under this Act.

SCHEDULE 8

Transitional relief

Part I
Interpretation of Schedule

1—(1) For the purposes of this Schedule, personal data are 'eligible data' at any time if, and to the extent that, they are at that time subject to processing which was already under way immediately before 24th October 1998.

(2) In this Schedule –

'eligible automated data' means eligible data which fall within paragraph (a) or (b) of the definition of 'data' in section 1(1);

'eligible manual data' means eligible data which are not eligible automated data;

'the first transitional period' means the period beginning with the commencement of this Schedule and ending with 23rd October 2001;

'the second transitional period' means the period beginning with 24th October 2001 and ending with 23rd October 2007.

Part II
Exemptions available before 24th October 2001

Manual data

2—(1) Eligible manual data, other than data forming part of an accessible record, are exempt from the data protection principles and Parts II and III of this Act during the first transitional period.

(2) This paragraph does not apply to eligible manual data to which paragraph 4 applies.

3—(1) This paragraph applies to –

  (a) eligible manual data forming part of an accessible record, and

  (b) personal data which fall within paragraph (d) of the definition of 'data' in section 1(1) but which, because they are not subject to processing which was already under way immediately before 24th October 1998, are not eligible data for the purposes of this Schedule.

(2) During the first transitional period, data to which this paragraph applies are exempt from –

  (a) the data protection principles, except the sixth principle so far as relating to sections 7 and 12A,

  (b) Part II of this Act, except –

     (i) section 7 (as it has effect subject to section 8) and section 12A, and

     (ii) section 15 so far as relating to those sections, and

  (c) Part III of this Act.

4—(1) This paragraph applies to eligible manual data which consist of information relevant to the financial standing of the data subject and in respect of which the data controller is a credit reference agency.

(2) During the first transitional period, data to which this paragraph applies are exempt from –

(a) the data protection principles, except the sixth principle so far as relating to sections 7 and 12A,

(b) Part II of this Act, except –
 (i) section 7 (as it has effect subject to sections 8 and 9) and section 12A, and
 (ii) section 15 so far as relating to those sections, and

(c) Part III of this Act.

Processing otherwise than by reference to the data subject

5 During the first transitional period, for the purposes of this Act (apart from paragraph 1), eligible automated data are not to be regarded as being 'processed' unless the processing is by reference to the data subject.

Payrolls and accounts

6—(1) Subject to sub-paragraph (2), eligible automated data processed by a data controller for one or more of the following purposes –

(a) calculating amounts payable by way of remuneration or pensions in respect of service in any employment or office or making payments of, or of sums deducted from, such remuneration or pensions, or

(b) keeping accounts relating to any business or other activity carried on by the data controller or keeping records of purchases, sales or other transactions for the purpose of ensuring that the requisite payments are made by or to him in respect of those transactions or for the purpose of making financial or management forecasts to assist him in the conduct of any such business or activity,

are exempt from the data protection principles and Parts II and III of this Act during the first transitional period.

(2) It shall be a condition of the exemption of any eligible automated data under this paragraph that the data are not processed for any other purpose, but the exemption is not lost by any processing of the eligible data for any other purpose if the data controller shows that he had taken such care to prevent it as in all the circumstances was reasonably required.

(3) Data processed only for one or more of the purposes mentioned in sub-paragraph (1)(a) may be disclosed –

(a) to any person, other than the data controller, by whom the remuneration or pensions in question are payable,

(b) for the purpose of obtaining actuarial advice,

(c) for the purpose of giving information as to the persons in any employment or office for use in medical research into the health of, or injuries suffered by, persons engaged in particular occupations or working in particular places or areas,

(d) if the data subject (or a person acting on his behalf) has requested or consented to the disclosure of the data either generally or in the circumstances in which the disclosure in question is made, or

(e) if the person making the disclosure has reasonable grounds for believing that the disclosure falls within paragraph (d).

(4) Data processed for any of the purposes mentioned in sub-paragraph (1) may be disclosed –

(a) for the purpose of audit or where the disclosure is for the purpose only of giving information about the data controller's financial affairs, or

(b) in any case in which disclosure would be permitted by any other provision of this Part of this Act if sub-paragraph (2) were included among the non-disclosure provisions.

(5) In this paragraph 'remuneration' includes remuneration in kind and 'pensions' includes gratuities or similar benefits.

Unincorporated members' clubs and mailing lists

7 Eligible automated data processed by an unincorporated members' club and relating only to the members of the club are exempt from the data protection principles and Parts II and III of this Act during the first transitional period.

8 Eligible automated data processed by a data controller only for the purposes of distributing, or recording the distribution of, articles or information to the data subjects and consisting only of their names, addresses or other particulars necessary for effecting the distribution, are exempt from the data protection principles and Parts II and III of this Act during the first transitional period.

9 Neither paragraph 7 nor paragraph 8 applies to personal data relating to any data subject unless he has been asked by the club or data controller whether he objects to the data relating to him being processed as mentioned in that paragraph and has not objected.

10 It shall be a condition of the exemption of any data under paragraph 7 that the data are not disclosed except as permitted by paragraph 11 and of the exemption under paragraph 8 that the data are not processed for any purpose other than that mentioned in that paragraph or as permitted by paragraph 11, but –

(a) the exemption under paragraph 7 shall not be lost by any disclosure in breach of that condition, and
(b) the exemption under paragraph 8 shall not be lost by any processing in breach of that condition,

if the data controller shows that he had taken such care to prevent it as in all the circumstances was reasonably required.

11 Data to which paragraph 10 applies may be disclosed –

(a) if the data subject (or a person acting on his behalf) has requested or consented to the disclosure of the data either generally or in the circumstances in which the disclosure in question is made,
(b) if the person making the disclosure has reasonable grounds for believing that the disclosure falls within paragraph (a), or
(c) in any case in which disclosure would be permitted by any other provision of this Part of this Act if paragraph 8 were included among the non-disclosure provisions.

Back-up data

12 Eligible automated data which are processed only for the purpose of replacing other data in the event of the latter being lost, destroyed or impaired are exempt from section 7 during the first transitional period.

Exemption of all eligible automated data from certain requirements

13—(1) During the first transitional period, eligible automated data are exempt from the following provisions –

(a) the first data protection principle to the extent to which it requires compliance with –
  (i) paragraph 2 of Part II of Schedule 1,
  (ii) the conditions in Schedule 2, and
  (iii) the conditions in Schedule 3,

(b) the seventh data protection principle to the extent to which it requires compliance with paragraph 12 of Part II of Schedule 1;

(c) the eighth data protection principle,

(d) in section 7(1), paragraphs (b), (c)(ii) and (d),

(e) sections 10 and 11,

(f) section 12, and

(g) section 13, except so far as relating to –

    (i) any contravention of the fourth data protection principle,

    (ii) any disclosure without the consent of the data controller,

    (iii) loss or destruction of data without the consent of the data controller, or

    (iv) processing for the special purposes.

(2) The specific exemptions conferred by sub-paragraph (1)(a), (c) and (e) do not limit the data controller's general duty under the first data protection principle to ensure that processing is fair.

Part III
Exemptions available after 23rd October 2001 but before 24th October 2007

14—(1) This paragraph applies to –

(a) eligible manual data which were held immediately before 24th October 1998, and

(b) personal data which fall within paragraph (d) of the definition of 'data' in section 1(1) but do not fall within paragraph (a) of this sub-paragraph,

but does not apply to eligible manual data to which the exemption in paragraph 16 applies.

(2) During the second transitional period, data to which this paragraph applies are exempt from the following provisions –

(a) the first data protection principle except to the extent to which it requires compliance with paragraph 2 of Part II of Schedule 1,

(b) the second, third, fourth and fifth data protection principles, and

(c) section 14(1) to (3).

Part IV
Exemptions after 23rd October 2001 for historical research

15 In this Part of this Schedule 'the relevant conditions' has the same meaning as in section 33.

16—(1) Eligible manual data which are processed only for the purpose of historical research in compliance with the relevant conditions are exempt from the provisions specified in sub-paragraph (2) after 23rd October 2001.

(2) The provisions referred to in sub-paragraph (1) are –

(a) the first data protection principle except in so far as it requires compliance with paragraph 2 of Part II of Schedule 1,

(b) the second, third, fourth and fifth data protection principles, and

(c) section 14(1) to (3).

17—(1) After 23rd October 2001 eligible automated data which are processed only for the purpose of historical research in compliance with the relevant conditions are exempt from the first data protection principle to the extent to which it requires compliance with the conditions in Schedules 2 and 3.

(2) Eligible automated data which are processed –

(a) only for the purpose of historical research,

(b) in compliance with the relevant conditions, and

(c) otherwise than by reference to the data subject,

are also exempt from the provisions referred to in sub-paragraph (3) after 23rd October 2001.

(3) The provisions referred to in sub-paragraph (2) are –

(a) the first data protection principle except in so far as it requires compliance with paragraph 2 of Part II of Schedule 1,

(b) the second, third, fourth and fifth data protection principles, and

(c) section 14(1) to (3).

18 For the purposes of this Part of this Schedule personal data are not to be treated as processed otherwise than for the purpose of historical research merely because the data are disclosed –

(a) to any person, for the purpose of historical research only,

(b) to the data subject or a person acting on his behalf,

(c) at the request, or with the consent, of the data subject or a person acting on his behalf, or

(d) in circumstances in which the person making the disclosure has reasonable grounds for believing that the disclosure falls within paragraph (a), (b) or (c).

Part V
Exemption from section 22

19 Processing which was already under way immediately before 24th October 1998 is not assessable processing for the purposes of section 22.

SCHEDULE 9

Powers of entry and inspection

Issue of warrants

1—(1) If a circuit judge is satisfied by information on oath supplied by the Commissioner that there are reasonable grounds for suspecting –

(a) that a data controller has contravened or is contravening any of the data protection principles, or

(b) that an offence under this Act has been or is being committed,

and that evidence of the contravention or of the commission of the offence is to be found on any premises specified in the information, he may, subject to sub-paragraph (2) and paragraph 2, grant a warrant to the Commissioner.

(2) A judge shall not issue a warrant under this Schedule in respect of any personal data processed for the special purposes unless a determination by the Commissioner under section 45 with respect to those data has taken effect.

(3) A warrant issued under sub-paragraph (1) shall authorise the Commissioner or any of his officers or staff at any time within seven days of the date of the warrant to enter the premises, to search them, to inspect, examine, operate and test any equipment found there which is used or intended to be used for the processing of personal data and to inspect and seize any documents or other material found there which may be such evidence as is mentioned in that sub-paragraph.

2—(1) A judge shall not issue a warrant under this Schedule unless he is satisfied –

    (a) that the Commissioner has given seven days' notice in writing to the occupier of the premises in question demanding access to the premises, and

    (b) that either –

        (i)   access was demanded at a reasonable hour and was unreasonably refused, or

        (ii)   although entry to the premises was granted, the occupier unreasonably refused to comply with a request by the Commissioner or any of the Commissioner's officers or staff to permit the Commissioner or the officer or member of staff to do any of the things referred to in paragraph 1(3), and

    (c) that the occupier, has, after the refusal, been notified by the Commissioner of the application for the warrant and has had an opportunity of being heard by the judge on the question whether or not it should be issued.

(2) Sub-paragraph (1) shall not apply if the judge is satisfied that the case is one of urgency or that compliance with those provisions would defeat the object of the entry.

3 A judge who issues a warrant under this Schedule shall also issue two copies of it and certify them clearly as copies.

Execution of warrants

4 A person executing a warrant issued under this Schedule may use such reasonable force as may be necessary.

5 A warrant issued under this Schedule shall be executed at a reasonable hour unless it appears to the person executing it that there are grounds for suspecting that the evidence in question would not be found if it were so executed.

6 If the person who occupies the premises in respect of which a warrant is issued under this Schedule is present when the warrant is executed, he shall be shown the warrant and supplied with a copy of it; and if that person is not present a copy of the warrant shall be left in a prominent place on the premises.

7—(1) A person seizing anything in pursuance of a warrant under this Schedule shall give a receipt for it if asked to do so.

(2) Anything so seized may be retained for so long as is necessary in all the circumstances but the person in occupation of the premises in question shall be given a copy of anything that is seized if he so requests and the person executing the warrant considers that it can be done without undue delay.

Matters exempt from inspection and seizure

8 The powers of inspection and seizure conferred by a warrant issued under this Schedule shall not be exercisable in respect of personal data which by virtue of section 28 are exempt from any of the provisions of this Act.

9—(1) Subject to the provisions of this paragraph, the powers of inspection and seizure conferred by a warrant issued under this Schedule shall not be exercisable in respect of –

(a) any communication between a professional legal adviser and his client in connection with the giving of legal advice to the client with respect to his obligations, liabilities or rights under this Act, or

(b) any communication between a professional legal adviser and his client, or between such an adviser or his client and any other person, made in connection with or in contemplation of proceedings under or arising out of this Act (including proceedings before the Tribunal) and for the purposes of such proceedings.

(2) Sub-paragraph (1) applies also to –

(a) any copy or other record of any such communication as is there mentioned, and

(b) any document or article enclosed with or referred to in any such communication if made in connection with the giving of any advice or, as the case may be, in connection with or in contemplation of and for the purposes of such proceedings as are there mentioned.

(3) This paragraph does not apply to anything in the possession of any person other than the professional legal adviser or his client or to anything held with the intention of furthering a criminal purpose.

(4) In this paragraph references to the client of a professional legal adviser include references to any person representing such a client.

10 If the person in occupation of any premises in respect of which a warrant is issued under this Schedule objects to the inspection or seizure under the warrant of any material on the grounds that it consists partly of matters in respect of which those powers are not exercisable, he shall, if the person executing the warrant so requests, furnish that person with a copy of so much of the material as is not exempt from those powers.

Return of warrants

11 A warrant issued under this Schedule shall be returned to the court from which it was issued –

(a) after being executed, or

(b) if not executed within the time authorised for its execution;

and the person by whom any such warrant is executed shall make an endorsement on it stating what powers have been exercised by him under the warrant.

Offences

12 Any person who –

(a) intentionally obstructs a person in the execution of a warrant issued under this Schedule, or

(b) fails without reasonable excuse to give any person executing such a warrant such assistance as he may reasonably require for the execution of the warrant,

is guilty of an offence.

Vessels, vehicles etc

13 In this Schedule 'premises' includes any vessel, vehicle, aircraft or hovercraft, and references to the occupier of any premises include references to the person in charge of any vessel, vehicle, aircraft or hovercraft.

Scotland and Northern Ireland

14 In the application of this Schedule to Scotland –

(a) for any reference to a circuit judge there is substituted a reference to the sheriff,

(b) for any reference to information on oath there is substituted a reference to evidence on oath, and

(c) for the reference to the court from which the warrant was issued there is substituted a reference to the sheriff clerk.

15 In the application of this Schedule to Northern Ireland –

(a) for any reference to a circuit judge there is substituted a reference to a county court judge, and

(b) for any reference to information on oath there is substituted a reference to a complaint on oath.

SCHEDULE 10

Further provisions relating to assistance under section 53

1 In this Schedule 'applicant' and 'proceedings' have the same meaning as in section 53.

2 The assistance provided under section 53 may include the making of arrangements for, or for the Commissioner to bear the costs of –

(a) the giving of advice or assistance by a solicitor or counsel, and

(b) the representation of the applicant, or the provision to him of such assistance as is usually given by a solicitor or counsel –

(i) in steps preliminary or incidental to the proceedings, or

(ii) in arriving at or giving effect to a compromise to avoid or bring an end to the proceedings.

3 Where assistance is provided with respect to the conduct of proceedings –

(a) it shall include an agreement by the Commissioner to indemnify the applicant (subject only to any exceptions specified in the notification) in respect of any liability to pay costs or expenses arising by virtue of any judgment or order of the court in the proceedings,

(b) it may include an agreement by the Commissioner to indemnify the applicant in respect of any liability to pay costs or expenses arising by virtue of any compromise or settlement arrived at in order to avoid the proceedings or bring the proceedings to an end, and

(c) it may include an agreement by the Commissioner to indemnify the applicant in respect of any liability to pay damages pursuant to an undertaking given on the grant of interlocutory relief (in Scotland, an interim order) to the applicant.

4 Where the Commissioner provides assistance in relation to any proceedings, he shall do so on such terms, or make such other arrangements, as will secure that a person against whom the proceedings have been or are commenced is informed that assistance has been or is being provided by the Commissioner in relation to them.

5 In England and Wales or Northern Ireland, the recovery of expenses incurred by the Commissioner in providing an applicant with assistance (as taxed or assessed in such manner as may be prescribed by rules of court) shall constitute a first charge for the benefit of the Commissioner –

(a)   on any costs which, by virtue of any judgment or order of the court, are payable to the applicant by any other person in respect of the matter in connection with which the assistance is provided, and

(b)   on any sum payable to the applicant under a compromise or settlement arrived at in connection with that matter to avoid or bring to an end any proceedings.

6 In Scotland, the recovery of such expenses (as taxed or assessed in such manner as may be prescribed by rules of court) shall be paid to the Commissioner, in priority to other debts –

(a)   out of any expenses which, by virtue of any judgment or order of the court, are payable to the applicant by any other person in respect of the matter in connection with which the assistance is provided, and

(b)   out of any sum payable to the applicant under a compromise or settlement arrived at in connection with that matter to avoid or bring to an end any proceedings.

SCHEDULE 11

Educational records

Meaning of 'educational record'

1 For the purposes of section 68 'educational record' means any record to which paragraph 2, 5 or 7 applies.

England and Wales

2 This paragraph applies to any record of information which –

(a)   is processed by or on behalf of the governing body of, or a teacher at, any school in England and Wales specified in paragraph 3,

(b)   relates to any person who is or has been a pupil at the school, and

(c)   originated from or was supplied by or on behalf of any of the persons specified in paragraph 4,

other than information which is processed by a teacher solely for the teacher's own use.

3 The schools referred to in paragraph 2(a) are –

(a)   a school maintained by a local education authority, and

(b)   a special school, as defined by section 6(2) of the Education Act 1996, which is not so maintained.

4 The persons referred to in paragraph 2(c) are –

(a)   an employee of the local education authority which maintains the school,

(b)   in the case of –

(i)   a voluntary aided, foundation or foundation special school (within the meaning of the School Standards and Framework Act 1998), or

(ii)   a special school which is not maintained by a local education authority,

a teacher or other employee at the school (including an educational psychologist engaged by the governing body under a contract for services),

(c) the pupil to whom the record relates, and

(d) a parent, as defined by section 576(1) of the Education Act 1996, of that pupil.

Scotland

5 This paragraph applies to any record of information which is processed –

(a) by an education authority in Scotland, and

(b) for the purpose of the relevant function of the authority,

other than information which is processed by a teacher solely for the teacher's own use.

6 For the purposes of paragraph 5 –

(a) 'education authority' means an education authority within the meaning of the Education (Scotland) Act 1980 ('the 1980 Act') or, in relation to a self-governing school, the board of management within the meaning of the Self-Governing Schools etc. (Scotland) Act 1989 ('the 1989 Act'),

(b) 'the relevant function' means, in relation to each of those authorities, their function under section 1 of the 1980 Act and section 7(1) of the 1989 Act, and

(c) information processed by an education authority is processed for the purpose of the relevant function of the authority if the processing relates to the discharge of that function in respect of a person –

  (i)   who is or has been a pupil in a school provided by the authority, or

  (ii) who receives, or has received, further education (within the meaning of the 1980 Act) so provided.

Northern Ireland

7—(1) This paragraph applies to any record of information which –

(a) is processed by or on behalf of the Board of Governors of, or a teacher at, any grant-aided school in Northern Ireland,

(b) relates to any person who is or has been a pupil at the school, and

(c) originated from or was supplied by or on behalf of any of the persons specified in paragraph 8,

other than information which is processed by a teacher solely for the teacher's own use.

(2) In sub-paragraph (1) 'grant-aided school' has the same meaning as in the Education and Libraries (Northern Ireland) Order 1986.

8 The persons referred to in paragraph 7(1) are –

(a) a teacher at the school,

(b) an employee of an education and library board, other than such a teacher,

(c) the pupil to whom the record relates, and

(d) a parent (as defined by Article 2(2) of the Education and Libraries (Northern Ireland) Order 1986) of that pupil.

England and Wales: transitory provisions

9—(1) Until the appointed day within the meaning of section 20 of the School Standards and Framework Act 1998, this Schedule shall have effect subject to the following modifications.

(2) Paragraph 3 shall have effect as if for paragraph (b) and the 'and' immediately preceding it there were substituted –

'(aa) a grant-maintained school, as defined by section 183(1) of the Education Act 1996,

(ab) a grant-maintained special school, as defined by section 337(4) of that Act, and

(b) a special school, as defined by section 6(2) of that Act, which is neither a maintained special school, as defined by section 337(3) of that Act, nor a grant-maintained special school.'

(3) Paragraph 4(b)(i) shall have effect as if for the words from 'foundation', in the first place where it occurs, to '1998)' there were substituted 'or grant-maintained school'.

SCHEDULE 12

Accessible public records

Meaning of 'accessible public record'

1 For the purposes of section 68 'accessible public record' means any record which is kept by an authority specified –

(a)   as respects England and Wales, in the Table in paragraph 2,

(b)   as respects Scotland, in the Table in paragraph 4, or

(c)   as respects Northern Ireland, in the Table in paragraph 6,

and is a record of information of a description specified in that Table in relation to that authority.

Housing and social services records: England and Wales

2 The following is the Table referred to in paragraph 1(a).

TABLE OF AUTHORITIES AND INFORMATION

The authorities	*The accessible information*
Housing Act local authority.	Information held for the purpose of any of the authority's tenancies.
Local social services authority.	Information held for any purpose of the authority's social services functions.

3—(1) The following provisions apply for the interpretation of the Table in paragraph 2.

(2) Any authority which, by virtue of section 4(e) of the Housing Act 1985, is a local authority for the purpose of any provision of that Act is a 'Housing Act local authority' for the purposes of this Schedule, and so is any housing action trust established under Part III of the Housing Act 1988.

(3) Information contained in records kept by a Housing Act local authority is 'held for the purpose of any of the authority's tenancies' if it is held for any purpose of the relationship of landlord and tenant of a dwelling which subsists, has subsisted or may subsist between the authority and any individual who is, has been or, as the case may be, has applied to be, a tenant of the authority.

(4) Any authority which, by virtue of section 1 or 12 of the Local Authority Social Services Act 1970, is or is treated as a local authority for the purposes of that Act is a 'local social services

authority' for the purposes of this Schedule; and information contained in records kept by such an authority is 'held for any purpose of the authority's social services functions' if it is held for the purpose of any past, current or proposed exercise of such a function in any case.

(5) Any expression used in paragraph 2 or this paragraph and in Part II of the Housing Act 1985 or the Local Authority Social Services Act 1970 has the same meaning as in that Act.

Housing and social services records: Scotland

4 The following is the Table referred to in paragraph 1(b).

TABLE OF AUTHORITIES AND INFORMATION

The authorities	*The accessible information*
Local authority. Scottish Homes.	Information held for the purpose of any of the body's tenancies.
Social work authority.	Information held for any purpose of the authority's functions under the Social Work (Scotland) Act 1968 and the enactments referred to in section 5(1B) of that Act.

5—(1) The following provisions apply for the interpretation of the Table in paragraph 4.

(2) 'Local authority' means –

(a) a council constituted under section 2 of the Local Government etc. (Scotland) Act 1994,
(b) a joint board or joint committee of two or more of those councils, or
(c) any trust under the control of such a council.

(3) Information contained in records kept by a local authority or Scottish Homes is held for the purpose of any of their tenancies if it is held for any purpose of the relationship of landlord and tenant of a dwelling-house which subsists, has subsisted or may subsist between the authority or, as the case may be, Scottish Homes and any individual who is, has been or, as the case may be, has applied to be a tenant of theirs.

(4) 'Social work authority' means a local authority for the purposes of the Social Work (Scotland) Act 1968; and information contained in records kept by such an authority is held for any purpose of their functions if it is held for the purpose of any past, current or proposed exercise of such a function in any case.

Housing and social services records: Northern Ireland

6 The following is the Table referred to in paragraph 1(c).

TABLE OF AUTHORITIES AND INFORMATION

The authorities	*The accessible information*
The Northern Ireland Housing Executive.	Information held for the purpose of any of the Executive's tenancies.
A Health and Social Services Board.	Information held for the purpose of any past, current or proposed exercise by the Board of any function exercisable, by virtue of directions under Article 17(1) of the Health and Personal Social Services (Northern Ireland) Order 1972, by the Board on behalf of the Department of Health and Social Services with respect to the administration of personal social services under –
	(a) the Children and Young Persons Act (Northern Ireland) 1968; (b) the Health and Personal Social Services (Northern Ireland) Order 1972; (c) Article 47 of the Matrimonial Causes (Northern Ireland) Order 1978; (d) Article 11 of the Domestic Proceedings (Northern Ireland) Order 1980; (e) the Adoption (Northern Ireland) Order 1987, or (f) the Children (Northern Ireland) Order 1995.
An HSS trust	Information held for the purpose of any past, current or proposed exercise by the trust of any function exercisable, by virtue of an authorisation under Article 3(1) of the Health and Personal Social Services (Northern Ireland) Order 1994, by the trust on behalf of a Health and Social Services Board with respect to the administration of personal social services under any statutory provision mentioned in the last preceding entry.

7—(1) This paragraph applies for the interpretation of the Table in paragraph 6.

(2) Information contained in records kept by the Northern Ireland Housing Executive is 'held for the purpose of any of the Executive's tenancies' if it is held for any purpose of the relationship of landlord and tenant of a dwelling which subsists, has subsisted or may subsist

between the Executive and any individual who is, has been or, as the case may be, has applied to be, a tenant of the Executive.

SCHEDULE 13

Modifications of Act having effect before 24th October 2007

1 After section 12 there is inserted –

'12A Rights of data subjects in relation to exempt manual data
(1) A data subject is entitled at any time by notice in writing –

(a) to require the data controller to rectify, block, erase or destroy exempt manual data which are inaccurate or incomplete, or
(b) to require the data controller to cease holding exempt manual data in a way incompatible with the legitimate purposes pursued by the data controller.

(2) A notice under subsection (1)(a) or (b) must state the data subject's reasons for believing that the data are inaccurate or incomplete or, as the case may be, his reasons for believing that they are held in a way incompatible with the legitimate purposes pursued by the data controller.

(3) If the court is satisfied, on the application of any person who has given a notice under subsection (1) which appears to the court to be justified (or to be justified to any extent) that the data controller in question has failed to comply with the notice, the court may order him to take such steps for complying with the notice (or for complying with it to that extent) as the court thinks fit.

(4) In this section "exempt manual data" means –

(a) in relation to the first transitional period, as defined by paragraph 1(2) of Schedule 8, data to which paragraph 3 or 4 of that Schedule applies, and
(b) in relation to the second transitional period, as so defined, data to which paragraph 14 of that Schedule applies.

(5) For the purposes of this section personal data are incomplete if, and only if, the data, although not inaccurate, are such that their incompleteness would constitute a contravention of the third or fourth data protection principles, if those principles applied to the data.'

2 In section 32 –

(a) in subsection (2) after 'section 12' there is inserted –
'(dd) section 12A,', and
(b) in subsection (4) after '12(8)' there is inserted ', 12A(3)'.

3 In section 34 for 'section 14(1) to (3)' there is substituted 'sections 12A and 14(1) to (3).'

4 In section 53(1) after '12(8)' there is inserted ', 12A(3)'.

5 In paragraph 8 of Part II of Schedule 1, the word 'or' at the end of paragraph (c) is omitted and after paragraph (d) there is inserted 'or

(e) he contravenes section 12A by failing to comply with a notice given under subsection (1) of that section to the extent that the notice is justified.'

SCHEDULE 14

Transitional provisions and savings

Interpretation

1 In this Schedule –

'the 1984 Act' means the Data Protection Act 1984;

'the old principles' means the data protection principles within the meaning of the 1984 Act;

'the new principles' means the data protection principles within the meaning of this Act.

Effect of registration under Part II of 1984 Act

2—(1) Subject to sub-paragraphs (4) and (5) any person who, immediately before the commencement of Part III of this Act –

    (a) is registered as a data user under Part II of the 1984 Act, or
    (b) is treated by virtue of section 7(6) of the 1984 Act as so registered,

is exempt from section 17(1) of this Act until the end of the registration period or, if earlier, 24th October 2001.

(2) In sub-paragraph (1) 'the registration period', in relation to a person, means –

    (a) where there is a single entry in respect of that person as a data user, the period at the end of which, if section 8 of the 1984 Act had remained in force, that entry would have fallen to be removed unless renewed, and
    (b) where there are two or more entries in respect of that person as a data user, the period at the end of which, if that section had remained in force, the last of those entries to expire would have fallen to be removed unless renewed.

(3) Any application for registration as a data user under Part II of the 1984 Act which is received by the Commissioner before the commencement of Part III of this Act (including any appeal against a refusal of registration) shall be determined in accordance with the old principles and the provisions of the 1984 Act.

(4) If a person falling within paragraph (b) of sub-paragraph (1) receives a notification under section 7(1) of the 1984 Act of the refusal of his application, sub-paragraph (1) shall cease to apply to him –

    (a) if no appeal is brought, at the end of the period within which an appeal can be brought against the refusal, or
    (b) on the withdrawal or dismissal of the appeal.

(5) If a data controller gives a notification under section 18(1) at a time when he is exempt from section 17(1) by virtue of sub-paragraph (1), he shall cease to be so exempt.

(6) The Commissioner shall include in the register maintained under section 19 an entry in respect of each person who is exempt from section 17(1) by virtue of sub-paragraph (1); and each entry shall consist of the particulars which, immediately before the commencement of Part III of this Act, were included (or treated as included) in respect of that person in the register maintained under section 4 of the 1984 Act.

(7) Notification regulations under Part III of this Act may make provision modifying the duty referred to in section 20(1) in its application to any person in respect of whom an entry in the register maintained under section 19 has been made under sub-paragraph (6).

(8) Notification regulations under Part III of this Act may make further transitional provision in connection with the substitution of Part III of this Act for Part II of the 1984 Act (registration), including provision modifying the application of provisions of Part III in transitional cases.

Rights of data subjects

3—(1) The repeal of section 21 of the 1984 Act (right of access to personal data) does not affect the application of that section in any case in which the request (together with the information referred to in paragraph (a) of subsection (4) of that section and, in a case where it is required, the consent referred to in paragraph (b) of that subsection) was received before the day on which the repeal comes into force.

(2) Sub-paragraph (1) does not apply where the request is made by reference to this Act.

(3) Any fee paid for the purposes of section 21 of the 1984 Act before the commencement of section 7 in a case not falling within sub-paragraph (1) shall be taken to have been paid for the purposes of section 7.

4 The repeal of section 22 of the 1984 Act (compensation for inaccuracy) and the repeal of section 23 of that Act (compensation for loss or unauthorised disclosure) do not affect the application of those sections in relation to damage or distress suffered at any time by reason of anything done or omitted to be done before the commencement of the repeals.

5 The repeal of section 24 of the 1984 Act (rectification and erasure) does not affect any case in which the application to the court was made before the day on which the repeal comes into force.

6 Subsection (3)(b) of section 14 does not apply where the rectification, blocking, erasure or destruction occurred before the commencement of that section.

Enforcement and transfer prohibition notices served under Part V of 1984 Act

7—(1) If, immediately before the commencement of section 40 –

(a) an enforcement notice under section 10 of the 1984 Act has effect, and
(b) either the time for appealing against the notice has expired or any appeal has been determined,

then, after that commencement, to the extent mentioned in sub-paragraph (3), the notice shall have effect for the purposes of sections 41 and 47 as if it were an enforcement notice under section 40.

(2) Where an enforcement notice has been served under section 10 of the 1984 Act before the commencement of section 40 and immediately before that commencement either –

(a) the time for appealing against the notice has not expired, or
(b) an appeal has not been determined,

the appeal shall be determined in accordance with the provisions of the 1984 Act and the old principles and, unless the notice is quashed on appeal, to the extent mentioned in sub-paragraph (3) the notice shall have effect for the purposes of sections 41 and 47 as if it were an enforcement notice under section 40.

(3) An enforcement notice under section 10 of the 1984 Act has the effect described in sub-paragraph (1) or (2) only to the extent that the steps specified in the notice for complying with the old principle or principles in question are steps which the data controller could be required by an enforcement notice under section 40 to take for complying with the new principles or any of them.

8—(1) If, immediately before the commencement of section 40 –

(a) a transfer prohibition notice under section 12 of the 1984 Act has effect, and

(b) either the time for appealing against the notice has expired or any appeal has been determined,

then, on and after that commencement, to the extent specified in sub-paragraph (3), the notice shall have effect for the purposes of sections 41 and 47 as if it were an enforcement notice under section 40.

(2) Where a transfer prohibition notice has been served under section 12 of the 1984 Act and immediately before the commencement of section 40 either –

(a) the time for appealing against the notice has not expired, or

(b) an appeal has not been determined,

the appeal shall be determined in accordance with the provisions of the 1984 Act and the old principles and, unless the notice is quashed on appeal, to the extent mentioned in sub-paragraph (3) the notice shall have effect for the purposes of sections 41 and 47 as if it were an enforcement notice under section 40.

(3) A transfer prohibition notice under section 12 of the 1984 Act has the effect described in sub-paragraph (1) or (2) only to the extent that the prohibition imposed by the notice is one which could be imposed by an enforcement notice under section 40 for complying with the new principles or any of them.

Notices under new law relating to matters in relation to which 1984 Act had effect

9 The Commissioner may serve an enforcement notice under section 40 on or after the day on which that section comes into force if he is satisfied that, before that day, the data controller contravened the old principles by reason of any act or omission which would also have constituted a contravention of the new principles if they had applied before that day.

10 Subsection (5)(b) of section 40 does not apply where the rectification, blocking, erasure or destruction occurred before the commencement of that section.

11 The Commissioner may serve an information notice under section 43 on or after the day on which that section comes into force if he has reasonable grounds for suspecting that, before that day, the data controller contravened the old principles by reason of any act or omission which would also have constituted a contravention of the new principles if they had applied before that day.

12 Where by virtue of paragraph 11 an information notice is served on the basis of anything done or omitted to be done before the day on which section 43 comes into force, subsection (2)(b) of that section shall have effect as if the reference to the data controller having complied, or complying, with the new principles were a reference to the data controller having contravened the old principles by reason of any such act or omission as is mentioned in paragraph 11.

Self-incrimination, etc

13—(1) In section 43(8), section 44(9) and paragraph 11 of Schedule 7, any reference to an offence under this Act includes a reference to an offence under the 1984 Act.

(2) In section 34(9) of the 1984 Act, any reference to an offence under that Act includes a reference to an offence under this Act.

Warrants issued under 1984 Act

14 The repeal of Schedule 4 to the 1984 Act does not affect the application of that Schedule in any case where a warrant was issued under that Schedule before the commencement of the repeal.

Complaints under section 36(2) of 1984 Act and requests for assessment under section 42

15 The repeal of section 36(2) of the 1984 Act does not affect the application of that provision in any case where the complaint was received by the Commissioner before the commencement of the repeal.

16 In dealing with a complaint under section 36(2) of the 1984 Act or a request for an assessment under section 42 of this Act, the Commissioner shall have regard to the provisions from time to time applicable to the processing, and accordingly –

    (a) in section 36(2) of the 1984 Act, the reference to the old principles and the provisions of that Act includes, in relation to any time when the new principles and the provisions of this Act have effect, those principles and provisions, and

    (b) in section 42 of this Act, the reference to the provisions of this Act includes, in relation to any time when the old principles and the provisions of the 1984 Act had effect, those principles and provisions.

Applications under Access to Health Records Act 1990 or corresponding Northern Ireland legislation

17—(1) The repeal of any provision of the Access to Health Records Act 1990 does not affect –

    (a) the application of section 3 or 6 of that Act in any case in which the application under that section was received before the day on which the repeal comes into force, or

    (b) the application of section 8 of that Act in any case in which the application to the court was made before the day on which the repeal comes into force.

(2) Sub-paragraph (1)(a) does not apply in relation to an application for access to information which was made by reference to this Act.

18—(1) The revocation of any provision of the Access to Health Records (Northern Ireland) Order 1993 does not affect –

    (a) the application of Article 5 or 8 of that Order in any case in which the application under that Article was received before the day on which the repeal comes into force, or

    (b) the application of Article 10 of that Order in any case in which the application to the court was made before the day on which the repeal comes into force.

(2) Sub-paragraph (1)(a) does not apply in relation to an application for access to information which was made by reference to this Act.

Applications under regulations under Access to Personal Files Act 1987 or corresponding Northern Ireland legislation

19—(1) The repeal of the personal files enactments does not affect the application of regulations under those enactments in relation to –

    (a) any request for information,

    (b) any application for rectification or erasure, or

(c)   any application for review of a decision,

which was made before the day on which the repeal comes into force.

(2) Sub-paragraph (1)(a) does not apply in relation to a request for information which was made by reference to this Act.

(3) In sub-paragraph (1) 'the personal files enactments' means –

(a)   in relation to Great Britain, the Access to Personal Files Act 1987, and
(b)   in relation to Northern Ireland, Part II of the Access to Personal Files and Medical Reports (Northern Ireland) Order 1991.

Applications under section 158 of Consumer Credit Act 1974

20 Section 62 does not affect the application of section 158 of the Consumer Credit Act 1974 in any case where the request was received before the commencement of section 62, unless the request is made by reference to this Act.

SCHEDULE 15

Minor and consequential amendments

Public Records Act 1958 (c 51)

1—(1) In Part II of the Table in paragraph 3 of Schedule 1 to the Public Records Act 1958 (definition of public records) for 'the Data Protection Registrar' there is substituted 'the Data Protection Commissioner'.

(2) That Schedule shall continue to have effect with the following amendment (originally made by paragraph 14 of Schedule 2 to the Data Protection Act 1984).

(3) After paragraph 4(1)(n) there is inserted –

'(nn)   records of the Data Protection Tribunal'.

Parliamentary Commissioner Act 1967 (c 13)

2 In Schedule 2 to the Parliamentary Commissioner Act 1967 (departments etc. subject to investigation) for 'Data Protection Registrar' there is substituted 'Data Protection Commissioner'.

3 In Schedule 4 to that Act (tribunals exercising administrative functions), in the entry relating to the Data Protection Tribunal, for 'section 3 of the Data Protection Act 1984' there is substituted 'section 6 of the Data Protection Act 1998'.

Superannuation Act 1972 (c 11)

4 In Schedule 1 to the Superannuation Act 1972, for 'Data Protection Registrar' there is substituted 'Data Protection Commissioner'.

House of Commons Disqualification Act 1975 (c 24)

5—(1) Part II of Schedule 1 to the House of Commons Disqualification Act 1975 (bodies whose members are disqualified) shall continue to include the entry 'The Data Protection

Tribunal' (originally inserted by paragraph 12(1) of Schedule 2 to the Data Protection Act 1984).

(2) In Part III of that Schedule (disqualifying offices) for 'The Data Protection Registrar' there is substituted 'The Data Protection Commissioner'.

Northern Ireland Assembly Disqualification Act 1975 (c 25)

6—(1) Part II of Schedule 1 to the Northern Ireland Assembly Disqualification Act 1975 (bodies whose members are disqualified) shall continue to include the entry 'The Data Protection Tribunal' (originally inserted by paragraph 12(3) of Schedule 2 to the Data Protection Act 1984).

(2) In Part III of that Schedule (disqualifying offices) for 'The Data Protection Registrar' there is substituted 'The Data Protection Commissioner'.

Representation of the People Act 1983 (c 2)

7 In Schedule 2 of the Representation of the People Act 1983 (provisions which may be included in regulations as to registration etc), in paragraph 11A(2) –

    (a) for 'data user' there is substituted 'data controller', and
    (b) for 'the Data Protection Act 1984' there is substituted 'the Data Protection Act 1998'.

Access to Medical Reports Act 1988 (c 28)

8 In section 2(1) of the Access to Medical Reports Act 1988 (interpretation), in the definition of 'health professional', for 'the Data Protection (Subject Access Modification) Order 1987' there is substituted 'the Data Protection Act 1998'.

Football Spectators Act 1989 (c 37)

9—(1) Section 5 of the Football Spectators Act 1989 (national membership scheme: contents and penalties) is amended as follows.

(2) In subsection (5), for 'paragraph 1(2) of Part II of Schedule 1 to the Data Protection Act 1984' there is substituted 'paragraph 1(2) of Part II of Schedule 1 to the Data Protection Act 1998'.

(3) In subsection (6), for 'section 28(1) and (2) of the Data Protection Act 1984' there is substituted 'section 29(1) and (2) of the Data Protection Act 1998'.

Education (Student Loans) Act 1990 (c 6)

10 Schedule 2 to the Education (Student Loans) Act 1990 (loans for students) so far as that Schedule continues in force shall have effect as if the reference in paragraph 4(2) to the Data Protection Act 1984 were a reference to this Act.

Access to Health Records Act 1990 (c 23)

11 For section 2 of the Access to Health Records Act 1990 there is substituted –

'2 Health professionals
In this Act "health professional" has the same meaning as in the Data Protection 1998.'

12 In section 3(4) of that Act (cases where fee may be required) in paragraph (a), for 'the maximum prescribed under section 21 of the Data Protection Act 1984' there is substituted 'such maximum as may be prescribed for the purposes of this section by regulations under section 7 of the Data Protection Act 1998'.

13 In section 5(3) of that Act (cases where right of access may be partially excluded) for the words from the beginning to 'record' in the first place where it occurs there is substituted 'Access shall not be given under section 3(2) to any part of a health record'.

Access to Personal Files and Medical Reports (Northern Ireland) Order 1991 (1991/1707 (NI/14))

14 In Article 4 of the Access to Personal Files and Medical Reports (Northern Ireland) Order 1991 (obligation to give access), in paragraph (2) (exclusion of information to which individual entitled under section 21 of the Data Protection Act 1984) for 'section 21 of the Data Protection Act 1984' there is substituted 'section 7 of the Data Protection Act 1998'.

15 In Article 6(1) of that Order (interpretation), in the definition of 'health professional', for 'the Data Protection (Subject Access Modification) (Health) Order 1987' there is substituted 'the Data Protection Act 1998'.

Tribunals and Inquiries Act 1992 (c 53)

16 In Part 1 of Schedule 1 to the Tribunals and Inquiries Act 1992 (tribunals under direct supervision of Council on Tribunals), for paragraph 14 there is substituted –

'14. Data protection
(a) The Data Protection Commissioner appointed under section 6 of the Data Protection Act 1998;

(b) the Data Protection Tribunal constituted under that section, in respect of its jurisdiction under section 48 of that Act.'

Access to Health Records (Northern Ireland) Order 1993 (1993/1250 (NI 4))

17 For paragraphs (1) and (2) of Article 4 of the Access to Health Records (Northern Ireland) Order 1993 there is substituted –

'(1) In this Order "health professional" has the same meaning as in the Data Protection Act 1998.'

18 In Article 5(4) of that Order (cases where fee may be required) in sub-paragraph (a), for 'the maximum prescribed under section 21 of the Data Protection Act 1984' there is substituted 'such maximum as may be prescribed for the purposes of this Article by regulations under section 7 of the Data Protection Act 1998'.

19 In Article 7 of that Order (cases where right of access may be partially excluded) for the words from the beginning to 'record' in the first place where it occurs there is substituted 'Access shall not be given under Article 5(2) to any part of a health record'.

SCHEDULE 16

Repeals and revocations

Part I
Repeals

Chapter	Short title	Extent of repeal
1984 c 35.	The Data Protection Act 1984.	The whole Act.
1986 c 60.	The Financial Services Act 1986.	Section 190.
1987 c. 37.	The Access to Personal Files Act 1987.	The whole Act.
1988 c 40.	The Education Reform Act 1988.	Section 223.
1988 c 50.	The Housing Act 1988.	In Schedule 17, paragraph 80.
1990 c 23.	The Access to Health Records Act 1990.	In section 1(1), the words from 'but does not' to the end. In section 3, subsection (1)(a) to (e) and, in subsection (6)(a), the words 'in the case of an application made otherwise than by the patient'. Section 4(1) and (2). In section 5(1)(a)(i), the words 'of the patient or' and the word 'other'. In section 10, in subsection (2) the words 'or orders' and in subsection (3) the words 'or an order under section 2(3) above'. In section 11, the definitions of 'child' and 'parental responsibility'.
1990 c 37.	The Human Fertilisation and Embryology Act 1990.	Section 33(8).
1990 c 41.	The Courts and Legal Services Act 1990.	In Schedule 10, paragraph 58.
1992 c 13.	The Further and Higher Education Act 1992.	Section 86.
1992 c 37.	The Further and Higher Education (Scotland) Act 1992.	Section 59.

Chapter	Short title	Extent of repeal
1993 c 8.	The Judicial Pensions and Retirement Act 1993.	In Schedule 6, paragraph 50.
1993 c 10.	The Charities Act 1993.	Section 12.
1993 c 21.	The Osteopaths Act 1993.	Section 38.
1994 c 17.	The Chiropractors Act 1994.	Section 38.
1994 c 19.	The Local Government (Wales) Act 1994.	In Schedule 13, paragraph 30.
1994 c 33.	The Criminal Justice and Public Order Act 1994.	Section 161.
1994 c 39.	The Local Government etc. (Scotland) Act 1994.	In Schedule 13, paragraph 154.

Part II
Revocations

Number	Title	Extent of revocation
SI 1991/1142.	The Data Protection Registration Fee Order 1991.	The whole Order.
SI 1991/1707 (NI 14).	The Access to Personal Files and Medical Reports (Northern Ireland) Order 1991.	Part II. The Schedule.
SI 1992/3218	The Banking Co-ordination (Second Council Directive) Regulations 1992.	In Schedule 10, paragraphs 15 and 40.
SI 1993/1250 (NI 4)	The Access to Health Records (Northern Ireland) Order 1993.	In Article 2(2), the definitions of 'child' and 'parental responsibility'. In Article 3(1), the words from 'but does not include' to the end. In Article 5, paragraph (1)(a) to (d) and, in paragraph (6)(a), the words 'in the case of an application made otherwise than by the patient'. Article 6(1) and (2). In Article 7(1)(a)(i), the words 'of the patient or' and the word 'other'.
SI 1994/429 (NI 2).	The Health and Personal Social Services (Northern Ireland) Order 1994.	In Schedule 1, the entries relating to the Access to Personal Files and Medical Reports (Northern Ireland) Order 1991.
SI 1994/1696.	The Insurance Companies (Third Insurance Directives) Regulations 1994.	In Schedule 8, paragraph 8.
SI 1995/755 (NI 2).	The Children (Northern Ireland) Order 1995.	In Schedule 9, paragraphs 177 and 191.
SI 1995/3275	The Investment Services Regulations 1995.	In Schedule 10, paragraphs 3 and 15.
SI 1996/2827	The Open-Ended Investment Companies (Investment Companies with Variable Capital) Regulations 1996.	In Schedule 8, paragraphs 3 and 26.

Appendix 2

DIRECTIVE 95/46/EC OF THE EUROPEAN PARLIAMENT AND OF THE COUNCIL

of 24 October 1995

on the Protection of Individuals with regard to the Processing of Personal Data and on the Free Movement of such Data

THE EUROPEAN PARLIAMENT AND THE COUNCIL OF THE EUROPEAN UNION,

Having regard to the Treaty establishing the European Community, and in particular Article 100a thereof,

Having regard to the proposal from the Commission[1],

Having regard to the opinion of the Economic and Social Committee[2],

Acting in accordance with the procedure referred to in Article 189b of the Treaty[3],

(1) Whereas the objectives of the Community, as laid down in the Treaty, as amended by the Treaty on European Union, include creating an ever closer union among the peoples of Europe, fostering closer relations between the States belonging to the Community, ensuring economic and social progress by common action to eliminate the barriers which divide Europe, encouraging the constant improvement of the living conditions of its peoples, preserving and strengthening peace and liberty and promoting democracy on the basis of the fundamental rights recognised in the constitution and laws of the Member States and in the European Convention for the Protection of Human Rights and Fundamental Freedoms;

(2) Whereas data-processing systems are designed to serve man; whereas they must, whatever the nationality or residence of natural persons, respect their fundamental rights and freedoms, notably the right to privacy, and contribute to economic and social progress, trade expansion and the well-being of individuals;

(3) Whereas the establishment and functioning of an internal market in which, in accordance with Article 7a of the Treaty, the free movement of goods, persons, services and capital is ensured require not only that personal data should be able to flow freely from one Member State to another, but also that the fundamental rights of individuals should be safeguarded;

---

1 OJ No C 277, 5 November 1990, p 3 and OJ No C 311, 27 November 1992, p 30.
2 OJ No C 159, 17 June 1991, p 38.
3 Opinion of the European Parliament of 11 March 1992 (OJ No C 94, 13 April 1992, p 198), confirmed on 2 December 1993 (OJ No C 342, 20 December 1993, p 30); Council common position of 20 February 1995 (OJ No C 93, 13 April 1995, p 1) and Decision of the European Parliament of 15 June 1995 (OJ No C 166, 3 July 1995).

(4) Whereas increasingly frequent recourse is being had in the Community to the processing of personal data in the various spheres of economic and social activity; whereas the progress made in information technology is making the processing and exchange of such data considerably easier;

(5) Whereas the economic and social integration resulting from the establishment and functioning of the internal market within the meaning of Article 7a of the Treaty will necessarily lead to a substantial increase in cross-border flows of personal data between all those involved in a private or public capacity in economic and social activity in the Member States; whereas the exchange of personal data between undertakings in different Member States is set to increase, whereas the national authorities in the various Member States are being called upon by virtue of Community law to collaborate and exchange personal data so as to be able to perform their duties or carry out tasks on behalf of an authority in another Member State within the context of the area without internal frontiers as constituted by the internal market;

(6) Whereas, furthermore, the increase in scientific and technical cooperation and the coordinated introduction of new telecommunications networks in the Community necessitate and facilitate cross-border flows of personal data;

(7) Whereas the difference in levels of protection of the rights and freedoms of individuals, notably the right to privacy, with regard to the processing of personal data afforded in the Member States may prevent the transmission of such data from the territory of one Member State to that of another Member State; whereas this difference may therefore constitute an obstacle to the pursuit of a number of economic activities at Community level, distort competition and impede authorities in the discharge of their responsibilities under Community law; whereas this difference in levels of protection is due to the existence of a wide variety of national laws, regulations and administrative provisions;

(8) Whereas, in order to remove the obstacles to flows of personal data, the level of protection of the rights and freedoms of individuals with regard to the processing of such data must be equivalent in all Member States; whereas this objective is vital to the internal market but cannot be achieved by the Member States alone, especially in view of the scale of the divergences which currently exist between the relevant laws in the Member States and the need to coordinate the laws of the Member States so as to ensure that the cross-border flow of personal data is regulated in a consistent manner that is in keeping with the objective of the internal market as provided for in Article 7a of the Treaty; whereas Community action to approximate those laws is therefore needed;

(9) Whereas, given the equivalent protection resulting from the approximation of national laws, the Member States will no longer be able to inhibit the free movement between them of personal data on grounds relating to protection of the rights and freedoms of individuals, and in particular the right to privacy; whereas Member States will be left a margin for manoeuvre, which may, in the context of implementation of the Directive, also be exercised by the business and social partners; whereas Member States will therefore be able to specify in their national law the general conditions governing the lawfulness of data processing; whereas in doing so the Member States shall strive to improve the protection currently provided by their legislation; whereas, within the limits of this margin for manoeuvre and in accordance with Community law, disparities could arise in the implementation of the Directive, and this could have an effect on the movement of data within a Member State as well as within the Community;

(10) Whereas the object of the national laws on the processing of personal data is to protect fundamental rights and freedoms, notably the right to privacy, which is recognised both in Article 8 of the European Convention for the Protection of Human Rights and Fundamental Freedoms and in the general principles of Community law; whereas, for that reason, the approximation of those laws must not result in any lessening of the

protection they afford but must, on the contrary, seek to ensure a high level of protection in the Community;

(11) Whereas the principles of the protection of the rights and freedoms of individuals, notably the right to privacy, which are contained in this Directive, give substance to and amplify those contained in the Council of Europe Convention of 28 January 1981 for the Protection of Individuals with regard to Automatic Processing of Personal Data;

(12) Whereas the protection principles must apply to all processing of personal data by any person whose activities are governed by Community law; whereas there should be excluded the processing of data carried out by a natural person in the exercise of activities which are exclusively personal or domestic, such as correspondence and the holding of records of addresses;

(13) Whereas the activities referred to in Titles V and VI of the Treaty on European Union regarding public safety, defence, State security or the activities of the State in the area of criminal laws fall outside the scope of Community law, without prejudice to the obligations incumbent upon Member States under Article 56(2), Article 57 or Article 100a of the Treaty establishing the European Community; whereas the processing of personal data that is necessary to safeguard the economic well-being of the State does not fall within the scope of this Directive where such processing relates to State security matters;

(14) Whereas, given the importance of the developments under way, in the framework of the information society, of the techniques used to capture, transmit, manipulate, record, store or communicate sound and image data relating to natural persons, this Directive should be applicable to processing involving such data;

(15) Whereas the processing of such data is covered by this Directive only if it is automated or if the data processes are contained or are intended to be contained in a filing system structured according to specific criteria relating to individuals, so as to permit easy access to the personal data in question;

(16) Whereas the processing of sound and image data, such as in cases of video surveillance, does not come within the scope of this Directive if it is carried out for the purposes of public security, defence, national security or in the course of State activities relating to the area of criminal law or of other activities which do not come within the scope of Community law;

(17) Whereas, as far as the processing of sound and image data carried out for purposes of journalism or the purposes of literary or artistic expression is concerned, in particular in the audiovisual field, the principles of the Directive are to apply in a restricted manner according to the provisions laid down in Article 9;

(18) Whereas, in order to ensure that individuals are not deprived of the protection to which they are entitled under this Directive, any processing of personal data in the Community must be carried out in accordance with the law of one of the Member States; whereas, in this connection, processing carried out under the responsibility of a controller who is established in a Member Stare should be governed by the law of that State;

(19) Whereas establishment on the territory of a Member State implies the effective and real exercise of activity through stable arrangements; whereas the legal form of such an establishment, whether simply branch or a subsidiary with a legal personality, is not the determining factor in this respect; whereas, when a single controller is established on the territory of several Member States, particularly by means of subsidiaries, he must ensure, in order to avoid any circumvention of national rules, that each of the establishments fulfils the obligations imposed by the national law applicable to its activities;

(20) Whereas the fact that the processing of data is carried out by a person established in a third country must not stand in the way of the protection of individuals provided for in this Directive; whereas in these cases, the processing should be governed by the law of

the Member State in which the means used are located, and there should be guarantees to ensure that the rights and obligations provided for in this Directive are respected in practice;

(21) Whereas this Directive is without prejudice to the rules of territoriality applicable in criminal matters;

(22) Whereas Member States shall more precisely define in the laws they enact or when bringing into force the measures taken under this Directive the general circumstances in which processing is lawful; whereas in particular Article 5, in conjunction with Articles 7 and 8, allows Member States, independently of general rules, to provide for special processing conditions for specific sectors and for the various categories of data covered by Article 8;

(23) Whereas Member States are empowered to ensure the implementation of the protection of individuals both by means of a general law on the protection of individuals as regards the processing of personal data and by sectorial laws such as those relating, for example, to statistical institutes;

(24) Whereas the legislation concerning the protection of legal persons with regard to the processing data which concerns them is not affected by this Directive;

(25) Whereas the principles of protection must be reflected, on the one hand, in the obligations imposed on persons, public authorities, enterprises, agencies or other bodies responsible for processing, in particular regarding data quality, technical security, notification to the supervisory authority, and the circumstances under which processing can be carried out, and, on the other hand, in the right conferred on individuals, the data on whom are the subject of processing, to be informed that processing is taking place, to consult the data, to request corrections and even to object to processing in certain circumstances;

(26) Whereas the principles of protection must apply to any information concerning an identified or identifiable person; whereas, to determine whether a person is identifiable, account should be taken of all the means likely reasonably to be used either by the controller or by any other person to identify the said person; whereas the principles of protection shall not apply to data rendered anonymous in such a way that the data subject is no longer identifiable; whereas codes of conduct within the meaning of Article 27 may be a useful instrument for providing guidance as to the ways in which data may be rendered anonymous and retained in a form in which identification of the data subject is no longer possible;

(27) Whereas the protection of individuals must apply as much to automatic processing of data as to manual processing; whereas the scope of this protection must not in effect depend on the techniques used, otherwise this would create a serious risk of circumvention; whereas, nonetheless, as regards manual processing, this Directive covers only filing systems, not unstructured files; whereas, in particular, the content of a filing system must be structured according to specific criteria relating to individuals allowing easy access to the personal data; whereas, in line with the definition in Article 2(c), the different criteria for determining the constituents of a structured set of personal data, and the different criteria governing access to such a set, may be laid down by each Member State; whereas files or sets of files as well as their cover pages, which are not structured according to specific criteria, shall under no circumstances fall within the scope of this Directive;

(28) Whereas any processing of personal data must be lawful and fair to the individuals concerned; whereas, in particular, the data must be adequate, relevant and not excessive in relation to the purposes for which they are processed; whereas such purposes must be explicit and legitimate and must be determined at the time of collection of the data; whereas the purposes of processing further to collection shall not be incompatible with the purposes as they were originally specified;

(29) Whereas the further processing of personal data for historical, statistical or scientific purposes is not generally to be considered incompatible with the purposes for which the data have previously been collected provided that Member States furnish suitable safeguards; whereas these safeguards must in particular rule out the use of the data in support of measures or decisions regarding any particular individual;

(30) Whereas, in order to be lawful, the processing of personal data must in addition be carried out with the consent of the data subject or be necessary for the conclusion or performance of a contract binding on the data subject, or as a legal requirement, or for the performance of a task carried out in the public interest or in the exercise of official authority, or in the legitimate interests of a natural or legal person, provided that the interests or the rights and freedoms of the data subject are not overriding; whereas, in particular, in order to maintain a balance between the interests involved while guaranteeing effective competition, Member States may determine the circumstances in which personal data may be used or disclosed to a third party in the context of the legitimate ordinary business activities of companies and other bodies; whereas Member States may similarly specify the conditions under which personal data may be disclosed to a third party for the purposes of marketing whether carried out commercially or by a charitable organisation or by any other association or foundation, of a political nature for example, subject to the provisions allowing a data subject to object to the processing of data regarding him, at no cost and without having to state his reasons;

(31) Whereas the processing of personal data must equally be regarded as lawful where it is carried out in order to protect an interest which is essential for the data subject's life;

(32) Whereas it is for national legislation to determine whether the controller performing a task carried out in the public interest or in the exercise of official authority should be a public administration or another natural or legal person governed by public law, or by private law such as a professional association;

(33) Whereas data which are capable by their nature of infringing fundamental freedoms or privacy should not be processed unless the data subject gives his explicit consent; whereas, however, derogations from this prohibition must be explicitly provided for in respect of specific needs, in particular where the processing of these data is carried out for certain health-related purposes by persons subject to a legal obligation of professional secrecy or in the course of legitimate activities by certain associations or foundations the purpose of which is to permit the exercise of fundamental freedoms;

(34) Whereas Member States must also be authorised, when justified by grounds of important public interest, to derogate from the prohibition on processing sensitive categories of data where important reasons of public interest so justify in areas such as public health and social protection – especially in order to ensure the quality and cost-effectiveness of the procedures used for settling claims for benefits and services in the health insurance system – scientific research and government statistics; whereas it is incumbent on them, however, to provide specific and suitable safeguards so as to protect the fundamental rights and the privacy of individuals;

(35) Whereas, moreover, the processing of personal data by official authorities for achieving aims, laid down in constitutional law or international public law, of officially recognised religious associations is carried out on important grounds of public interest;

(36) Whereas where, in the course of electoral activities, the operation of the democratic system requires in certain Member States that political parties compile data on people's political opinion, the processing of such data may be permitted for reasons of important public interest, provided that appropriate safeguards are established;

(37) Whereas the processing of personal data for purposes of journalism or for purposes of literary of artistic expression, in particular in the audiovisual field, should qualify for exemption from the requirements of certain provisions of this Directive in so far as this

is necessary to reconcile the fundamental rights of individuals with freedom of information and notably the right to receive and impart information, as guaranteed in particular in Article 10 of the European Convention for the Protection of Human Rights and Fundamental Freedoms; whereas Member States should therefore lay down exemptions and derogations necessary for the purpose of balance between fundamental rights as regards general measures on the legitimacy of data processing, measures on the transfer of data to third countries and the power of the supervisory authority; whereas this should not, however, lead Member States to lay down exemptions from the measures to ensure security of processing; whereas at least the supervisory authority responsible for this sector should also be provided with certain ex-post powers, eg to publish a regular report or to refer matters to the judicial authorities;

(38) Whereas, if the processing of data is to be fair, the data subject must be in a position to learn of the existence of a processing operation and, where data are collected from him, must be given accurate and full information, bearing in mind the circumstances of the collection;

(39) Whereas certain processing operations involve data which the controller has not collected directly from the data subject; whereas, furthermore, data can be legitimately disclosed to a third party, even if the disclosure was not anticipated at the time the data were collected from the data subject; whereas, in all these cases, the data subject should be informed when the data are recorded or at the latest when the data are first disclosed to a third party;

(40) Whereas, however, it is not necessary to impose this obligation of the data subject already has the information; whereas, moreover, there will be no such obligation if the recording or disclosure are expressly provided for by law or if the provision of information to the data subject proves impossible or would involve disproportionate efforts, which could be the case where processing is for historical, statistical or scientific purposes; whereas, in this regard, the number of data subjects, the age of the data, and any compensatory measures adopted may be taken into consideration;

(41) Whereas any person must be able to exercise the right of access to data relating to him which are being processed, in order to verify in particular the accuracy of the data and the lawfulness of the processing; whereas, for the same reasons, every data subject must also have the right to know the logic involved in the automatic processing of data concerning him, at least in the case of the automated decisions referred to in Article 15(1); whereas this right must not adversely affect trade secrets or intellectual property and in particular the copyright protecting the software, whereas these considerations must not, however, result in the data subject being refused all information;

(42) Whereas Member States may, in the interest of the data subject or so as to protect the rights and freedoms of others, restrict rights of access and information; whereas they may, for example, specify that access to medical data may be obtained only through a health professional;

(43) Whereas restrictions on the rights of access and information and on certain obligations of the controller may similarly be imposed by Member States in so far as they are necessary to safeguard, for example, national security, defence, public safety, or important economic or financial interests of a Member State or the Union, as well as criminal investigations and prosecutions and action in respect of breaches of ethics in the regulated professions; whereas the list of exceptions and limitations should include the tasks of monitoring, inspection or regulation necessary in the three last-mentioned areas concerning public security, economic or financial interests and crime prevention; whereas the listing of tasks in these three areas does not affect the legitimacy of exceptions or restrictions for reasons of State security or defence;

(44) Whereas Member States may also be led, by virtue of the provisions of Community law, to derogate from the provisions of this Directive concerning the right of access, the obligation to inform individuals, and the quality of data, in order to secure certain of the purposes referred to above;

(45) Whereas, in cases where data might lawfully be processed on grounds of public interest, official authority or the legitimate interests of a natural or legal person, any data subject should nevertheless be entitled, on legitimate and compelling grounds relating to his particular situation, to object to the processing of any data relating to himself; whereas Member States may nevertheless lay down national provisions to the contrary;

(46) Whereas the protection of the rights and freedoms of data subjects with regard to the processing of personal data requires that appropriate technical and organisational measures be taken, both at the time of the design of the processing system and at the time of the processing itself, particularly in order to maintain security and thereby to prevent any unauthorised processing; whereas it is incumbent on the Member States to ensure that controllers comply with these measures; whereas these measures must ensure an appropriate level of security, taking into account the state of the art and the costs of their implementation in relation to the risks inherent in the processing and the nature of the data to be protected;

(47) Whereas where a message containing personal data is transmitted by means of a telecommunications or electronic mail service, the sole purpose of which is the transmission of such messages, the controller in respect of the personal data contained in the message will normally be considered to be the person from whom the message originates, rather than the person offering the transmission services; whereas, nevertheless, those offering such services will normally be considered controllers in respect of the processing of the additional personal data necessary for the operation of the service;

(48) Whereas the procedures for notifying the supervisory authority are designed to ensure disclosure of the purposes and main features of any processing operation for the purpose of verification that the operation is in accordance with the national measures taken under this Directive;

(49) Whereas, in order to avoid unsuitable administrative formalities, exemptions from the obligation to notify and simplification of the notification required may be provided for by Member States in cases where processing is unlikely adversely to affect the rights and freedoms of data subjects, provided that it is in accordance with a measure taken by a Member State specifying its limits; whereas exemption or simplification may similarly be provided for by Member States where a person appointed by the controller ensures that the processing carried out is not likely adversely to affect the rights and freedoms of data subjects; whereas such a data protection official, whether or not an employee of the controller, must be in a position to exercise his functions in complete independence;

(50) Whereas exemption or simplification could be provided for in cases of processing operations whose sole purpose is the keeping of a register intended, according to national law, to provide information to the public and open to consultation by the public or by any person demonstrating a legitimate interest;

(51) Whereas, nevertheless, simplification or exemption from the obligation to notify shall not release the controller from any of the other obligations resulting from this Directive;

(52) Whereas, in this context, *ex post facto* verification by the competent authorities must in general be considered a sufficient measure;

(53) Whereas, however, certain processing operation are likely to pose specific risks to the rights and freedoms of data subjects by virtue of their nature, their scope or their purposes, such as that of excluding individuals from a right, benefit or a contract, or by

virtue of the specific use of new technologies; whereas it is for Member States, if they so wish, to specify such risks in their legislation;

(54) Whereas with regard to all the processing undertaken in society, the amount posing such specific risks should be very limited; whereas Member States must provide that the supervisory authority, or the data protection official in co-operation with the authority, check such processing prior to it being carried out; whereas following this prior check, the supervisory authority may, according to its national law, give an opinion or an authorisation regarding the processing; whereas such checking may equally take place in the course of the preparation either of a measure of the national parliament or of a measure based on such a legislative measure, which defines the nature of the processing and lays down appropriate safeguards;

(55) Whereas, if the controller fails to respect the rights of data subjects, national legislation must provide for a judicial remedy; whereas any damage which a person may suffer as a result of unlawful processing must be compensated for by the controller, who may be exempted from liability if he proves that he is not responsible for the damage, in particular in cases where he establishes fault on the part of the data subject or in case of *force majeure*; whereas sanctions must be imposed on any person, whether governed by private or public law, who fails to comply with the national measures taken under this Directive;

(56) Whereas cross-border flows of personal data are necessary to the expansion of international trade; whereas the protection of individuals guaranteed in the Community by this Directive does not stand in the way of transfers of personal data to third countries which ensure an adequate level of protection; whereas the adequacy of the level of protection afforded by a third country must be assessed in the light of all the circumstances surrounding the transfer operation or set of transfer operations;

(57) Whereas, on the other hand, the transfer of personal data to a third country which does not ensure an adequate level of protection must be prohibited;

(58) Whereas provisions should be made for exemptions from this prohibition in certain circumstances where the data subject has given his consent, where the transfer is necessary in relation to a contract or a legal claim, where protection of an important public interest so requires, for example in cases of international transfers of data between tax or customs administrations or between services competent for social security matters, or where the transfer is made from a register established by law and intended for consultation by the public or persons having a legitimate interest; whereas in this case such a transfer should not involve the entirety of the data or entire categories of the data contained in the register and, when the register is intended for consultation by persons having a legitimate interest, the transfer should be made only at the request of those persons or if they are to be the recipients;

(59) Whereas particular measures may be taken to compensate for the lack of protection in a third country in cases where the controller offers appropriate safeguards; whereas, moreover, provision must be made for procedures for negotiations between the Community and such third countries;

(60) Whereas, in any event, transfers to third countries may be effected only in full compliance with the provisions adopted by the Member States pursuant to this Directive, and in particular Article 8 thereof;

(61) Whereas Member States and the Commission, in their respective spheres of competence, must encourage the trade associations and other representative organisations concerned to draw up codes of conduct so as to facilitate the application of this Directive, taking account of the specific characteristics of the processing carried out in certain sectors, and respecting the national provisions adopted for its implementation;

(62) Whereas the establishment in Member States of supervisory authorities, exercising their functions with complete independence, is an essential component of the protection of individuals with regard to the processing of personal data;

(63) Whereas such authorities must have the necessary means to perform their duties, including powers of investigation and intervention, particularly in cases of complaints from individuals, and powers to engage in legal proceedings; whereas such authorities must help to ensure transparency of processing in the Member States within whose jurisdiction they fall;

(64) Whereas the authorities in the different Member States will need to assist one another in performing their duties so as to ensure that the rules of protection are properly respected throughout the European Union;

(65) Whereas, at Community level, a Working Party on the Protection of Individuals with regard to the Processing of Personal Data must be set up and be completely independent in the performance of its functions; whereas, having regard to its specific nature, it must advise the Commission and, in particular, contribute to the uniform application of the national rules adopted pursuant to this Directive;

(66) Whereas, with regard to the transfer of data to third countries, the application of this. Directive calls for the conferment of powers of implementation on the Commission and the establishment of a procedure as laid down in Council Decision 87/373/EEC[1];

(67) Whereas an agreement on a *modus vivendi* between the European Parliament, the Council and the Commission concerning the implementing measures for acts adopted in accordance with the procedure laid down in Article 189b of the EC Treaty was reached on 20 December 1994;

(68) Whereas the principles set out in this Directive regarding the protection of the rights and freedoms of individuals, notably their right to privacy, with regard to the processing of personal data may be supplemented or clarified, in particular as far as certain sectors are concerned, by specific rules based on those principles;

(69) Whereas Member States should be allowed a period of not more than three years from the entry into force of the national measures transposing this Directive in which to apply such new national rules progressively to all processing operations already under way; whereas, in order to facilitate their cost-effective implementation, a further period expiring 12 years after the date on which this Directive is adopted will be allowed to Member States to ensure the conformity of existing manual filing systems with certain of the Directive's provisions; whereas, where data contained in such filing systems are manually processed during this extended transition period, those systems must be brought into conformity with these provisions at the time of such processing;

(70) Whereas it is not necessary for the data subject to give his consent again so as to allow the controller to continue to process, after the national provisions taken pursuant to this Directive enter into force, any sensitive data necessary for the performance of a contract concluded on the basis of free and informed consent before the entry into force of these provisions;

(71) Whereas this Directive does not stand in the way of a Member State's regulating marketing activities aimed at consumers residing in territory in so far as such regulation does not concern the protection of individuals with regard to the processing of personal data;

(72) Whereas this Directive allows the principle of public access to official documents to be taken into account when implementing the principles set out in this Directive,

HAVE ADOPTED THIS DIRECTIVE:

---

1   OJ No L 197, 18 July 1987, p 33.

Chapter I
GENERAL PROVISIONS

Article 1
Object of the Directive

1. In accordance with this Directive, Member States shall protect the fundamental rights and freedoms of natural persons, and in particular their right to privacy with respect to the processing of personal data.
2. Member States shall neither restrict nor prohibit the free flow of personal data between Member States for reasons connected with the protection afforded under paragraph 1.

Article 2
Definitions

For the purposes of this Directive:

(a) 'personal data' shall mean any information relating to an identified or identifiable natural person ('data subject'); an identifiable person is one who can be identified, directly or indirectly, in particular by reference to an identification number or to one of more factors specific to his physical, physiological, mental, economic, cultural or social identity;

(b) 'processing of personal data' ('processing') shall mean any operation or set of operations which is performed upon personal data, whether or not by automatic means, such as collection, recording, organisation, storage, adaptation or alteration, retrieval, consultation, use, disclosure by transmission, dissemination or otherwise making available, alignment or combination, blocking, erasure or destruction;

(c) 'personal data filing system' ('filing system') shall mean any structured set of personal data which are accessible according to specific criteria, whether centralised, decentralised or dispersed on a functional or geographical basis;

(d) 'controller' shall mean the natural or legal person, public authority, agency or any other body which alone or jointly with others determines the purposes and means of the processing of personal data; where the purposes and means of processing are determined by national or Community laws or regulations, the controller or the specific criteria for his nomination may be designated by national or Community law;

(e) 'processor' shall mean a natural or legal person, public authority, agency or any other body which processes personal data on behalf of the controller;

(f) 'third party' shall mean any natural or legal person, public authority, agency or any other body other than the data subject, the controller, the processor and the persons who, under the direct authority of the controller or the processor, are authorised to process the data;

(g) 'recipient' shall mean a natural or legal person, public authority, agency or any other body to whom data are disclosed, whether a third party or not; however, authorities which may receive data in the framework of a particular inquiry shall not be regarded as recipients;

(h) 'the data subject's consent' shall mean any freely given specific and informed indication of his wishes by which the data subject signifies his agreement to personal data relating to him being processed.

Article 3

Scope

1. This Directive shall apply to the processing of personal data wholly or partly by automatic means, and to the processing otherwise than by automatic means of personal data which form part of a filing system or are intended to form part of a filing system.
2. This Directive shall not apply to the processing of personal data:

   – in the course of an activity which falls outside the scope of Community law, such as those provided for by Titles V and VI of the Treaty on European Union and in any case to processing operations concerning public security, defence, State security (including the economic well-being of the State when the processing operation relates to State security matters) and the activities of the State in areas of criminal law,
   – by a natural person in the course of a purely personal or household activity.

Article 4

National law applicable

1. Each Member State shall apply the national provisions it adopts pursuant to this Directive to the processing of personal data where:

   (a) the processing is carried out in the context of the activities of an establishment of the controller on the territory of the Member State; when the same controller is established on the territory of several Member States, he must take the necessary measures to ensure that each of these establishments complies with the obligations laid down by the national law applicable;
   (b) the controller is not established on the Member State's territory, but in a place where its national law applies by virtue of international public law;
   (c) the controller is not established on Community territory and, for purposes of processing personal data makes use of equipment, automated or otherwise, situated on the territory of the said Member State, unless such equipment is used only for purposes of transit through the territory of the Community.

2. In the circumstances referred to in paragraph 1(c), the controller must designate a representative established in the territory of that Member State, without prejudice to legal actions which could be initiated against the controller himself.

Chapter II

GENERAL RULES ON THE LAWFULNESS OF THE PROCESSING OF PERSONAL DATA

Article 5

Member States shall, within the limits of the provisions of this Chapter, determine more precisely the conditions under which the processing of personal data is lawful.

Section I
PRINCIPLES RELATING TO DATA QUALITY

Article 6

1. Member States shall provide that personal data must be:

   (a) processed fairly and lawfully;

   (b) collected for specified, explicit and legitimate purposes and not further processed in a way incompatible with those purposes. Further processing of data for historical, statistical or scientific purposes shall not be considered as incompatible provided that Member States provide appropriate safeguards;

   (c) adequate, relevant and not excessive in relation to the purposes for which they are collected and/or further processed;

   (d) accurate and, where necessary, kept up to date; every reasonable step must be taken to ensure that data which are inaccurate or incomplete, having regard to the purposes for which they were collected or for which they are further processed, are erased or rectified;

   (e) kept in a form which permits identification of data subjects for no longer than is necessary for the purposes for which the data were collected or for which they are further processed. Member States shall lay down appropriate safeguards for personal data stored for longer periods for historical, statistical or scientific use.

2. It shall be for the controller to ensure that paragraph 1 is complied with.

Section II
CRITERIA FOR MAKING DATA PROCESSING LEGITIMATE

Article 7

Member States shall provide that personal data may be processed only if:

(a) the data subject has unambiguously given his consent; or

(b) processing is necessary for the performance of a contract to which the data subject is party or in order to take steps at the request of the data subject prior to entering into a contract; or

(c) processing is necessary for compliance with a legal obligation to which the controller is subject; or

(d) processing is necessary in order to protect the vital interests of the data subject; or

(e) processing is necessary for the performance of a task carried out in the public interest or in the exercise of official authority vested in the controller or in a third party to whom the data are disclosed; or

(f) processing is necessary for the purposes of the legitimate interests pursued by the controller or by the third party or parties to whom the data are disclosed, except where such interests are overridden by the interests for fundamental rights and freedoms of the data subject which require protection under Article 1(1).

Section III
SPECIAL CATEGORIES OF PROCESSING

Article 8
The processing of special categories of data

1. Member States shall prohibit the processing of personal data revealing racial or ethnic origin, political opinions, religious or philosophical beliefs, trade-union membership, and the processing of data concerning health or sex life.
2. Paragraph 1 shall not apply where:

   (a) the data subject has given his explicit consent to the processing of those data, except where the laws of the Member State provide that the prohibition referred to in paragraph 1 may not be lifted by the data subject's giving his consent; or

   (b) processing is necessary for the purposes of carrying out the obligations and specific rights of the controller in the field of employment law in so far as it is authorised by national law providing for adequate safeguards; or

   (c) processing is necessary to protect the vital interests of the data subject or of another person where the data subject is physically or legally incapable of giving his consent; or

   (d) processing is carried out in the course of its legitimate activities with appropriate guarantees by a foundation, association or any other non-profit-seeking body with a political, philosophical, religious or trade-union aim and on condition that the processing relates solely to the members of the body or to persons who have regular contact with it in connection with its purposes and that the data are not disclosed to a third party without the consent of the data subjects; or

   (e) the processing relates to data which are manifestly made public by the data subject or is necessary for the establishment, exercise or defence of legal claims.

3. Paragraph 1 shall not apply where processing of the data is required for the purposes of preventive medicine, medical diagnosis, the provision of care or treatment or the management of health-care services, and where those data are processed by a health professional subject under national law or rules established by national competent bodies to the obligation of professional secrecy or by another person also subject to an equivalent obligation of secrecy.
4. Subject to the provision of suitable safeguards, Member States may, for reasons of substantial public interest, lay down exemptions in addition to those laid down in paragraph 2 either by national law or by decision of the supervisory authority.
5. Processing of data relating to offences, criminal convictions or security measures may be carried out only under the control of official authority, or if suitable specific safeguards are provided under national law, subject to derogations which may be granted by the Member State under national provisions providing suitable specific safeguards. However, a complete register of criminal convictions may be kept only under the control of official authority.

   Member States may provide that data relating to administrative sanctions or judgements in civil cases shall also be processed under the control of official authority.

6. Derogations from paragraph 1 provided for in paragraphs 4 and 5 shall be notified to the Commission.
7. Member States shall determine the conditions under which a national identification number or any other identifier of general application may be processed.

Article 9

Processing of personal data and freedom of expression

Member States shall provide for exemptions or derogations from the provisions of this Chapter, Chapter IV and Chapter VI for the processing of personal data carried out solely for journalistic purposes or the purpose of artistic or literary expression only if they are necessary to reconcile the right to privacy with the rules governing freedom of expression.

Section IV

INFORMATION TO BE GIVEN TO THE DATA SUBJECT

Article 10

Information in cases of collection of data from the data subject

Member States shall provide that the controller or his representative must provide a data subject from whom data relating to himself are collected with at least the following information, except where he already has it:

- (a) the identity of the controller and of his representative, if any;
- (b) the purposes of the processing for which the data are intended;
- (c) any further information such as

    - the recipients or categories of recipients of the data,
    - whether replies to the questions are obligatory or voluntary, as well as the possible consequences of failure to reply,
    - the existence of the right of access to and the right to rectify the data concerning him

in so far as such further information is necessary, having regard to the specific circumstances in which the data are collected to guarantee fair processing in respect of the data subject.

Article 11

Information where the data have not been obtained from the data subject

1. Where the data have not been obtained from the data subject, Member States shall provide that the controller or his representative must at the time of undertaking the recording of personal data or if a disclosure to a third party is envisaged, no later than the time when the data are first disclosed provide the data subject with at least the following information, except where he already has it:

    - (a) the identity of the controller and of his representative, if any;
    - (b) the purposes of the processing;
    - (c) any further information such as:

        - the categories of data concerned,
        - the recipients or categories of recipients,
        - the existence of the right of access to and the right to rectify the data concerning him

    in so far as such further information is necessary, having regard to the specific circumstances in which the data are processed, to guarantee fair processing in respect of the data subject.

2. Paragraph 1 shall not apply where, in particular for processing for statistical purposes or for the purposes of historical or scientific research, the provision of such information proves impossible or would involve a disproportionate effort or if recording or disclosure is expressly laid down by law. In these cases Member States shall provide appropriate safeguards.

Section V
THE DATA SUBJECT'S RIGHT OF ACCESS TO DATA

Article 12
Right of acess

Member States shall guarantee every data subject the right to obtain from the controller:

(a) without constraint at reasonable intervals and without excessive delay or expense:

- confirmation as to whether or not data relating to him are being processed and information at least as to the purposes of the processing, the categories of data concerned, and the recipients or categories of recipients to whom the data are disclosed,
- communication to him in an intelligible form of the data undergoing processing and of any available information as to their source,
- knowledge of the logic involved in any automatic processing of data concerning him at least in the case of the automated decisions referred to in Article 15(1);

(b) as appropriate the rectification, erasure or blocking of data the processing of which does not comply with the provisions of this Directive, in particular because of the incomplete or inaccurate nature of the data;

(c) notification to third parties to whom the data have been disclosed of any rectification, erasure or blocking carried out in compliance with (b), unless this proves impossible or involves a disproportionate effort.

Section VI
EXEMPTIONS AND RESTRICTIONS

Article 13
Exemptions and restrictions

1. Member States may adopt legislative measures to restrict the scope of the obligations and rights provided for in Articles 6(1), 10, 11(1), 12 and 21 when such a restriction constitutes a necessary measures to safeguard:

(a) national security;
(b) defence;
(c) public security;
(d) the prevention, investigation, detection and prosecution of criminal offences, or of breaches of ethics for regulated professions;
(e) an important economic or financial interest of a Member State or of the European Union, including monetary, budgetary and taxation matters;
(f) a monitoring, inspection or regulatory function connected, even occasionally, with the exercise of official authority in cases referred to in (c), (d) and (e);

(g)   the protection of the data subject or of the rights and freedoms of others.

2.   Subject to adequate legal safeguards, in particular that the data are not used for taking measures or decisions regarding any particular individual, Member States may, where there is clearly no risk of breaching the privacy of the data subject, restrict by a legislative measure the rights provided for in Article 12 when data are processed solely for purposes of scientific research or are kept in personal form for a period which does nor exceed the period necessary for the sole purpose of creating statistics.

Section VII
THE DATA SUBJECT'S RIGHT TO OBJECT

Article 14
The data subject's right to object

Member States shall grant the data subject the right:

(a)   at least in the cases referred to in Article 7(e) and (f), to object at any time on compelling legitimate grounds relating to his particular situation to the processing of data relating to him, save where otherwise provided by national legislation. Where there is a justified objection, the processing instigated by the controller may no longer involve those data;

(b)   to object, on request and free of charge, to the processing of personal data relating to him which the controller anticipates being processed for the purposes of direct marketing, or to be informed before personal data are disclosed for the first time to third parties or used on their behalf for the purposes of direct marketing, and to be expressly offered the right to object free of charge to such disclosures or uses.

Member States shall take the necessary measures to ensure that data subjects are aware of the existence of the right referred to in the first subparagraph of (b).

Article 15
Automated individual decisions

1.   Member States shall grant the right to every person not to be subject to a decision which produces legal effects concerning him or significantly affects him and which is based solely on automated processing of data intended to evaluate certain personal aspects relating to him, such as his performance at work, creditworthiness, reliability, conduct, etc.

2.   Subject to the other Article of this Directive, Member States shall provide that a person may be subjected to a decision of the kind referred to in paragraph 1 of that decision:

(a)   is taken in the course of the entering into or performance of a contract, provided the request for the entering into or the performance of the contract, lodged by the data subject, has been satisfied or that there are suitable measures to safeguard his legitimate interests, such as arrangements allowing him to put his point of view; or

(b)   is authorised by a law which also lays down measures to safeguard the data subject's legitimate interests.

Section VIII
CONFIDENTIALITY AND SECURITY OF PROCESSING

Article 16
Confidentiality of processing

Any person acting under the authority of the controller or of the processor, including the processor himself, who has access to personal data must not process them except on instructions from the controller, unless he is required to do so by law.

Article 17
Security of processing

1. Member States shall provide that the controller must implement appropriate technical and organisational measures to protect personal data against accidental or unlawful destruction or accidental loss, alteration, unauthorized disclosure or access, in particular where the processing involves the transmission of data over a network, and against all other unlawful forms of processing.

    Having regard to the state of the art and the cost of their implementation, such measures shall ensure a level of security appropriate to the risks represented by the processing and the nature of the data to be protected.

2. The Member States shall provide that the controller must, where processing is carried out on his behalf, choose a processor providing sufficient guarantees in respect of the technical security measures and organisational measures governing the processing to be carried out, and must ensure compliance with those measures.

3. The carrying out of processing by way of a processor must be governed by a contract or legal act binding the processor to the controller and stipulating in particular that:

    –   the processor shall act only on instructions from the controller,
    –   the obligations set out in paragraph 1, as defined by the law of the Member State in which the processor is established, shall also be incumbent on the processor.

4. For the purposes of keeping proof, the parts of the contract or the legal act relating to data protection and the requirements relating to the measures referred to in paragraph 1 shall be in writing or in another equivalent form.

Section IX
NOTIFICATION

Article 18
Obligation to notify the supervisory authority

1. Member States shall provide that the controller or his representative, if any, must notify the supervisory authority referred to in Article 28 before carrying out any wholly or partly automatic processing operation or set of such operations intended to serve a single purpose or several related purposes.

2. Member States may provide for the simplification of or exemption from notification only in the following cases and under the following conditions:

–   where, for categories of processing operations which are unlikely, taking account of the data to be processed, to affect adversely the rights and freedoms of data subjects, they specify the purposes of the processing, the data or categories of data undergoing processing, the category or categories of data subject, the recipients or categories of recipient to whom the data are to be disclosed and the length of time the data are to be stored, and/or

–   where the controller, in compliance with the national law which governs him, appoints a personal data protection official, responsible in particular:

   –   for ensuring in an independent manner the internal application of the national provisions taken pursuant to this Directive
   –   for keeping the register of processing operations carried out by the controller, containing the items of information referred to in Article 21(2),

   thereby ensuring that the rights and freedoms of the data subjects are unlikely to be adversely affected by the processing operations.

3.   Member States may provide that paragraph 1 does not apply to processing whose sole purpose is the keeping of a register which according to laws or regulations is intended to provide information to the public and which is open to consultation either by the public in general or by any person demonstrating a legitimate interest.

4.   Member States may provide for an exemption from the obligation to notify or a simplification of the notification in the case of processing operations referred to in Article 8(2)(d).

5.   Member States may stipulate that certain or all non-automatic processing operations involving personal data shall be notified, or provide for these processing operations to be subject to simplified notification.

Article 19

Contents of notification

1.   Member States shall specify the information to be given in the notification. It shall include at least:

   (a)   the name and address of the controller and of his representative, if any;
   (b)   the purpose or purposes of the processing;
   (c)   a description of the category or categories of data subject and of the data or categories of data relating to them;
   (d)   the recipients or categories of recipient to whom the data might be disclosed;
   (e)   proposed transfers of data to third countries;
   (f)   a general description allowing a preliminary assessment to be made of the appropriateness of the measures taken pursuant to Article 17 to ensure security of processing.

2.   Member States shall specify the procedures under which any change affecting the information referred to in paragraph 1 must be notified to the supervisory authority.

Article 20

Prior checking

1.   Member States shall determine the processing operations likely to present specific risks to the rights and freedoms of data subjects and shall check that these processing operations are examined prior to the start thereof.

2. Such prior checks shall be carried out by the supervisory authority following receipt of a notification from the controller or by the data protection official, who, in cases of doubt, must consult the supervisory authority.
3. Member States may also carry out such checks in the context of preparation either of a measure of the national parliament or of a measure based on such a legislative measure, which define the nature of the processing and lay down appropriate safeguards.

Article 21

Publicising of processing operations

1. Member States shall take measures to ensure that processing operations are publicised.
2. Member States shall provide that a register of processing operations notified in accordance with Article 18 shall be kept by the supervisory authority.

   The register shall contain at least the information listed in Article 19(1)(a) to (e).

   The register may be inspected by any person.

3. Member States shall provide, in relation to processing operations not subject to notification, that controllers or another body appointed by the Member States make available at least the information referred to in Article 19(1)(a) to (e) in an appropriate form to any person on request.

   Member States may provide that this provision does not apply to processing whose sole purpose is the keeping of a register which according to laws or regulations is intended to provide information to the public and which is open to consultation either by the public in general or by any person who can provide proof of a legitimate interest.

Chapter III

JUDICIAL REMEDIES, LIABILITY AND SANCTIONS

Article 22

Remedies

Without prejudice to any administrative remedy for which provision may be made, *inter alia* before the supervisory authority referred to in Article 28, prior to referral to the judicial authority, Member States shall provide for the right of every person to a judicial remedy for any breach of the rights guaranteed him by the national law applicable to the processing in question.

Article 23

Liability

1. Member States shall provide that any person who has suffered damage as a result of an unlawful processing operation or of any act incompatible with the national provisions adopted pursuant to this Directive is entitled to receive compensation from the controller for the damage suffered.
2. The controller may be exempted from this liability, in whole or in part, if he proves that he is not responsible for the event giving rise to the damage.

Article 24
Sanctions

The Member States shall adopt suitable measures to ensure the full implementation of the provisions of this Directive and shall in particular lay down the sanctions to be imposed in case of infringement of the provisions adopted pursuant to this Directive.

Chapter IV
TRANSFER OF PERSONAL DATA TO THIRD COUNTRIES

Article 25
Principles

1. The Member States shall provide that the transfer to a third country of personal data which are undergoing processing or are intended for processing after transfer may take place only if, without prejudice to compliance with the national provisions adopted pursuant to the other provisions of this Directive, the third country in question ensures an adequate level of protection.
2. The adequacy of the level of protection afforded by a third country shall be assessed in the light of all the circumstances surrounding a data transfer operation or set of data transfer operations; particular consideration shall be given to the nature of the data, the purpose and duration of the proposed processing operation or operations, the country of origin and country of final destination, the rules of law, both general and sectoral, in force in the third country in question and the professional rules and security measures which are complied with in that country.
3. The Member States and the Commission shall inform each other of cases where they consider that a third country does not ensure an adequate level of protection within the meaning of paragraph 2.
4. Where the Commission finds, under the procedure provided for in Article 31(2), that a third country does not ensure an adequate level of protection within the meaning of paragraph 2 of this Article, Member States shall take the measures necessary to prevent any transfer of data of the same type to the third country in question.
5. At the appropriate time, the Commission shall enter into negotiations with a view to remedying the situation resulting from the finding made pursuant to paragraph 4.
6. The Commission may find, in accordance with the procedure referred to in Article 31(2), that a third country ensures an adequate level of protection within the meaning of paragraph 2 of this Article, by reason of its domestic law or of the international commitments it has entered into, particularly upon conclusion of the negotiations referred to in paragraph 5, for the protection of the private lives and basic freedoms and rights of individuals.

    Member States shall take the measures necessary to comply with the Commission's decision.

Article 26
Derogations

1. By way of derogation from Article 25 and save where otherwise provided by domestic law governing particular cases, Member States shall provide that a transfer or a set of transfers of personal data to a third country which does not ensure an adequate level of protection within the meaning of Article 25(2) may take place on condition that:

(a) the data subject has given his consent unambiguously to the proposed transfer; or

(b) the transfer is necessary for the performance of a contract between the data subject and the controller or the implementation of precontractual measures: taken in response to the data subject's request; or

(c) the transfer is necessary for the conclusion or performance of a contract concluded in the interest of the data subject between the controller and a third party; or

(d) the transfer is necessary or legally required on important public interest grounds, or for the establishment, exercise or defence of legal claims; or

(e) the transfer is necessary in order to protect the vital interests of the data subject; or

(f) the transfer is made from a register which according to laws or regulations is intended to provide information to the public and which is open to consultation either by the public in general or by any person who can demonstrate legitimate interest, to the extent that the conditions laid down in law for consultation are fulfilled in the particular case.

2. Without prejudice to paragraph 1, a Member State may authorise a transfer or a set of transfers of personal data to a third country which does not ensure an adequate level of protection within the meaning of Article 25(2), where the controller adduces adequate safeguards with respect to the protection of the privacy and fundamental rights and freedoms of individuals and as regards the exercise of the corresponding rights; such safeguards may in particular result from appropriate contractual clauses.

3. The Member State shall inform the Commission and the other Member States of the authorisations it grants pursuant to paragraph 2.

If a Member State or the Commission objects on justified grounds involving the protection of the privacy and fundamental rights and freedoms of individuals, the Commission shall take appropriate measures in accordance with the procedure laid down in Article 31(2).

Member States shall take the necessary measures to comply with the Commission's decision.

4. Where the Commission decides, in accordance with the procedure referred to in Article 31(2), that certain standard contractual clauses offer sufficient safeguards as required by paragraph 2, Member States shall take the necessary measures to comply with the Commission's decision.

Chapter V
CODES OF CONDUCT

Article 27

1. The Member States and the Commission shall encourage the drawing up of codes of conduct intended to contribute to the proper implementation of the national provisions adopted by the Member States pursuant to this Directive, taking account of the specific features of the various sectors.

2. Member States shall make provision for trade associations and other bodies representing other categories of controllers which have drawn up draft national codes or which have the intention of amending or extending existing national codes to be able to submit them to the opinion of the national authority.

Member States shall make provision for this authority to ascertain, among other things, whether the drafts submitted to it are in accordance with the national provisions adopted pursuant to this Directive. If it sees fit, the authority shall seek the views of data subjects or their representatives.

3.   Draft Community codes, and amendments or extensions to existing Community codes, may be submitted to the Working Party referred to in Article 29. This Working Party shall determine, among other things, whether the drafts submitted to it are in accordance with the national provisions adopted pursuant to this Directive. If it sees fit, the authority shall seek the views of data subjects or their representatives. The Commission may ensure appropriate publicity for the codes which have been approved by the Working Party.

Chapter VI

SUPERVISORY AUTHORITY AND WORKING PARTY ON THE PROTECTION OF INDIVIDUALS WITH REGARD TO THE PROCESSING OF PERSONAL DATA

Article 28

Supervisory authority

1.   Each Member State shall provide that one or more public authorities are responsible for monitoring the application within its territory of the provisions adopted by the Member States pursuant to this Directive.

These authorities shall act with complete independence in exercising the functions entrusted to them.

2.   Each Member State shall provide that the supervisory authorities are consulted when drawing up administrative measures or regulations relating to the protection of individuals' rights and freedoms with regard to the processing of personal data.

3.   Each authority shall in particular be endowed with:

   –   investigative powers, such as powers of access to data forming the subject-matter of processing operations and powers to collect all the information necessary for the performance of its supervisory duties,

   –   effective powers of intervention such as, for example, that of delivering opinions before processing operations are carried out, in accordance with Article 20, and ensuring appropriate publication of such opinions, of ordering the blocking, erasure or destruction of data, of imposing a temporary or definitive ban on processing, of warning or admonishing the controller, or that of referring the matter to national parliaments or other political institutions,

   –   the power to engage in legal proceedings where the national provisions adopted pursuant to this Directive have been violated or to bring these violations to the attention of the judicial authorities.

Decisions by the supervisory authority which give rise to complaints may be appealed against through the courts.

4.   Each supervisory authority shall hear claims lodged by any person, or by an association representing that person, concerning the protection of his rights and freedoms in regard to the processing of personal data. The person concerned shall be informed of the outcome of the claim.

Each supervisory authority shall, in particular, hear claims for checks on the lawfulness of data processing lodged by any person when the national provision adopted pursuant to Article 13 of this Directive apply. The person shall at any rate be informed that a check has taken place.

5. Each supervisory authority shall draw up a report on its activities at regular intervals. The report shall be made public.

6. Each supervisory authority is competent, whatever the national law applicable to the processing in question, to exercise, on the territory of its own Member State, the powers conferred on it in accordance with paragraph 3. Each authority may be requested to exercise its powers by an authority of another Member State.

   The supervisory authorities shall cooperate with one another to the extent necessary for the performance of their duties, in particular by exchanging all useful information.

7. Member States shall provide that the members and staff of the supervisory authority, even after their employment has ended, are to be subject to a duty of professional secrecy with regard to confidential information to which they have access.

Article 29

Working Party on the Protection of Individuals with regard to the Processing of Personal Data

1. A Working Party on the Protection of Individuals with regard to the Processing of Personal Data, hereinafter referred to as 'the Working Party', is hereby set up.

   It shall have advisory status and act independently.

2. The Working Party shall be composed of a representative of the supervisory authority or authorities designated by each Member State and of a representative of the authority or authorities established for the Community institutions and bodies, and of a representative of the Commission.

   Each member of the Working Party shall be designated by the institution, authority or authorities which he represents. Where a Member State has designated more than one supervisory authority, they shall nominate a joint representative. The same shall apply to the authorities established for Community institutions and bodies.

3. The Working Party shall take decisions by a simple majority of the representatives of the supervisory authorities.

4. The Working Party shall elect its chairman. The chairman's term of office shall be two years. His appointment shall be renewable.

5. The Working Party's secretariat shall be provided by the Commission.

6. The Working Party shall adopt its own rules of procedure.

7. The Working Party shall consider items placed on its agenda by its chairman, either on his own initiative or at the request of a representative of the supervisory authorities or at the Commission's request.

Article 30

1. The Working Party shall:

   (a) examine any question covering the application of the national measures adopted under this Directive in order to contribute to the uniform application of such measures;

   (b) give the Commission an opinion on the level of protection in the Community and in third countries;

   (c) advise the Commission on any proposed amendment of this Directive, on any additional or specific measures to safeguard the rights and freedoms of natural persons with regard to the processing of personal data and on any other proposed Community measures affecting such rights and freedoms;

(d)   give an opinion on codes of conduct drawn up at Community level.

2.   If the Working Party finds that divergences likely to affect the equivalence of protection for persons with regard to the processing of personal data in the Community are arising between the laws or practices of Member States, it shall inform the Commission accordingly.

3.   The Working Party may, on its own initiative, make recommendations on all matters relating to the protection of persons with regard to the processing of personal data in the Community.

4.   The Working Party's opinions and recommendations shall be forwarded to the Commission and to the committee referred to in Article 31.

5.   The Commission shall inform the Working Party of the action it has taken in response to its opinions and recommendations. It shall do so in a report which shall also be forwarded to the European Parliament and the Council. The report shall be made public.

6.   The Working Party shall draw up an annual report on the situation regarding the protection of natural persons with regard to the processing of personal data in the Community and in third countries, which it shall transmit to the Commission, the European Parliament and the Council. The report shall be made public.

Chapter VII
COMMUNITY IMPLEMENTING MEASURES

Article 31
The Committee

1.   The Commission shall be assisted by a committee composed of the representatives of the Member States and chaired by the representative of the Commission.

2.   The representative of the Commission shall submit to the committee a draft of the measures to be taken. The committee shall deliver its opinion on the draft within a time limit which the chairman may lay down according to the urgency of the matter.

The opinion shall be delivered by the majority laid down in Article 148(2) of the Treaty. The votes of the representatives of the Member States within the committee shall be weighted in the manner set out in that Article. The chairman shall not vote.

The Commission shall adopt measures which shall apply immediately. However, if these measures are not in accordance with the opinion of the committee, they shall be communicated by the Commission to the Council forthwith. It that event:

–   the Commission shall defer application of the measures which it has decided for a period of three months from the date of communication,

–   the Council, acting by a qualified majority, may take a different decision within the time limit referred to in the first indent.

FINAL PROVISIONS

Article 32

1.   Member States shall bring into force the laws, regulations and administrative provisions necessary to comply with this Directive at the latest at the end of a period of three years from the date of its adoption.

When Member States adopt these measures, they shall contain a reference to this Directive or be accompanied by such reference on the occasion of their official publication. The methods of making such reference shall be laid down by the Member States.

2.   Member States shall ensure that processing already under way on the date the national provisions adopted pursuant to this Directive enter into force, is brought into conformity with these provisions within three years of this date.

By way of derogation from the preceding subparagraph, Member States may provide that the processing of data already held in manual filing systems on the date of entry into force of the national provisions adopted in implementation of this Directive shall be brought into conformity with Articles 6, 7 and 8 of this Directive within 12 years of the date on which it is adopted. Member States shall, however, grant the data subject the right to obtain, at his request and in particular at the time of exercising his right of access, the rectification, erasure or blocking of data which are incomplete, inaccurate or stored in a way incompatible with the legitimate purposes pursued by the controller.

3.   By way of derogation from paragraph 2, Member States may provide, subject to suitable safeguards, that data kept for the sole purpose of historical research need not be brought into conformity with Articles 6, 7 and 8 of this Directive.

4.   Member States shall communicate to the Commission the text of the provisions of domestic law which they adopt in the field covered by this Directive.

Article 33

The Commission shall report to the Council and the European Parliament at regular intervals, starting not later than three years after the date referred to in Article 32(1), on the implementation of this Directive, attaching to its report, if necessary, suitable proposals for amendments. The report shall be made public.

The Commission shall examine, in particular, the application of this Directive to the data processing of sound and image data relating to natural persons and shall submit any appropriate proposals which prove to be necessary, taking account of developments in information technology and in the light of the state of progress in the information society.

Article 34

This Directive is addressed to the Member States.

Done at Luxembourg, 24 October 1995.

Appendix 3

DIRECTIVE 97/66/EC OF THE EUROPEAN PARLIAMENT AND OF THE COUNCIL

of 15 December 1997

concerning the Processing of Personal Data and the Protection of Privacy in the Telecommunications Sector

THE EUROPEAN PARLIAMENT AND THE COUNCIL OF THE EUROPEAN UNION,

Having regard to the Treaty establishing the European Community, and in particular Article 100a thereof,

Having regard to the proposal from the Commission[1],

Having regard to the opinion of the Economic and Social Committee[2],

Acting in accordance with the procedure laid down in Article 189b of the Treaty[3], in the light of the joint text approved by the Conciliation Committee on 6 November 1997,

(1) Whereas Directive 95/46/EC of the European Parliament and of the Council of 24 October 1995 on the protection of individuals with regard to the processing of personal data and on the free movement of such data[4] requires Member States to ensure the rights and freedoms of natural persons with regard to the processing of personal data, and in particular their right to privacy, in order to ensure the free flow of personal data in the Community;

(2) Whereas confidentiality of communications is guaranteed in accordance with the international instruments relating to human rights (in particular the European Convention for the Protection of Human Rights and Fundamental Freedoms) and the constitutions of the Member States;

(3) Whereas currently in the Community new advanced digital technologies are introduced in public telecommunications networks, which give rise to specific requirements concerning the protection of personal data and privacy of the user; whereas the development of the information society is characterised by the introduction of new telecommunications services; whereas the successful cross-border development of these services, such as video-on-demand, interactive television, is partly dependent on the confidence of the users that their privacy will not be at risk;

---

1 OJ C 200, 22 July 1994, p 4.
2 OJ C 159, 17 June 1991, p 38.
3 Opinion of the European Parliament of 11 March 1992 (OJ C 94, 13 April 1992, p 198). Council Common Position of 12 September 1996 (OJ C 315, 24 October 1996, p 30) and Decision of the European Parliament of 16 January 1997 (OJ C 33, 3 February 1997, p 78). Decision of the European Parliament of 20 November 1997 (OJ C 371, 8 December 1997). Council Decision of 1 December 1997.
4 OJ L 281, 23 November 1995, p 31.

(4) Whereas this is the case, in particular, with the introduction of the Integrated Services Digital Network (ISDN) and digital mobile networks;

(5) Whereas the Council, in its Resolution of 30 June 1988 on the development of the common market for telecommunications services and equipment up to 1992[1], called for steps to be taken to protect personal data, in order to create an appropriate environment for the future development of telecommunications in the Community; whereas the Council re-emphasised the importance of the protection of personal data and privacy in its Resolution of 18 July 1989 on the strengthening of the coordination for the introduction of the Integrated Services Digital Network (ISDN) in the European Community up to 1992[2];

(6) Whereas the European Parliament has underlined the importance of the protection of personal data and privacy in the telecommunications networks, in particular with regard to the introduction of the Integrated Services Digital Network (ISDN);

(7) Whereas, in the case of public telecommunications networks, specific legal, regulatory, and technical provisions must be made in order to protect fundamental rights and freedoms of natural persons and legitimate interests of legal persons, in particular with regard to the increasing risk connected with automated storage and processing of data relating to subscribers and users;

(8) Whereas legal, regulatory, and technical provisions adopted by the Member States concerning the protection of personal data, privacy and the legitimate interest of legal persons, in the telecommunications sector, must be harmonised in order to avoid obstacles to the internal market for telecommunications in conformity with the objective set out in Article 7a of the Treaty; whereas the harmonisation is limited to requirements that are necessary to guarantee that the promotion and development of new telecommunications services and networks between Member States will not be hindered;

(9) Whereas the Member States, providers and users concerned, together with the competent Community bodies, should cooperate in introducing and developing the relevant technologies where this is necessary to apply the guarantees provided for by the provisions of this Directive.

(10) Whereas these new services include interactive television and video on demand;

(11) Whereas, in the telecommunications sector, in particular for all matters concerning protection of fundamental rights and freedoms, which are not specifically covered by the provisions of this Directive, including the obligations on the controller and the rights of individuals, Directive 95/46/EC applies; whereas Directive 95/46/EC applies to non-publicly available telecommunications services;

(12) Whereas this Directive, similarly to what is provided for by Article 3 of Directive 95/46/EC, does not address issues of protection of fundamental rights and freedoms related to activities which are not governed by Community law; whereas it is for Member States to take such measures as they consider necessary for the protection of public security, defence, State security (including the economic well-being of the State when the activities relate to State security matters) and the enforcement of criminal law; whereas this Directive shall not affect the ability of Member States to carry out lawful interception of telecommunications, for any of these purposes;

(13) Whereas subscribers of a publicly available telecommunications service may be natural or legal persons; whereas the provisions of this Directive are aimed to protect, by supplementing Directive 95/46/EC, the fundamental rights of natural persons and particularly their right to privacy, as well as the legitimate interests of legal persons; whereas these provisions may in no case entail an obligation for Member States to

---

1   OJ C 257, 4 October 1988, p 1.
2   OJ C 196, 1 August 1989, p 4.

extend the application of Directive 95/46/EC to the protection of the legitimate interests of legal persons; whereas this protection is ensured within the framework of the applicable Community and national legislation;

(14) Whereas the application of certain requirements relating to presentation and restriction of calling and connected line identification and to automatic call forwarding to subscriber lines connected to analogue exchanges must not be made mandatory in specific cases where such application would prove to be technically impossible or would require a disproportionate economic effort; whereas it is important for interested parties to be informed of such cases and the Member States should therefore notify them to the Commission;

(15) Whereas service providers must take appropriate measures to safeguard the security of their services, if necessary in conjunction with the provider of the network, and inform subscribers of any special risks of a breach of the security of the network; whereas security is appraised in the light of the provision of Article 17 of Directive 95/46/EC;

(16) Whereas measures must be taken to prevent the unauthorised access to communications in order to protect the confidentiality of communications by means of public telecommunications networks and publicly available telecommunications services; whereas national legislation in some Member States only prohibits intentional unauthorised access to communications;

(17) Whereas the data relating to subscribers processed to establish calls contain information on the private life of natural persons and concern the right to respect for their correspondence or concern the legitimate interests of legal persons; whereas such data may only be stored to the extent that is necessary for the provision of the service for the purpose of billing and for interconnection payments, and for a limited time; whereas any further processing which the provider of the publicly available telecommunications services may want to perform for the marketing of its own telecommunications services may only be allowed if the subscriber has agreed to this on the basis of accurate and full information given by the provider of the publicly available telecommunications services about the types of further processing he intends to perform;

(18) Whereas the introduction of itemised bills has improved the possibilities for the subscriber to verify the correctness of the fees charged by the service provider; whereas, at the same time, it may jeopardise the privacy of the users of publicly available telecommunications services; whereas therefore, in order to preserve the privacy of the user, Member States must encourage the development of telecommunications service options such as alternative payment facilities which allow anonymous or strictly private access to publicly available telecommunications services, for example calling cards and facilities for payment by credit card; whereas, alternatively, Member States may, for the same purpose, require the deletion of a certain number of digits from the called numbers mentioned in itemised bills;

(19) Whereas it is necessary, as regards calling line identification to protect the right of the calling party to withhold the presentation of the identification of the line from which the call is being made and the right of the called party to reject calls from unidentified lines; whereas it is justified to override the elimination of calling line identification presentation in specific cases; whereas certain subscribers, in particular helplines and similar organisations, have an interest in guaranteeing the anonymity of their callers; whereas it is necessary, as regards connected line identification to protect the right and the legitimate interest of the called party to withhold the presentation of the identification of the line to which the calling party is actually connected, in particular in the case of forwarded calls; whereas the providers of publicly available telecommuni-cations services must inform their subscribers of the existence of calling and connected line identification in the network and of all services which are offered on the basis of calling and connected line identification and about the privacy options which are

available; whereas this will allow the subscribers to make an informed choice about the privacy facilities they may want to use; whereas the privacy options which are offered on a per-line basis do not necessarily have to be available as an automatic network service but may be obtainable through a simple request to the provider of the publicly available telecommunications service;

(20) Whereas safeguards must be provided for subscribers against the nuisance which may be caused by automatic call forwarding by others; whereas, in such cases, it must be possible for subscribers to stop the forwarded calls being passed on to their terminals by simple request to the provider of the publicly available telecommunications service;

(21) Whereas directories are widely distributed and publicly available; whereas the right to privacy of natural persons and the legitimate interest of legal persons require that subscribers are able to determine the extent to which their personal data are published in a directory; whereas Member States may limit this possibility to subscribers who are natural persons;

(22) Whereas safeguards must be provided for subscribers against intrusion into their privacy by means of unsolicited calls and telefaxes; whereas Member States may limit such safeguards to subscribers who are natural persons;

(23) Whereas it is necessary to ensure that the introduction of technical features of telecommunications equipment for data protection purposes is harmonised in order to be compatible with the implementation of the internal market;

(24) Whereas in particular, similarly to what is provided for by Article 13 of Directive 95/46/EC, Member States can restrict the scope of subscribers' obligations and rights in certain circumstances, for example by ensuring that the provider of a publicly available telecommunications service may override the elimination of the presentation of calling line identification in conformity with national legislation for the purpose of prevention or detection of criminal offences or State security;

(25) Whereas where the rights of the users and subscribers are not respected, national legislation must provide for judicial remedy; whereas sanctions must be imposed on any person, whether governed by private or public law, who fails to comply with the national measures taken under this Directive;

(26) Whereas it is useful in the field of application of this Directive to draw on the experience of the Working Party on the protection of individuals with regard to the processing of personal data composed of representatives of the supervisory authorities of the Member States, set up by Article 29 of Directive 95/46/EC;

(27) Whereas, given the technological developments and the attendant evolution of the services on offer, it will be necessary technically to specify the categories of data listed in the Annex to this Directive for the application of Article 6 of this Directive with the assistance of the Committee composed of representatives of the Member States set up in Article 31 of Directive 95/46/EC in order to ensure a coherent application of the requirements set out in this Directive regardless of changes in technology; whereas this procedure applies solely to specifications necessary to adapt the Annex to new technological developments, taking into consideration changes in market and consumer demand; whereas the Commission must duly inform the European Parliament of its intention to apply this procedure and whereas, otherwise, the procedure laid down in Article 100a of the Treaty shall apply;

(28) Whereas, to facilitate compliance with the provisions of this Directive, certain specific arrangements are needed for processing of data already under way on the date that national implementing legislation pursuant to this Directive enters into force,

HAVE ADOPTED THIS DIRECTIVE:

Article 1

Object and scope

1. This Directive provides for the harmonisation of the provisions of the Member States required to ensure an equivalent level of protection of fundamental rights and freedoms and in particular the right to privacy, with respect to the processing of personal data in the telecommunications sector and to ensure the free movement of such data and of telecommunications equipment and services in the Community.

2. The provisions of this Directive particularise and complement Directive 95/46/EC for the purposes mentioned in paragraph 1. Moreover, they provide for protection of legitimate interests of subscribers who are legal persons.

3. This Directive shall not apply to the activities which fall outside the scope of Community law, such as those provided for by Titles V and VI of the Treaty on European Union, and in any case to activities concerning public security, defence, State security (including the economic well-being of the State when the activities relate to State security matters) and the activities of the State in areas of criminal law.

Article 2

Definitions

In addition to the definitions given in Directive 95/46/EC, for the purposes of this Directive:

(a) 'subscriber' shall mean any natural or legal person who or which is party to a contract with the provider of publicly available telecommunications services for the supply of such services;

(b) 'user' shall mean any natural person using a publicly available telecommunications service, for private or business purposes, without necessarily having subscribed to this service;

(c) 'public telecommunications network' shall mean transmission systems and, where applicable, switching equipment and other resources which permit the conveyance of signals between defined termination points by wire, by radio, by optical or by other electromagnetic means, which are used, in whole or in part, for the provision of publicly available telecommunications services;

(d) 'telecommunications service' shall mean services whose provision consists wholly or partly in the transmission and routing of signals on telecommunications networks, with the exception of radio and television broadcasting.

Article 3

Services concerned

1. This Directive shall apply to the processing of personal data in connection with the provision of publicly available telecommunications services in public telecommunications networks in the Community, in particular via the Integrated Services Digital Network (ISDN) and public digital mobile networks.

2. Articles 8, 9 and 10 shall apply to subscriber lines connected to digital exchanges and, where technically possible and if it does not require a disproportionate economic effort, to subscriber lines connected to analogue exchanges.

3. Cases where it would be technically impossible or require a disproportionate investment to fulfil the requirements of Articles 8, 9 and 10 shall be notified to the Commission by the Member States.

Article 4

Security

1. The provider of a publicly available telecommunications service must take appropriate technical and organisational measures to safeguard security of its services, if necessary in conjunction with the provider of the public telecommunications network with respect to network security. Having regard to the state of the art and the cost of their implementation, these measures shall ensure a level of security appropriate to the risk presented.
2. In case of a particular risk of a breach of the security of the network, the provider of a publicly available telecommunications service must inform the subscribers concerning such risk and any possible remedies, including the costs involved.

Article 5

Confidentiality of the communications

1. Member States shall ensure via national regulations the confidentiality of communications by means of a public telecommunications network and publicly available telecommunications services. In particular, they shall prohibit listening, tapping, storage or other kinds of interception or surveillance of communications, by others than users, without the consent of the users concerned, except when legally authorised, in accordance with Article 14(1).
2. Paragraph 1 shall not affect any legally authorised recording of communications in the course of lawful business practice for the purpose of providing evidence of a commercial transaction or of any other business communication.

Article 6

Traffic and billing data

1. Traffic data relating to subscribers and users processed to establish calls and stored by the provider of a public telecommunications network and/or publicly available telecommunications service must be erased or made anonymous upon termination of the call without prejudice to the provisions of paragraphs 2, 3 and 4.
2. For the purpose of subscriber billing and interconnection payments, data indicated in the Annex may be processed. Such processing is permissible only up to the end of the period during which the bill may lawfully be challenged or payment may be pursued.
3. For the purpose of marketing its own telecommunications services, the provider of a publicly available telecommunications service may process the data referred to in paragraph 2, if the subscriber has given his consent.
4. Processing of traffic and billing data must be restricted to persons acting under the authority of providers of the public telecommunications networks and/or publicly available telecommunications services handling billing or traffic management, customer enquiries, fraud detection and marketing the provider's own telecommunications services and it must be restricted to what is necessary for the purposes of such activities.
5. Paragraphs 1, 2, 3 and 4 shall apply without prejudice to the possibility for competent authorities to be informed of billing or traffic data in conformity with applicable legislation in view of settling disputes, in particular interconnection or billing disputes.

Article 7
Itemised billing

1. Subscribers shall have the right to receive non-itemised bills.
2. Member States shall apply national provisions in order to reconcile the rights of subscribers receiving itemised bills with the right to privacy of calling users and called subscribers, for example by ensuring that sufficient alternative modalities for communications or payments are available to such users and subscribers.

Article 8
Presentation and restriction of calling and connected line identification

1. Where presentation of calling-line identification is offered, the calling user must have the possibility via a simple means, free of charge, to eliminate the presentation of the calling-line identification on a per-call basis. The calling subscriber must have this possibility on a per-line basis.
2. Where presentation of calling-line identification is offered, the called subscriber must have the possibility via a simple means, free of charge for reasonable use of this function, to prevent the presentation of the calling line identification of incoming calls.
3. Where presentation of calling line identification is offered and where the calling line identification is presented prior to the call being established, the called subscriber must have the possibility via a simple means to reject incoming calls where the presentation of the calling line identification has been eliminated by the calling user or subscriber.
4. Where presentation of connected line identification is offered, the called subscriber must have the possibility via a simple means, free of charge, to eliminate the presentation of the connected line identification to the calling user.
5. The provisions set out in paragraph 1 shall also apply with regard to calls to third countries originating in the Community; the provisions set out in paragraphs 2, 3 and 4 shall also apply to incoming calls originating in third countries.
6. Member States shall ensure that where presentation of calling and/or connected line identification is offered, the providers of publicly available telecommunications services inform the public thereof and of the possibilities set out in paragraphs 1, 2, 3 and 4.

Article 9
Exceptions

Member States shall ensure that there are transparent procedures governing the way in which a provider of a public telecommunications network and/or a publicly available telecommunications service may override the elimination of the presentation of calling line identification:

(a) on a temporary basis, upon application of a subscriber requesting the tracing of malicious or nuisance calls; in this case, in accordance with national law, the data containing the identification of the calling subscriber will be stored and be made available by the provider of a public telecommunications network and/or publicly available telecommunications service;
(b) on a per-line basis for organisations dealing with emergency calls and recognised as such by a Member State, including law enforcement agencies, ambulance services and fire brigades, for the purpose of answering such calls.

Article 10

Automatic call forwarding

Member States shall ensure that any subscriber is provided, free of charge and via a simple means, with the possibility to stop automatic call forwarding by a third party to the subscriber's terminal.

Article 11

Directories of subscribers

1. Personal data contained in printed or electronic directories of subscribers available to the public or obtainable through directory enquiry services should be limited to what is necessary to identify a particular subscriber, unless the subscriber has given his unambiguous consent to the publication of additional personal data. The subscriber shall be entitled, free of charge, to be omitted from a printed or electronic directory at his or her request, to indicate that his or her personal data may not be used for the purpose of direct marketing to have his or her address omitted in part and not to have a reference revealing his or her sex, where this is applicable linguistically.
2. Notwithstanding paragraph 1, Member States may allow operators to require a payment from subscribers wishing to ensure that their particulars are not entered in a directory, provided that the sum involved does not act as a disincentive to the exercise of this right, and that, taking account of the quality requirements of the public directory in the light of the universal service, it is limited to the actual costs incurred by the operator for the adaptation and updating of the list of subscribers not to be included in the public directory.
3. The rights conferred by paragraph 1 shall apply to subscribers who are natural persons. Member States shall also guarantee, in the framework of Community law and applicable national legislation, that the legitimate interests of subscribers other than natural persons with regard to their entry in public directories are sufficiently protected.

Article 12

Unsolicited calls

1. The use of automated calling systems without human intervention (automatic calling machine) or facsimile machines (fax) for the purposes of direct marketing may only be allowed in respect of subscribers who have given their prior consent.
2. Member States shall take appropriate measures to ensure that, free of charge, unsolicited calls for purposes of direct marketing, by means other than those referred to in paragraph 1, are not allowed either without the consent of the subscribers concerned or in respect of subscribers who do not wish to receive these calls, the choice between these options to be determined by national legislation.
3. The rights conferred by paragraphs 1 and 2 shall apply to subscribers who are natural persons. Member States shall also guarantee, in the framework of Community law and applicable national legislation, that the legitimate interests of subscribers other than natural persons with regard to unsolicited calls are sufficiently protected.

Article 13

Technical features and standardisation

1. In implementing the provisions of this Directive, Member States shall ensure, subject to paragraphs 2 and 3, that no mandatory requirements for specific technical features are imposed on terminal or other telecommunications equipment which could impede the

placing of equipment on the market and the free circulation of such equipment in and between Member States.

2. Where provisions of this Directive can be implemented only by requiring specific technical features, Member States shall inform the Commission according to the procedures provided for by Directive 83/189/EEC[1] which lays down a procedure for the provision of information in the field of technical standards and regulations.

3. Where required, the Commission will ensure the drawing up of common European standards for the implementation of specific technical features, in accordance with Community legislation on the approximation of the laws of the Member States concerning telecommunications terminal equipment, including the mutual recognition of their conformity, and Council Decision 87/95/EEC of 22 December 1986 on standardisation in the field of information technology and telecommunications[2].

Article 14
Extension of the scope of application of certain provisions of Directive 95/46/EC

1. Member States may adopt legislative measures to restrict the scope of the obligations and rights provided for in Articles 5, 6 and Article 8(1), (2), (3) and (4), when such restriction constitutes a necessary measure to safeguard national security, defence, public security, the prevention, investigation, detection and prosecution of criminal offences or of unauthorised use of the telecommunications system, as referred to in Article 13(1) of Directive 95/46/EC.

2. The provisions of Chapter III on judicial remedies, liability and sanctions of Directive 95/46/EC shall apply with regard to national provisions adopted pursuant to this Directive and with regard to the individual rights derived from this Directive.

3. The Working Party on the Protection of Individuals with regard to the Processing of Personal Data establishes according to Article 29 of Directive 95/46/EC shall carry out the tasks laid down in Article 30 of the abovementioned Directive also with regard to the protection of fundamental rights and freedoms and of legitimate interests in the telecommunications sector, which is the subject of this Directive.

4. The Commission, assisted by the Committee established by Article 31 of Directive 95/46/EC, shall technically specify the Annex according to the procedure mentioned in this Article. The aforesaid Committee shall be convened specifically for the subjects covered by this Directive.

Article 15
Implementation of the Directive

1. Member States shall bring into force the laws, regulations and administrative provisions necessary for them to comply with this Directive not later than 24 October 1998.

By way of derogation from the first subparagraph, Member States shall bring into force the laws, regulations and administrative provisions necessary for them to comply with Article 5 of this Directive not later than 24 October 2000.

When Member States adopt these measures, they shall contain a reference to this Directive or shall be accompanied by such a reference at the time of their official publication. The procedure for such reference shall be adopted by Member States.

---

1   OJ L 109, 26 April 1983, p 8. Directive as last amended by Directive 94/10/EC (OJ L 100, 19 April 1994, p 30).

2   OJ L 36, 7 February 1987, p 31. Decision as last amended by the 1994 Act of Accession.

2. By way of derogation from Article 6(3), consent is not required with respect to processing already under way on the date the national provisions adopted pursuant to this Directive enter into force. In those cases the subscribers shall be informed of this processing and if they do not express their dissent within a period to be determined by the Member State, they shall be deemed to have given their consent.
3. Article 11 shall not apply to editions of directories which have been published before the national provisions adopted pursuant to this Directive enter into force.
4. Member States shall communicate to the Commission the text of the provisions of national law which they adopt in the field governed by this Directive.

Article 16
Addressees

This Directive is addressed to the Member States.

Done at Brussels, 15 December 1997.

ANNEX
List of data

For the purpose referred to in Article 6(2) the following data may be processed:
Data containing the:

— number or identification of the subscriber station,
— address of the subscriber and the type of station,
— total number of units to be charged for the accounting period,
— called subscriber number,
— type, starting time and duration of the calls made and/or the data volume transmitted,
— date of the call/service,
— other information concerning payments such as advance payment, payments by instalments, disconnection and reminders.

Appendix 4

DRAFT TELECOMMUNICATIONS (DATA PROTECTION AND PRIVACY) REGULATIONS 1998

(31 JULY 1998)

PART I

General

1. Citation and commencement

These Regulations may be cited as the Telecommunications (Data Protection and Privacy Regulations 1998 and shall come into force on . . . 1998.

2. Interpretation

(1) In these Regulations—

'the Act of 1984' means the Telecommunications Act 1984[1];
'bill' includes an invoice, account, statement or other instrument of the like character and 'billing' shall be construed accordingly;
'corporate subscriber', means a subscriber who is not an individual, that is to say, a subscriber who is—

(a) a company within the meaning of section 735(1) of the Companies Act 1985;
(b) a company incorporated in pursuance of a royal charter or letters patent;
(c) a partnership in Scotland;
(d) a corporation sole; or
(e) any other body corporate or other entity which is a legal person distinct from the persons (if any) of which it is composed;

'the Data Protection Commissioner' and 'the Commissioner' both mean the Commissioner appointed under section 6 of the Data Protection Act 1998[2];
'the Directive' means Directive 97/66/EC of the European Parliament and of the Council of the European Union[3];
'the Director' means the Director General of Telecommunications appointed under section 1 of the Act of 1984;
'individual' means a living individual;
'public telecommunications network' means any transmission system, and any associated switching equipment and other facilities which—

---

1   1984 c 12.
2   1998 c 29
3   OJ L 24, 30 January 1998, p 1.

(a) permit of the conveyance of signals between different termination points by wire, by wireless telegraphy, or by optical or other electro-magnetic means, and

(b) are used, in whole or in part, for the provision of publicly available telecommunication services;

'relevant telecommunications network', in relation to a telecommunications service provider, means a public telecommunications network which is used by that service provider for the provision of publicly available telecommunications services;

'relevant telecommunications service provider' means—

(a) in relation to a user, the provider of the services he uses, and

(b) in relation to a subscriber, the provider who provides him with services;

'subscriber' means a person who is a party to a contract with a telecommunications service provider for the supply of publicly available telecommunications services;

'telecommunications network provider' means a person who provides a public telecommunications network (whether or not he is also a telecommunications service provider);

'telecommunications service provider' means a person who provides publicly available telecommunications services (whether or not he is also a telecommunications network provider);

'telecommunications services' means services the provision of which consists, in whole or in part, of the transmission and routing of signals on telecommunication networks, not being services by way of radio or television broadcasting;

'user' means an individual using a publicly available telecommunications service (whether or not he is a subscriber).

(2) Section 1 of the Data Protection Act 1998 (basic interpretative provisions) shall have effect for the purposes of these Regulations as it has effect for the purposes of that Act.

(3) Subject to paragraphs (1) and (2) and except where the context otherwise requires, expressions used in these Regulations which are also used in the Directive have the same meanings in these Regulations as they have in the Directive.

(4) In a case in which signals are conveyed to telecommunications equipment used by a subscriber, wholly or partly otherwise than by line, any reference in these Regulations to a line shall be construed as including a reference to what, in that case, functionally corresponds to a line and 'connected', in relation to a line, shall be construed accordingly.

3. Requirements of Regulations

(1) Notwithstanding that the requirements of these Regulations are requirements imposed by law, where a person is required, in the case of a subscriber, to provide, or ensure the provision of, a facility he may make a reasonable charge in respect thereof save in so far as is otherwise provided in regulations 10(2), 11(2) and (3), 17(1) and 18(1).

(2) To the extent that any term in a contract between a subscriber to, and the provider of, publicly available telecommunications services would be inconsistent with a requirement of these Regulations, that term shall be void.

4. Consents, notices and notifications for purposes of Regulations

(1) A consent, notice or notification for the purposes of these Regulations may be in general or more limited terms and may be subject to conditions and, so long as it remains in force, shall have effect according to its tenor.

(2) A consent, notice or notification for the purposes of these Regulations may (without prejudice to any other method of transmission) be sent by post.

PART II

Traffic and Billing Data

5. Limitation on processing certain traffic data

(1) This regulation relates to data which—

   (a) are in respect of traffic handled by a telecommunications network provider or a telecommunications service provider;

   (b) are processed to secure the connection of a call and stored by the provider of a network or service concerned, and

   (c) constitute personal data which relate to a subscriber to, or user of, any publicly available telecommunications service or, in the case of a corporate subscriber, would constitute such personal data if that subscriber were an individual.

(2) Upon the termination of the call in question, save as provided in regulations 8(2) and 9, such data as are mentioned in paragraph (1) shall be erased or shall be depersonalised by the person by whom they are stored, that is to say the data shall be so dealt with, that they cease to be such data as are mentioned in paragraph (1)(c).

6. Limitation on processing certain billing data

(1) This regulation relates to the processing of any such data as are mentioned in Schedule 1 and are stored by a telecommunications network provider or a telecommunications service provider for purposes connected with the payment of sums falling to be paid—

   (a) by a subscriber, or

   (b) by way of interconnection charges.

(2) Notwithstanding anything in regulation 5 where the data are, in whole or in part, also such data as are mentioned in paragraph (1) of that regulation, such data as are mentioned in paragraph (1) of this regulation may, and may only, be processed for the purposes there mentioned until the expiry of the period during which legal proceedings may be brought in respect of the payments due, or alleged to be due, or, where such proceedings are brought within that period, until those proceedings are finally determined and, for the purposes hereof, the proceedings shall not be taken to be finally determined—

   (a) so long as either party has a right of appeal, or

   (b) pending the determination of any appeal brought.

7. Processing of billing data for certain marketing purposes of telecommunications service provider

(1) This regulation relates to the processing of such data as are mentioned in Schedule 1 which—

   (a) are stored by a telecommunications service provider, and

   (b) constitute personal data in the case of a subscriber to that service or, in the case of a corporate subscriber, would constitute such data if that subscriber were an individual.

(2)   Notwithstanding anything in regulation 5 where the data are, in whole or in part, also such data as are mentioned in paragraph (1) of that regulation, such data as are mentioned in paragraph (1) of this regulation may be processed by the provider of a publicly available telecommunications service concerned for the purposes of marketing telecommunications services which he provides if, but only if, the subscriber concerned has given his consent.

8.   Further provisions relating to the processing of traffic and billing data

(1)   This regulation relates to the processing by either a telecommunications network provider or a telecommunications service provider ('the relevant person') of data to which regulation 5 or 6 relates.

(2)   The processing by the relevant person of such data as are mentioned in paragraph (1) shall, without prejudice to any other restriction contained in this Part, be restricted to what is necessary for the purposes of such an activity as is mentioned in paragraph (3) and shall only be carried out by a person—

(a)   acting under the authority of the relevant person, and
(b)   whose other activities under that authority include such an activity as is so mentioned.

(3)   The activities referred to in paragraph (2) are activities relating to—

(a)   the management of billing or traffic;
(b)   customer enquiries;
(c)   the detection of fraud, and
(d)   the marketing of any telecommunications services provided by the relevant person.

9.   Savings relating to the settling of disputes

(1)   This regulation relates to any provision relating to the settling of disputes (by way of legal proceedings or otherwise), which is contained in, or made by virtue of, any enactment.

(2)   Nothing in this Part shall preclude the furnishing of billing or traffic data to a person who is a competent authority for the purposes of any such provision as is mentioned in paragraph (1).

PART III

Calling or called line identification

10.   Prevention of calling line identification – outgoing calls

(1)   This regulation relates to outgoing calls on a line.

(2)   The relevant telecommunications service provider shall ensure that a user originating a call has, subject to regulations 12 and 13, as respects that call, a simple means to prevent, without charge, the presentation on the called line of the identity of the calling line.

(3)   The relevant telecommunications service provider shall ensure that a subscriber has, subject to regulations 12 and 13, as respects his line and all calls originating therefrom, a simple means to prevent, without charge, the presentation on any called line of the identity of his line.

11. Prevention of called or calling line identification – incoming calls

(1) This regulation relates to incoming calls on a line.

(2) Where the presentation on the called line of the identity of the calling line is available, the relevant telecommunications service provider shall ensure that the subscriber has, as respects his line, a simple means to prevent, without charge for the reasonable use of the facility, such presentation thereon of the identity of a calling line.

(3) Where the presentation on the calling line of the identity of the connected line is available, the relevant telecommunications service provider shall ensure that the subscriber has, as respects that line, a simple means to prevent, without charge, such presentation on a calling line of the identity of that line.

(4) Where the presentation on the called line of the identity of the calling line, before the establishment of a call, is available, the relevant telecommunications service provider shall ensure that the subscriber has, as respects all or particular calls in the case of which such presentation on his line of the identity of the calling line has been prevented as mentioned in regulation 10(2) or (3), a simple means to reject the calls in question.

12. 999 or 112 calls

(1) This regulation relates to calls to the emergency services made using either of the emergency call numbers 999 or 112 ('999 or 112 calls').

(2) In order to facilitate responses to such calls—

    (a) all 999 or 112 calls shall be excluded from the calls referred to in regulation 10, and

    (b) in relation to 999 or 112 calls, no person shall be entitled to prevent the presentation on the called line of the identity of the calling line.

13. Tracing of malicious or nuisance calls

(1) This regulation shall apply where the relevant telecommunications service provider has been notified by a subscriber that he requests the tracing of malicious or nuisance calls received on his line.

(2) Until such time as action in pursuance of such a request has ceased, the relevant telecommunications service provider or the provider of a relevant telecommunications network, where the subscriber has made application in that behalf, may—

    (a) in relation to calls in relation to which the subscriber's line is the called line, and

    (b) so far as it appears to the provider in question necessary or expedient for the purposes of such action,

override anything done to prevent the presentation of the identity of the calling line.

(3) Any term of a contract for the provision of telecommunications services which relates to such prevention shall have effect subject to the provisions of paragraph (2).

(4) In relation to such calls as are mentioned in paragraph (2)(a), nothing in these Regulations or in the Data Protection Act 1998 shall preclude the relevant telecommunications service provider, or a provider of a relevant telecommunications network, from storing, and making available to a person with a legitimate interest therein, data containing the identification of a calling subscriber which were obtained while paragraph (2) applied.

14.   Facilities for calling or called line identification to be publicised

A telecommunications service provider who offers facilities for calling or called line identification shall take all reasonable steps to publicise that he does so and of the effect of this Part in relation thereto.

15.   Supplementary provisions

(1)   Any other telecommunications service provider and any telecommunications network provider shall comply with any reasonable requests made by a relevant telecommunications service provider for the purposes of regulation 10, 11 or 13.

(2)   Where a subscriber has two or more lines, regulations 10 and 11 shall, in his case, have effect separately as respects each line as if that line were his only line.

PART IV

Directories of subscribers

16.   Directories to which Part IV applies

(1)   This Part applies in relation to a directory of subscribers to publicly available telecommunications services, whether in printed form or in electronic form—

(a)   which is made available to the public or a section of the public, or

(b)   information from which is provided by a directory enquiry service.

(2)   In this Part any reference to a directory is a reference to such a directory as is mentioned in paragraph (1), 'production' in relation to a directory means its publication or preparation and 'producer' shall be construed accordingly.

17.   Entries relating to individuals

(1)   This regulation applies in relation to a directory which includes entries which relate to subscribers who are individuals and any person who produces such a directory shall, without charge to any such subscriber, ensure that it complies with this regulation.

(2)   Except to the extent, if any, to which the subscriber in question has consented otherwise, such a directory shall not contain any personal data in relation to a subscriber who is an individual other than data which are necessary to identify him and the number allocated to him.

(3)   Without prejudice to paragraph (2), where a subscriber who is an individual has so requested the producer of such a directory then, in his case—

(a)   no entry relating a number specified in the request shall be included in that directory;

(b)   no entry therein shall contain a reference which reveals his sex, and

(c)   no such entry shall contain such part of his address as is so specified.

(4)   Where, in connection with the production of a directory, information relating to a particular subscriber is supplied to the producer thereof by some other person—

(a)   where that other person has in his possession such a request by that subscriber as is mentioned in paragraph (3) (to whomsoever made), he shall transmit that request to the producer of the directory, and

(b)   any request so transmitted shall be treated for the purposes of paragraph (3) as if it had been made to that producer.

18. Entries relating to corporate subscribers

(1) This regulation applies in relation to a directory which includes entries which relate to corporate subscribers and any person who produces such a directory shall, without charge to any such subscriber, ensure that it complies with this regulation.

(2) Where a corporate subscriber has so requested the producer of directory, then, in its case, no entry relating to a number specified in the request shall be included in that directory.

(3) Paragraph (4) of regulation 17 shall have effect for the purposes of this regulation as if any reference therein to paragraph (3) of that regulation were a reference to paragraph (2) of this regulation.

19. Supplementary provisions relating to directory enquiry services

Where a person directs an enquiry relating to a particular subscriber to a directory enquiry service but there is no entry relating to that subscriber in a directory used by that service, nothing in this Part shall be taken to preclude the person in question being told the reason, or possible reason, why there is no such entry.

PART V

Use of telecommunications services for direct marketing purposes

20. Application of Part V

(1) This Part shall apply in relation to the use of publicly available telecommunications services for direct marketing purposes.

(2) Any reference in this Part to direct marketing is a reference to the communication of any advertising or marketing material on a particular line.

21. Use of fax and automated calling systems for direct marketing purposes – communications on lines of subscribers who are individuals

(1) This regulation applies in relation to the use of publicly available telecommunications services for the communication of material, for direct marketing purposes, by means of—

    (a) facsimile transmission, or

    (b) an automated calling system, that is to say, a system which, when activated, operates to make calls without human intervention,

where the called line is that of a subscriber who is an individual.

(2) A person shall not use publicly available telecommunications services, and a subscriber to such services shall not permit them to be used, as mentioned in paragraph (1), except where the called line is that of a subscriber who has previously notified the caller that he consents to such communications as are there mentioned being made by the caller in question on that line.

22. Use of fax for direct marketing purposes – unsolicited communications on lines of corporate subscribers

(1) This regulation applies in relation to the use of publicly available telecommunications services for the unsolicited communication of material, for direct marketing purposes, by means of facsimile transmission, where the called line is that of a corporate subscriber.

(2) A person shall not use publicly available telecommunications services, and a subscriber to such services shall not permit them to be used, as mentioned in paragraph (1) where—

  (a) the called line is that of a corporate subscriber who has previously notified the caller that such unsolicited communications as are there mentioned should not be made on that line, or

  (b) the number allocated to a corporate subscriber in respect of the called line is one listed in the record kept under paragraph (4).

(3) For the purposes of paragraph (1) and (2), the communication of material as mentioned in paragraph (1) shall not be treated as unsolicited where the called line is that of a corporate subscriber which has notified the caller that it does not object to receiving on that line such communications as are so mentioned from the caller in question.

(4) For the purposes of this regulation, the Secretary of State shall—

  (a) maintain and keep up-to-date, in printed form or in electronic form, a record of the numbers allocated to corporate subscribers, in respect of particular lines, who have notified him that they do not for the time being wish to receive such communications as are mentioned in paragraph (1) on the lines in question, and

  (b) on the request of—

    (i) a person wishing to send such communications or

    (ii) a subscriber wishing to permit the use of his line for the sending of such communications,

and the payment by him of such fee as is required by the Secretary of State, make that record available to that person or that subscriber.

(5) For the purposes of paragraph (4)(b) the Secretary of State may require different fees for making the record available in different forms but the fees required by him shall be such as are designed to secure, as nearly as may be and taking one year with another, that the aggregate fees received, or reasonably expected to be received, equal the costs incurred, or reasonably expected to be incurred, by the Secretary of State in discharging his duties under paragraph (4).

(6) The functions of the Secretary of State under paragraph (4), other than the function of determining the fees to be required for the purposes of sub-paragraph (b) thereof, may be discharged on his behalf by some other person in pursuance of arrangements in that behalf made by the Secretary of State with that other person.

23. Unsolicited calls for direct marketing purposes on lines of subscribers who are individuals

(1) Except where regulation 21 applies, this regulation applies in relation to the use of publicly available telecommunications services for the purposes of making unsolicited calls, for direct marketing purposes, where the called line is that of a subscriber who is an individual.

(2) A person shall not use publicly available telecommunications services, and a subscriber to such services shall not permit them to be used, as mentioned in paragraph (1) where—

  (a) the called line is that of a subscriber who has previously notified the caller that such unsolicited calls as are there mentioned should not be made on that line, or

  (b) the number allocated to a subscriber in respect of the called line is one listed in the record kept under paragraph (4).

(3) For the purposes of paragraphs (1) and (2), a call on a subscriber's line shall not be treated as an unsolicited call if that subscriber has notified the caller that he does not object to receiving on that line calls from the caller in question made for direct marketing purposes.

(4) For the purposes of this regulation, the Secretary of State shall—

    (a) maintain and keep up-to-date, in printed form or in electronic form, a record of the numbers allocated to subscribers who are individuals, in respect of particular lines, who have notified him that they do not for the time being wish to receive unsolicited calls made for direct marketing purposes on the lines in question, and

    (b) on the request of—

        (i) a person wishing to make such calls on the lines of subscribers who are individuals, or

        (ii) a subscriber wishing to permit the use of his line for the making of such calls as aforesaid,

    and the payment by him of such fee as is required by the Secretary of State, make that record available to that person or that subscriber,

(5) For the purpose of paragraph (4)(b) the Secretary of State may require different fees for making the record available in different forms but the fees required by him shall be such as are designed to secure, as nearly as may be and taking one year with another, that the aggregate fees received, or reasonably expected to be received, equal the costs incurred, or reasonably expected to be incurred, by the Secretary of State in discharging his duties under paragraph (4).

(6) The functions of the Secretary of State under paragraph (4), other than the function of determining the fees to be required for the purposes of sub-paragraph (b) thereof, may be discharged on his behalf by some other person in pursuance of arrangements in that behalf made by the Secretary of State with that other person.

24. Supplementary provisions

(1) In this regulation, 'relevant regulation' means regulation 21, 22 or 23, as the case may require and in this Part, 'caller' means a person using publicly available telecommunications services as mentioned in paragraph (1) of a relevant regulation.

(2) Where publicly available telecommunications services are used as mentioned in paragraph (1) of a relevant regulation, the caller shall include in the material communicated—

    (a) his name and address, or

    (b) a freephone telephone number on which he can be reached.

(3) Where such services are so used by the caller at the instigation of some other person—

    (a) the caller shall, without prejudice to paragraph (2), include in the material communicated the name and address of that other person or a freephone telephone number on which that person can be reached;

    (b) where that other person has in his possession such a notification as is mentioned in paragraph (2) of the relevant regulation (to whomsoever it is addressed) he shall transmit it to the caller in question and any notification so transmitted shall be treated for the purposes of paragraph (2) of the relevant regulation as if it had been given to that caller, and

    (c) that other person shall take all reasonable steps to ensure that the caller in question complies with the requirements of the relevant regulation and those of this regulation.

PART VI

Miscellaneous provisions

25. Security of telecommunications services

(1) Subject to paragraph (2), a telecommunications service provider shall take technical and organisational measures which are appropriate to secure the security of the service he provides, in particular as respects the risk of communications in a readily intelligible form being misdirected to, or readily accessible by, persons other than those to whom they were directed by the originator thereof.

(2) If necessary, the measures required by paragraph (1) shall be taken by a telecommunications service provider in conjunction with the provider of the relevant telecommunications network who shall comply with any reasonable requests made by the service provider for the purposes hereof.

(3) Where, notwithstanding the taking of measures required hereby, there is a significant risk to the security of the relevant telecommunications network the telecommunications service provider shall inform the subscribers concerned of—

   (a) that risk;
   (b) any measures appropriate to afford safeguards against that risk which they themselves might take, and
   (c) the costs involved in the taking of such measures.

(4) For the purposes of this regulation, measures shall only be taken to be appropriate if, having regard to—

   (a) the state of technological development, and
   (b) the cost of implementing the measures,

   they are proportionate to the risks against which they would afford safeguards.

(5) For the purposes of this regulation the security of a public telecommunications service or network shall not be taken to be at risk by reason of the intentional disclosure, or possibility of such disclosure of any matter falling within subsection (1)(a) or (b) of section 45 of the Act of 1984[1] by a telecommunications service or network provider in a case or circumstances in which he would not be guilty of an offence under that section if—

   (a) the reference therein to a person engaged in the running of a public telecommunication system were a reference to such a provider, and
   (b) any reference therein to a message were a reference to a communication.

26. Right to bills which are not itemised

At the request of the subscriber concerned, a telecommunications service provider shall only submit to him bills which are not itemised.

27. Itemised billing and privacy

(1) The Secretary of State and the Director shall each have a duty, when exercising any function assigned to him by a provision of the Act of 1984 specified in paragraph (2), to have regard to the need to reconcile the rights of subscribers receiving itemised bills with the rights to privacy of calling users and called subscribers, for example by

---

1   Section 45 was amended by section 11(1) of the Interception of Communications Act 1985 (c 56).

ensuring that sufficient alternative means for the making of calls or methods of paying therefor are available to such users and subscribers.

(2) For the purposes of paragraph (1), the specified provisions of the Act of 1984 are sections 3, 7, 8, 12, 13, 15, 16, 17, 18, 47, 48, 49 and 50.

28. Termination of unwanted automatic call forwarding

Where calls originally directed to another line are being automatically forwarded to a subscriber's line as a result of action taken by a third party and the subscriber so requests the relevant telecommunications service provider ('the subscriber's provider'), that provider shall ensure, without charge, that such forwarding ceases without any avoidable delay; and any other telecommunications service provider and any telecommunications network provider shall comply with any reasonable requests made by the subscriber's provider for the purposes of this regulation.

29. National security

(1) Nothing in any of the provisions of these Regulations shall require a telecommunications service or network provider to do, or refrain from doing, anything (including the processing of data) if, in any case, exemption from a requirement of that provision is required for the purpose of safeguarding national security.

(2) Subject to paragraph (4), a certificate signed by a Minister of the Crown certifying that exemption from any requirement of these Regulations is or at any time was required for the purpose of safeguarding national security shall be conclusive evidence of that fact.

(3) A certificate under paragraph (2) may identify the cases to which it applies by means of a general description and may be expressed to have prospective effect.

(4) Any person directly affected by the issuing of a certificate under paragraph (2) may appeal to the Tribunal against the certificate.

(5) If on an appeal under paragraph (4), the Tribunal finds that, applying the principles applied by a court on an application for judicial review, the Minister did not have reasonable grounds for issuing the certificate, the Tribunal may allow the appeal and quash the certificate.

(6) Where in any proceedings under or by virtue of these Regulations it is claimed by a telecommunications service or network provider that a certificate under paragraph (2) which identifies the cases to which it applies by means of a general description applies to any case, any other party to the proceedings may appeal to the Tribunal on the ground that the certificate does not apply to the case in question and, subject to any determination under paragraph (7), the certificate shall be conclusively presumed so to apply.

(7) On any appeal under paragraph (6), the Tribunal may determine that the certificate does not so apply.

(8) In this Regulation 'the Tribunal' means the Data Protection Tribunal referred to in section 6 of the Data Protection Act 1998 and subsections (8), (9), (10) and (12) of section 28 of that Act and Schedule 6 thereto shall apply for the purposes of, and in connection with, this regulation as if any references therein to subsection (2), (4) or (6) of the said section 28 were, respectively, references to paragraph (2), (4) or (6) of this regulation.

30. Law enforcement etc

Nothing in any of the provisions of these Regulations shall require a telecommunications service or network provider to do, or refrain from doing, anything (including the processing of data), if that is necessary or expedient for the purposes of—

(a)   the prevention or detection of crime;
(b)   any criminal proceedings;
(c)   compliance with the order of a court, or
(d)   compliance with a warrant issued by the Secretary of State under section 2 of the
       Interception of Communications Act 1985[1].

31.   Incidental and consequential amendments

The amendments set out in Schedule 2 shall have effect.

32.   Transitory provisions

The transitory provisions in Schedule 3 shall have effect.

PART VII

Compensation and enforcement

33.   Compensation for failure to comply with requirements of Regulations

(1)   A person who suffers damage by reason of any contravention of any of the requirements
       of these regulations by any other person shall be entitled to compensation from that
       other person for that damage.
(2)   In proceedings brought against a person by virtue of this regulation it shall be a defence
       to prove that he had taken such care as in all the circumstances was reasonably required
       to comply with the requirement concerned.

34.   Enforcement – application of Part V of the Data Protection Act 1998

(1)   Subject to the exceptions and modifications set out in Schedule 4, the provisions of Part
       V of the Data Protection Act 1998 and of Schedules 6 and 9 thereto shall apply for the
       purposes of the enforcement of these Regulations and connected purposes.
(2)   In this regulation and in regulations 35 and 36, 'enforcement functions' means the
       functions of the Commissioner under the said provisions as so applied.
(3)   The provisions of this regulation and those of regulation 33 are without prejudice to
       each other.

35.   Request that Commissioner exercise his enforcement functions

Where it is alleged that there has been contravention of any of the requirements of these
Regulations either the Director or a person aggrieved by the alleged contravention may request
the Commissioner to exercise his enforcement functions in respect of that contravention; but
those functions shall be exercisable by him whether or not he has been so requested.

36.   Technical advice to Commissioner

The Director shall comply with any reasonable request made by the Commissioner, in
connection with his enforcement functions, for advice on technical and similar matters relating
to telecommunications.

---

1   1985 c 56.

SCHEDULE 1

Regulations 6(1) and 7(1)

Data referred to in Regulations 6 and 7

1. The data referred to in regulations 6(1) and 7(1) are data which constitute personal data in the case of a subscriber to, or user of, any publicly available telecommunications service or, in the case of a corporate subscriber, would constitute such data if that subscriber were an individual, and which comprise information in respect of all or any of the following matters, namely—

   (a) the number or other identification of the subscriber's station;
   (b) the subscriber's address and the type of the station;
   (c) the total number of units of use by reference to which the sum payable in respect of an accounting period is calculated;
   (d) the type, date, starting time and duration of calls and the volume of data transmissions in respect of which sums are payable by the subscriber and the numbers or other identification of the stations to which they were made;
   (e) the date of the provision of any service not falling within sub-paragraph (d), and
   (f) other matters concerning payments including, in particular, advance payments, payments by instalments, reminders and disconnections.

2. The reference in paragraph 1(c) to an accounting period is, in relation to sums of any description payable to a telecommunications network provider or a telecommunications service provider, a reference to a period in respect of which the relevant person normally sends out bills for sums of that description payable to him.

SCHEDULE 2

Regulation 31

Incidental and consequential amendments

1. The Telecommunications Act 1984

At the end of section 1(6) of the Act of 1984 (payment out of money provided by Parliament) there shall be added the words 'or in consequence of the provisions of the Telecommunications (Data Protection and Privacy) Regulations 1998'.

2. At the end of section 7(5)(a) of the Act of 1984 (power to licence systems) then shall be added the words 'or by regulation 30 of the Telecommunications (Data Protection and Privacy) Regulations 1998'.

3. The Data Protection Act 1998

At the end of section 11 of the Data Protection Act 1998 (right to prevent processing for purposes of direct marketing) there shall be added the following subsection—

'(5) This section shall not apply in relation to the processing of such data as are mentioned in paragraph (1) of regulation 7 of the Telecommunications (Data Protection and Privacy) Regulations 1998 (processing of telecommunications billing data for marketing purposes) for the purposes mentioned in paragraph (2) of that regulation.'.

4. The Telecommunications (Open Network Provision (Voice Telephony) Regulations 1998

In regulation 2(1) of the Telecommunications (Open Network Provision) (Voice Telephony) Regulations 1998[1] (interpretation), for the definition of 'relevant data protection legislation' there shall be substituted the following definition—

' "relevant data protection legislation" means the Data Protection Act 1998 and the Telecommunications (Data Protection and Privacy) Regulations 1998;'.

SCHEDULE 3

Regulation 32

Transitory provisions

1. Provisions relating to regulation 7

(1) This paragraph applies where—

    (a) immediately before the coming into force of these regulations, any such data as mentioned in regulation 7(1) were being processed by a telecommunications service provider for the purposes of marketing telecommunications services which he provides ('the existing data'), and

    (b) that service provider has given a subscriber concerned written notice of that processing and of the effect of this paragraph ('a notified subscriber').

(2) Subject to sub-paragraph (3), for the purposes of regulation 7(2) in relation to the continued processing of existing data which constitutes personal data in the case of a notified subscriber, or, in the case of a notified corporate subscriber, would constitute such data if that subscriber were an individual, the notified subscriber shall be deemed to have given his consent.

(3) If, within 2 months of a notified subscriber having been given the notice referred to in sub-paragraph (1)(b), he expresses his dissent by written notice given to the telecommunications service provider concerned, then, in the case of that subscriber, the provider concerned shall cease, as soon as is reasonably practicable the continued processing of existing data in pursuance of sub-paragraph (2).

2. Provisions relating to Part IV

(1) This paragraph shall apply in relation to any edition published before the coming into force of these Regulations of such a directory as is mentioned in regulation 16(1).

(2) Part IV shall not apply in relation to such a directory which is comprised in an edition so published.

---

1   SI 1998/1580.

SCHEDULE 4

Regulation 34(1)

Exceptions and modifications to Part V of the Data Protection Act 1998 and Schedules 6 and 9 thereto as extended by Regulation 34

1. In section 40—

(a) in subsection (1), for the words 'data protection principles' there shall be substituted the words 'requirements of the Telecommunications (Data Protection and Privacy) Regulations 1998 (in this Part referred to as 'a relevant requirement')' and for the words 'principle or principles' there shall be substituted the words 'requirement or requirements';

(b) in subsection (2), the words 'or distress' shall be omitted.

(c) subsections (3), (4), (8) and (9) shall be omitted, and

(d) in subsection (5)(a) for the words 'data protection principle or principles' there shall be substituted the words 'relevant requirement or requirements'.

2. In section 41, for the words 'data protection principle or principles', in both places where they occur, there shall be substituted the words 'relevant requirement or requirements'.

3. Section 42 shall be omitted.

4. In section 43—

(a) in subsection (1), for the words preceding 'within such time' there shall be substituted the words 'If the Commissioner reasonably requires any information for the purpose of determining whether a person has complied or complying with the relevant requirements he may serve that person';

(b) for subsection (2), there shall be substituted the following provision—

'(2) An information notice must contain a statement that the Commissioner regards the specified information as relevant for the purpose of determining whether the person has complied, or is complying, with the relevant requirements and his reason for regarding it as relevant for that purpose';

(c) in subsection (7)(a), after the word 'under' there shall be inserted the words 'the Telecommunications (Data Protection and Privacy) Regulations 1998 or'; and

(d) subsection (11) shall be omitted.

5. Sections 44, 45 and 46 shall be omitted.

6. In section 47(1) and (2), for the words 'an information notice or a special information notice', in both places where they occur, there shall be substituted the words 'or an information notice'.

7. In section 48—

(a) in subsections (1) and (3), for the words 'an information notice or a special information notice', in both places where they occur, there shall be substituted the words 'or an information notice';

(b) in subsection (3) for the words '43(6) or 44(7)' there shall be substituted the words 'or 43(6)'; and

(c) subsection (4) shall be omitted.

8. In section 49, subsection (5) shall be omitted.

9. In paragraph 4(1) of Schedule 6, for the words '(2) or (4)' there shall be substituted the words 'or (2)'.

10.   In paragraph 1 of Schedule 9—

(a)   for sub-paragraph (1)(a) there shall be substituted the following provision—

'(a)   that a person has contravened or is contravening any of the requirements of the Telecommunications (Data Protection and Privacy) Regulations 1998 (in this Schedule referred to as "the 1998 Regulations"), or',

and (b) sub-paragraph (2) shall be omitted.

11.   In paragraph 9 of Schedule 9—

(a)   in sub-paragraph (1)(a), after the words 'rights under' there shall be inserted the words 'the 1998 Regulations or', and

(b)   in sub paragraph (1)(b), after the words 'arising out of' there shall be inserted the words 'the 1998 Regulations or'.

INDEX

References are to paragraph numbers.